INTRODUCTION TO RELIGIOUS STUDIES

Harvey J. Sindima

University Press of America,® Inc.
Lanham · Boulder · New York · Toronto · Plymouth, UK

Copyright © 2009 by
University Press of America,® Inc.
4501 Forbes Boulevard
Suite 200
Lanham, Maryland 20706
UPA Acquisitions Department (301) 459-3366

Estover Road
Plymouth PL6 7PY
United Kingdom

Library of Congress Control Number: 2009932195
ISBN: 978-0-7618-4760-1 (clothbound : alk. paper)
ISBN: 978-0-7618-4761-8 (paperback : alk. paper)
eISBN: 978-0-7618-4762-5

™
⊖⊖ The paper used in this publication meets the minimum
requirements of American National Standard for Information
Sciences—Permanence of Paper for Printed Library Materials,
ANSI Z39.48-1992

To all my nephews and nieces

Contents

Introduction   vii

1. Why Study Religion   1
2. What is Religion   19
3. The Elements of Religion   29
4. Celebration and Divination   49
5. Scripture   71
6. Religions Functionaries   89
7. Magic, Sorcery, and Witchcraft   119
8. Sacred Time, Objects, and Space   143
9. Living Within the Sacred   157

Works Cited   167
Index   175

how they organise their life accordingly. To know what other people value as important, is to be a well-educated and a well-informed person.

In what ways does one become a well-rounded and productive citizen by studying religion? With the aggressive evangelism campaigns of Christianity and Islam—in their effort to spread their beliefs to all parts of the world—one is likely to come across individuals of other religions than one's own. Christianity and Islam are recruiting heavily in the cities and villages in most parts of the world. It is very common now for people to find that their friends, relatives, or even a family member(s) have converted to a different religion. It is now possible for one to go to school, college, university, or work beside someone of a different religion. It is common in some villages in Kenya, Tanzania, Malawi, and Mozambique for people to have Christian neighbours in a Muslim village, or Muslim neighbours in a predominately Christian village. Marriages, resettlements, and jobs are bringing people of various religions together, or in frequent close contact. This is happening all over the world, especially in cities. Having some knowledge of the religions of others will certainly go a long way towards creating an atmosphere of harmony by overcoming ignorance, prejudice, and bigotry.

To illustrate, since the attack in the United States of America on 11 September, 2001, and the subsequent wars in Afghanistan and Iraq, radio and television stations have made people in Europe, the United States of America, Australia, and even some in Africa associate Islam with violence. Many people are convinced that Islam is a violent religion; that it preaches hatred towards non-Muslims. Many people do not know that the *Qur'an* teaches the fellowship and equality of all people and that Islam abhors prejudice of any type. Many people are not aware that Islam teaches compassion and kindness. For example, that a Muslim must contribute at least two and one half percent of his or her income to the poor. Instead, Muslims are seen and treated as evil or bad people. Many Muslims in the U.S.A. suffered violent attacks following the tragedy of the Twin Towers in New York City on 11 September, 2001. Elsewhere in the world, Muslim leaders became suspects, some were arrested, investigated, and interrogated for connections with Al-Quida. Non Muslims too, suffered. Sikh men were attacked because they had turbans as Taliban Muslims. In New York City, a Sikh truck driver was pulled out of his vehicle and beaten. Two teenage boys and a girl in a small town in central New York state burned to the ground a Sikh holy place. They believed the Sikh men were terrorists because they wore turbans. Anyone who wore a turban was and still is a suspect in America because he is considered a Taliban, therefore a terrorist, although the Taliban never attacked the U.S.A.

All these acts of violence happened because of ignorance about what Islam teaches, and the lack of knowledge of Sikh religion. For sure, there are some verses in the *Qur'an* that may be used as the basis for violence, but such verses are to be found in the *Tanak* (the Jewish scriptures), or the Christian Bible too. One has only to read the history of the Jews in Hebrew scriptures to discover that it is a history written with blood as Jews fought and conquered non-Jews. Two references will do:

Introduction

This is a general survey of religions and religious practises around the world. This book was suggested by a friend and a former colleague who wanted me to put Africa right at the centre of religious studies. For the longest time, religious studies referred to topics related to Christianity. This is to say that religious studies evolved from Biblical studies taught in departments of religion in colleges and universities. Very often religious studies were taught by Christians with theological training from divinity schools or seminaries.

In the early days most of the professors in departments of religion were Christian ordained men. Only slowly did the composition of the faculty in religious studies change. The change occurred when the faculty being opened to the idea of including eastern religions in the curriculum as studies in Sanskrit became of academic interest. The academic interest in Sanskrit started in studies in philology, or linguistics with such scholars as Max Müller, then scholars in sociology and history developed an interest in Sanskrit. The academic interest went beyond Sanskrit, to studies in religion and social structure with scholars like Max Weber and Karl Marx. Although research in anthropology brought attention to religions other than eastern religions, studies in religion did not find those of scholarly interest. So religious studies meant learning about Christianity versa visa eastern religions. The method used was a comparative approach. The curriculum rationale for comparative methodology was to show the superiority of the Christian faith to other faiths, because of its revelation, considered the fullest of all.

It is interesting to note though, that although religious studies developed from Christian biblical studies, Judaism was not taught in departments of religion. It was only after liberal scholars no longer wanted to appear anti-Semitic that Judaism was included in a college and university curriculum on religion. This was in the late 1970s. By now, religious studies offerings included Christianity, Hinduism, Buddhism, and Judaism. The rest of world religions were not included because they lacked the minimal revelation of the eastern religions, and certainly that of Judaism, not to mention the fullness of Christian revelation.

The study of religion evolved in juxtaposition to Christian biblical and theological studies. The worthiness, or truth of other all religions is measured in relation to the revelation in Christianity. Revelation here seems to be the determining factor. It also seems that at the heart of revelation is the issue of salvation. It can therefore be argued that religious studies took interest in religions of salvation. The lack of interest in other religions was because they concentrated in the here and now, "the worldly religions" and not world fleeing religions, as Weber would have identified them.

The inclusion of other religions in religious studies is credited to the work of anthropologists who brought to the academic a great deal of religious materials from other cultures. Although the religions of those cultures were this worldly, or what in this book are called religions of structure, scholars brought a wealth of religious material that would benefit comparative studies. It was through anthropologists that religions of native peoples of North America and Australia begun to be remotely considered religions within religious studies and therefore included along with African religions. At the time of writing, religious studies treat native religions as peripheral.

Very often introductory books to the study of religion treat native religions as either an appendage, or tack native and African religions in a few pages somewhere towards the end of the book. My friend and colleague wanted an introductory book that gives students a global perspective of the religious believes and practise. He also wanted a book that discussed other less known religions, such as Native American and the other less popular religions of Asia. This book has been written to contribute towards a global understanding of religion.

I thank my colleagues at Colgate University for reading and setting time as a department to discuss an earlier draft manuscript of this book. I am grateful for their comments, suggestions, books offered, and encouragement for me to publish the book in Africa and the United States of America to ensure that students in both areas are offered a world perspective of religious studies. I am also grateful to the department's Administrative Assistant for reading the manuscript.

1

Why Study Religion

1. For a Good Education

As a professor of Religion and Philosophy, I am often asked by parents and student alike: Why study religion? Behind the question is the view that one cannot do much with a degree in religion unless one wants to be a cleric (a priest, a pastor, a rabbi, an *imam*), or a teacher, or professor. People want to acquire knowledge that they can use, knowledge that is profitable to them. Religion does not seem profitable for even the professions for which the study of religion may be a good preparation, are low-paying: clergy or teaching. Religion may not be as profitable as economics, but do not students study mathematics or chemistry even if they are not going to become teachers or work in a laboratory? Why do students learn different subjects when they will not apply directly the knowledge they acquire from all the courses they take? The answer may be that they take all those courses in order to meet the requirements for a full certificate or degree. Certainly, students do take a course in religion to meet certificate or degree requirements. What both students and parents do not realise, however, is that all the courses students take, make them well-rounded individuals and therefore useful citizens. Social studies, chemistry, physical science, political science, and all other disciplines of learning make individuals better citizens. Imagine how useful an individual would be in life if he or she studied only mathematics and nothing else? The person would indeed be educated, but would be narrow in his or her understanding of life and the world. When something is learned for the sake of knowledge, it broadens the horizon of one's mind, therefore one's view of life and the world. Intellectual growth is important, for it makes an individual a productive citizen. Perhaps there is no other discipline of inquiry that makes one more well-rounded than a course that teaches people how to become well versed in human values. This is what religion is all about: human values; things of great importance; things that make people who they are and why the live in a certain manner. Religion is about core values at their deepest level. To study religion is to know people at the core of their very being. One should study religion for the sake of knowledge, that is, to know what is important to others and

> I will deliver the inhabitants of the land into your hand, and you shall drive them out before you. You shall make no covenant with them or their gods. They shall not dwell in their land, lest they make you sin against me; for if you serve their gods it will surely be a snare to you (Exodus 23:31b–33).

> When the Lord your God brings you into the land which you are entering to take possession of it, and clear away many nations before you, the Hittites, the Girgashites, the Amorites, the Canaanites, the Perizzites, the Hivites, and the Jebusites, seven nations greater and mightier than yourselves, and when the Lord your God gives them over to you and you defeat them; then you must utterly destroy them; you shall make no covenant with them, and show no mercy to them (Deuteronomy 7:1,2).

Christian history is as full of blood too, it forced people to convert as the papal Bulls recommended, or during the Crusades and beyond. I have given elsewhere some accounts of Christian violence in Africa. I will use the account of Portuguese Franciscans plundering and setting fire on Kilwa on 24 July, 1805. I quoted from an eye witness account recorded by Hans Meyer (1858–1929), a German who travelled with Portuguese in their flagship, *Sam Rafel*.

> The Vical-General and some of the Franciscan Fathers came ashore carrying two crosses in procession singing *Te Deum*. They went to the palace and the crosses were put down and the Grand Captain prayed. Then everyone started to plunder the town of its merchandise and provisions. [de Almeida set the town on fire two days after they started the plunder.]

A similar account was written about the plunder of Mombasa:

> Then everyone [the Portuguese Franciscans] started to plunder the town and to search the houses, forcing open the doors with axes and iron bars. There was a large quantity of cloth from Sofala in the town. . . . So the Grand captain got a good deal of the trade from Sofala himself. A large quantity of silk and gold embroidered clothes were seized, and carpets also; one of these which was without equal beauty, was sent to the king of Portugal together with many other valuables.[1]

One cannot clear Judaism, Christianity, or Islam of violence, but Christians see the evil in Muslims ignoring the violence in their own religion. The study of religion enlightens people and prevents them from making general and sometimes ignorant remarks about other religions or their followers.

It would be wrong to think that the study of religion is good only for preparing to live with those who belong or convert to other religions. All people need to know about their spirituality because it is the foundation of their values, ethical principles, and sometimes the laws of their land. Non-Western people need to know more about their religion, because those who are educated, or have joined foreign religions—Christianity, Islam, Judaism, Bahai and others—have no respect for those who still follow and practise the spirituality of their ancestors. A serious study of traditional spirituality will help one to give respect and dignity to those who have decided to keep the traditions of the elders. Indigenous people everywhere—the

Americas, Australia, or Asia and places in between—never disrespected religions of others. Long before Christianity and Islam established themselves on the African continent, Africans respected the religion of others. Africa has always been a continent of many religions and people of different religions have always lived in harmony with each other. The study of religion will help people regain that lost virtue in African religious experience, namely, respect for all ways of living.

Religion as a Classic. Finally, a well-rounded person is one who is also well educated. To be well educated, is to study the classics of one's culture and others. The word "classic" refers to the arts, especially literature, music, art (drawings and paintings), and dances that have endured the test of time. Classics reveal the values and virtues of those who hold them. Whether they are the rock paintings in Malawi that go back to the Stone Age, or Hindu music that reveals 2,500 years of Indian history, one will find that classics are routed in the religion of the people. Religion is an ancient discipline, but also a classical discipline of the highest order, for it is the mother of all disciplines of inquiry, and still going strong. A well-educated person will study religion to understand better the foundations of a particular culture. For example, what an excellent way would there be to understand Chinese culture than to study Confucian scripture, "The Four Books and Five Classics?" These books still define the social order, behaviour and virtues of Chinese society in spite of the official view of religion. Let us look at two other examples. To grasp the essence of Jewish culture one would do well to read Hebrew scripture, the *Tanak*. So too, the study of the *Qur'an* would help one understand Islamic culture and society better. No one fully understands the roots and ethical principles of Western civilization, without reading the Bible, or at least parts of it. All these books are the classics of the society that produced them. A well-educated person must be well-versed in the classics of a culture, and religion, the oldest of all disciplines of learning houses classics of society. The artifacts, music, stories of creation and divinities, and architecture, all these are classics that open windows into the values and virtues of society that any person desiring to be well-educated would do well to study them in their proper setting, that is, religion.

2. Religion Shapes History

The discussion on Islam reveals another reason for studying religion, namely, that religion is a force that shapes social and political reality in the world. In short religion is a force in history. The fact that religion is a force that shapes local and world history may not be clear among native peoples. For example, in many parts of Africa, people never fought over religion, neither did religious beliefs influence fuel a conflict. This changed with the coming of Christianity and Islam on the continent. Up to the time of Roman persecutions of Christians that started in the second century of the Common Era (C.E.), no one died in Africa because of religion, profession faith, defence of the faith, or forcing others to join one's religion. Under Roman persecutions we find the first Christian martyrs in 180, and many were to follow under the persecutions of emperors Marcus Aurelius (160–180), Severus (202–203) Decian (249–251) Valerian (253–259) and others.[2]

The entry of Islam into Africa from the Arabian peninsula in 641, led Africans to die in *jihads*, holy wars that claimed African lives as Islam advanced across north Africa and down to west Africa, establishing Islamic empires there.[3] During the fourth Crusades, Africans died in Egypt, Nubia (Sudan), and parts of Uganda in 1275 under leadership of Sultan Saladin, the Muslim ruler of Egypt. Coptic Christians in Egypt were killed by Sultan Ali-Salih as he imposed Islamic rule over the Copts. West Africa is well familiar with the history of Usman Dan Fodio who wanted to purify Islam in the region.[4] From the twentieth century there have been many interreligious and religiously driven conflicts between Muslims and Christians notably in Nigeria and Sudan. Muslim and Christian students at universities in northern Nigeria have fought and others died because of religion. As a matter of fact, it is almost impossible to talk about the politics of Nigeria and Sudan without talking about religion.

Religion has shaped the history of the whole African continent. The entry of Christianity in Egypt and Ethiopia in the first century, and the Muslim evangelisation of the Maghreb (North Africa) changed North and West African history and greatly affected African culture and religion in those regions. The Christian evangelisation of the rest of Africa, led to colonisation. The history of Africa has been shaped by both Christianity and Islam through evangelisation and colonisation. Religion has changed the identity of Africa: the Islamic north identifies more with the Arab world, so that many people there and in northern Sudan think of themselves as Arabs first, before they are Africans. Christian Africa does not identify itself with the West, because of race differences, but Western countries are considered "traditional allies" and "friends" of Christian African countries.

3. Religion is history

One understands history much deeper by understanding religion. The history of Africa cannot be fully understood and appreciated without looking at the role religion played in the making of contemporary Africa. It is not only the history of colonisation, but also of trade. In pre-colonial Africa there was a network of long distance trade from north Africa to west Africa to present day Gambia, Senegal, Mali, Ghana, or the Soghay Empire. The network of trade routes in the east African trade went from Persia to Zanzibar, Kilwa, and Mombasa in Kenya from mainland Tanzania into the hinterland of Malawi and south Mozambique. Although all these trade networks were lead and built by Africans themselves, long before the coming of Islam, Muslims exploited them as they preached their religion and traded in gold, iron, ivory, or humans. The religious rationalisation of European trade in humans from Africa to the West Indies and the Americas have been well documented by many scholars.

The history of colonisation and education in Africa can only be fully understood through the lens of religion. For example, it was the presence of Scottish missionaries in Malawi that led to the British colonisation of the country. The missionaries wrote home for people to urge Scottish representatives in British Parliament to agitate and request the British government to declare Malawi a British Protectorate.[5] The struggle to independence is best understood by knowing the role religion played. When the struggle for independence started in 1914 in Malawi, it was by a Baptist pastor, the Reverend John Chilembwe (1860s–1915). Clergymen were involved in the struggle for independence elsewhere in Africa. The Reverend Ndabaningi Sithole (1920–2000) was an active politician in the struggle against white rule in Zimbabwe; so was the Reverend Canaan Banana (1936–2003) who became the first ceremonial President of Zimbabwe.

4. To understand Politics

The struggle for independence in some African countries is best understood when approached from the influence of religion. Before majority rule in South Africa in 1994, the white regime drew from religion support for its racist system of "separate development", or apartheid as they called it. Long before 1948, when South African whites voted themselves into power and thus out British control, white Christian clergy and theologians developed the theology of chosenness, or the idea that white people were chosen by God—just as God had chosen the Israelites— to be a light to the nations.[6] Professor Simon Maimela argued against the theology of chosenness saying, "Perhaps the most serious problem about this theology—this is true for English and Afrikaans Churches—is that it is devoid of the conception of a dynamic God who actively involves humans now in the present in order to transform the natural and social environment".[7]

Here religion was used for political goals. It was religion too that rallied the African majority in South Africa when their leaders were in prison. South African clergy, mostly Africans, denounced the system of apartheid as evil and against God. Archbishop Desmond Tutu (1931–), Reverend Doctor Allan Boesak (1945–) and many other Christian leaders led the Christian resistence to apartheid. Boesak told the world that "apartheid is more than an ideology, more than something that has been thought up to form the content of a particular political policy. Apartheid is also pseudo-gospel. It was born in the Church". He said:

> The struggle against apartheid . . . is, therefore, more than merely a struggle against an evil ideology. It is more than a struggle for the liberation and wholeness of people, white as well as Black, in South Africa. It is also finally a struggle for the integrity of the Gospel of Jesus Christ.[8]

So we find that the religion was used by both whites and Africans to establish political positions.

Examples of using religion in politics could be multiplied elsewhere in Africa and the world. The struggle of Black people in the United States of America cannot be fully understood without looking at the role of religion in Black society. The civil rights movement was born on white plantations among enslaved Africans as they cried out to their God for liberation. It was the Black church that was the vanguard of the civil rights movement. Black clerics spearheaded the movement in the 1960s, the most notable being Reverend Doctor Martin Luther King, Jr. (1929–1968).

The United States of America prides itself of its practise of separation of church and state. In a preface to my book on church and state I argued that there is really no separation in practise:

> Christian symbols abound in public places, including the legislature, a chaplain in the houses of Congress, and the display of the nativity scene, or the cross in public places during high holy days. Laws passed by Congress often reflect the Jewish-Christian influence of the American heritage. The Christian right influences American politics. It is general knowledge that the Christian right was a strong factor in the 1980 presidential elections and that they led Ronald Regan to the White House. The Republican platform at the 1996 Convention, in San Diego, California reflected the values of the Christian right.[9]

Indeed, the election of George Bush, Jr. in 1999 and his reelecting in 2004 were both advanced by Christian conservatives.

5. To Understand Culture

Culture is about how people organise themselves into societies according to their values. People who share the same values belong to the same culture. People speak of a "football culture", that is, people who order or plan their lives around the values of football. For them football is the overarching symbol of life or the fulness of life. They talk and think about the values associated with football. Each culture produces what it likes, or what is called artifacts. It may be a certain type of drum, drawings on clay pots, a certain type of dance or musical instruments. For example, the drum is very particular to Africans. In almost all traditional African music the tom-tom beat of the drum can be heard. Africans dance to the drum, but they also celebrate God with the drum. The drum defines and distinguishes African culture.

Culture lies deep in people's life or values. Look at Africans who have joined Christianity or Islam. Their cultural values influence the way they worship in these new religions. Think of African Christians: no matter how beautiful the organ music may be, it is the tom-tom beat of the drum played to Christian hymns that speaks to their souls. Missionaries failed to suppress the drum and other African values which they condemned as non-Christian. Descendants of Africa in the Americas did not forget the drum in the new world. In American colonies, the Maryland legislature by law prohibited the use of drums for any kind of festivity because drums reminded enslaved Africans of their African heritage and that made them stubborn. To improvise for the drum, enslaved Africans started thumbing and hand clamping that they still do today in Black worship.[10] Whites in the Americas and missionaries in Africa insisted on the people giving up their African values, names, and practises in order to become Christian, which actually meant to become Europeanised. African culture was considered the work of the devil and his evil practises.[11] True religion was Christianity and the Western culture in which it was dressed. That Europeans failed, is demonstrated by the persistence of African cultural practises in African society today in both Africa and mainline America. In Africa, it is at critical times that African cultural practises dominant. Look at what happens when a Christian dies in Africa. In most places a vigil commences and it goes on until the day of the burial. During the vigil mourners and sympathisers sing Christian hymns to African tunes and style which often include the song leader throwing into the hymn words expressing his or her personal feelings. During the funeral service itself though, when the priest or pastor is present, they sing the same hymns to Western tunes and not African traditional singing style. For to sing the hymns to traditional tunes and manner would be considered non-Christian by the priest or minister, who often tend to take Western styles as Christian styles. Then there are traditional funeral rituals of mourning which the family does in private, that is, out of sight of the clergy and other church leaders. It has taken a long time for Christians in Africa to accept the fact that people cannot be separated from their culture. Culture defines who people are, their identity, where and to whom they belong.

It is not only in Christianity that Africans have brought their culture to reshape and redefine the new religion. African Islam has some practises that reflect African culture. The early Muslims in Africa were mostly traders. They did not insist on Africans giving up their cultural values and practises to become Muslims. Of course, early Muslim did not bring trade and Islam alone, but also Arab culture. In a way, the Islamisation of Africa was in fact Arabisation of the continent. African converts did not only become Muslims, but also African Arabs. They developed interest in Arab culture, dress, and food. Some even learned Arabic leaving their African languages such as some of the tribes of northern Sudan who are thoroughly Arabised in religion, language, and culture. In East Africa too, Arab culture was seen in dress as well with men wearing flowing gowns and a fez and women covering their heads. Perhaps the most significant was the development of Swahili, a language with sixty percent Arabic words and forty percent deriving from African languages. The current attempts in Islam by the Wahhabi to purify Islam in Africa, its teachings and practise, will only further the Arabasation of African Muslims for purification of Islam will mean getting rid of African cultural practises in African Islam. The Wahhabi attempts to purify African Islam will fail as Christianity has failed to Europeanise African Christianity, or as mainline America has had to accept Black music among its youth.

Culture runs deep in society. It is in people's hearts because culture concerns what people care about the most. Culture is a guide to what makes sense, or what is meaningful in life. Religion is about values and meaning in life and as it has been shown above, religion is woven in the very fabric of culture. Religion is the thread that makes culture hung together as a tapestry of values. Therefore, the study of religion enables one to understand people's culture at the deepest level. This is true in most societies, such as in Africa where religion is a way of life and there is no separation between religion and culture holy and unholy things. Moreover, all religions are born in culture and they bear the marks and characteristics of their cultures. This is why a student of religion is in a better position to have a much richer knowledge and respect of other people's culture.

6. To understand Morals

The question that concerns most individuals and societies is how one should live for life to be meaningful. The question assumes there is a certain way of life, a standard, or a set of values proper to living in the world. Morals are about the standard, or the values proper to life together. Morals are about those values that protect life, or individuals and bind people together. Morality is about human values that separate and distinguish people from animals. That is why sometimes Africans will refer to someone as "an animal", meaning that the individual does not behave or live as one with values that fit human life. Usually, Africans will call someone "an animal" when the individual does not have compassion, kindness, respect for others, or when the individual is unfriendly. These are values or virtues that are considered very important for living together in African culture and society. These are the virtues which Malawians call *umunthu*, or humanness. Anyone who does not have these qualities of life is called *chinyama*, "an animal".[12]

When these qualities are examined, one finds that they are rooted in religion because religion is about highest values. It is stated above that culture is about how people organise themselves and according to shared values. Most often those values have their roots in religion. Not only do values develop from religion, but religion also holds up the high values. This is to argue that religion is the foundation of the qualities of the values, the norms, or standard for shared life. To study religion is to dig deep into the foundation of morals in order to gain deeper knowledge, or to learn what brings and holds people together.

To say that morals are rooted in religion does not imply that without religion there would be no values, or to imply that those who do not have religion, atheists, cannot be moral people. Neither is it to claim that religion is nothing but morality. No! Morality by itself, or mere morality is about doing that which is lawful, right, or proper to do, and it is a duty. As such, morality is about people; it is self-interested. That is to say, people do moral things for themselves, to live in harmony, for instance. The morality we are talking about here, the morality that is rooted in religion, is simply not about people, it is a way for people to connect themselves with the holy or ultimate reality. Religious morals are not about "being good", but a way for people to reach beyond themselves to something greater, something higher than themselves. The morality of atheists is about human beings and nothing beyond. Atheists do good things to be good people. Their morality is self-interested; there is no reaching beyond themselves. This reaching beyond self, is understood as deliverance or redemption in the religions that focus on salvation: Christianity, Judaism, Hinduism, Islam, Jainism, among others. In religions without salvation, such as African religions, morality is still a way of connecting with the ideals of the ancestors sanctioned by divinity blessed.

7. For Practical Purposes

Religion is the most practical of all disciplines of study. It does not matter what one wants to do in life, studying religion will be beneficial to the student. Here we have seen that historians, anthropologists, politicians, ethicists all can use religious knowledge to deepen their understanding of their field. Talking about politics, think much a politician would need to be aware of the religious sensitivities of people in a religiously pluralistic society, whether the politician is in India, east or west Africa, London, or in New York City. The aides and speech writers of politician, journalists, advertisers, or artists all have to be aware of religious sensitivities of their people. There are products that would offend some religious communities; just as there is art that would violate the religious beliefs of others. For instance, what would it benefit an artist to make artistic pieces in a community whose religion prohibits images such as Judaism or Islam? In the recent past Muslims were angered by depictions of Prophet Muhammad in Western newspapers that showed him wearing a turban with missals on his head. As advertisers and artists, diplomats would do well to study religion for they would avoid saying or doing something that would be religiously offensive to their host country.

That economics and religion go hand in hand was demonstrated by Max Weber in *Protestantism and the Spirit of Capitalism*. It was the virtue or work ethic of Protestants—constant and hard work—(the Protestant or Puritan work ethic) that spearheaded the rise of capitalism. The Protestant ethic, makes work an obligation, a duty that one has to society, and for which God rewards or blesses individuals. Work produces more money or capital and wealth. Today, the study of religion is important too, to those working in the financial world of this ever-shrinking global economy. A person working for a major international or regional investment banking or financial institution, will start off his or career in one country or region, and end up going to several places before retirement. There used to be a time when people in financial world would work at the same place, the headquarters until retirement. Today one starts work in New York, the company next sends him or her to London, Tokyo, and to Dubai, the new financial capital of the world, and tomorrow to South Africa. Young men and women working for nonprofit international organsations and business conglomerates, start their careers at one place and they go to places they never thought of. They go from Dakar in Sengal to Nairobi, Kenya. Africans are known to study and work in Arab Emirates, China, and India. In all these places, taking a course in the study of religions would prepare the individual to understand, or at least appreciate the values of the locals, and that would be good for business. The Chair of my department once publicised the courses of the department with words that summarise why one should study religion: "No educated person can afford not to study religion".

CONDITIONS FOR STUDYING RELIGION

Just as there are instructions for doing or learning something, here are the necessary conditions, or instructions for being a good student in religious studies:

1. Tolerance

Studying religion helps one become sympathetic and appreciative of others, and thereby become a world citizen. Therefore, a student of religion makes tolerance a guiding principle, or a virtue. Tolerance in religious studies does not mean "anything goes". On the contrary, tolerance means reserving judgement, not allowing oneself to say some uncritical and superficial things against the religion of others. Often uninformed, uncritical, and superficial comments arise out of little or lack of knowledge of other people's religion. A student of religion needs to develop a disciplined mind and tongue, to watch what he or she says about religion of others.

2. Openness

We note then that religious studies help students become open-minded people, nonjudgemental, and without prejudice. Open-mindedness removes arrogance and pride that stand in the way of relationships. Open-mindedness provides possibilities for "understanding" individuals and communities leading to establishing unity among people. Understanding is here in quotes because one can never fully understand the other; we understand only in part, so our knowledge of others is usually partial.

3. Truth

Knowledge is a quest for truth. This is necessarily true in religious studies where the focus and primary intention is to learn the truth about various religions. One may wonder that given all the religions in the world, which is the true one? Some, without any hesitation will say their own is true religion and they will give many reasons to prove the point. Indeed truth is one; there are not many truths and neither is truth relative? All religions are true in the sense that they are ways of going beyond self, or what in religion is called transcendence. Religion in its purest form is never about individuals or communities, as one earlier French sociologist, Emil Durkheim (1858–1917) claimed.[13] Religion is about a transcendent power, a power beyond individuals and communities. The focus of inquiry in religious studies is about this transcendent power or reality: how it is approached and how individuals and common life are influenced by it.

4. **Critical reading**

Studying religion is different from mathematics or science where one uses formulas to solve a problem. There are theories in religious studies for sure, but they do not lead to understanding religious behaviour or practise. It is critical reading of a text, or critical analysis of a text or a social context, a practise that is needed in religious studies. A student of religion must not only be able to read critically and evaluate the evidence, but must also carefully observe and weigh the evidence, placing patterns of behaviour side by side for coherence to discern meaning. Critical reading and analysis call for that type of reading that asks what, who, why, and where? Critical reading aims at grasping what is said, "the said", the question, the arguement in a text, or in a religious narrative or discourse. Without critical reading skills a text can easily be misunderstood or misinterpreted. Such mistakes happen far too many times by both insiders and outsiders of a religion who use scriptures to advance, defend, or discredit a particular point of view.

5. **Critical thinking**

Critical thinking is essential in religious studies. Critical thinking is disciplined thinking, or that activity of the mind towards a reflection that focuses ordering and analysing ideas. Critical thinking does not mean making negative remarks, or comments on ideas about others. It is not negative criticism, but evaluating ideas. Critical thinking is the kind of thinking—about any subject, content, or do-main—that improves itself through disciplined analysis and assessment. Analysis requires knowledge of the elements of thought; assessment requires knowledge of standards for thought. Critical thinking involves: gathering and assessing information; raising vital questions and problems within the text, formulating them clearly and precisely to see how they hang together; and looking for significance. This is to say that critical thinking does not only look for patterns of behaviour or practise, but seeks to understand the significance of those patterns and practises.

6. **Critical learning**

Critical reading and thinking lead to critical learning. A student of religion must develop the habit of being precise, or using correctly religious terms of a particular religious tradition. The student of religion must pay special attention to religious terms because they are important and meaningful to the people in the particular tradition. Care must be taken not to lose or misuse religious terms lest the student offends individuals of a particular religion. A student of religion must strive to learn as correctly as possibly the values, terms, the symbols, and the signs of a particular religion.

THE STUDY OF RELIGION

The study of religion is about learning different religions, their beliefs and practises. There are many religions in the world so only a few are selected to attempt to understand them. Religion is studied through various ways: by observing and describing them, by comparing their beliefs and practises, examining their function in society, or by merely interpreting their world views. A student of religion learns about other religions without any personal commitment or faith interest in the religion. The academic study of religion is not to convert individuals, neither is religious study a form of religious instruction. A student of religion does not get into a course to seek ideas or practises to use in his or her faith, or to develop faith. One's faith may indeed be enriched by learning about others religious belief practises, but that is not the focus of the study of religion. Religious studies are a way of increasing one's knowledge and an attempt to understand people of different faiths and how they live according to their faith. To know only one religion, one's own, is good, but to know more than one's own is to know more about the world. One of the early scholars of the study of religion, Max Müller (1823–1900), often said, "He who knows one, knows none".[14] To study other religions is to see oneself as part of larger human family and to recognise the humanity of others in the family.

The emphasis in religious studies is on the words *"attempt to understand"*. These are very important words to remember always in studying religion because it is not possible for an outsider to fully understand other people's religion. As pointed out above, we understand only in part. People and their religions are not so opaque as to fully understand them. Humans and their beliefs and practises are very complex for an analysis of any kind to be fully known. Non-Western people know very well how too often they have been misunderstood and misjudged by some "sympathetic" foreigners, especially Western scholars, missionaries, and government officials who took time to learn about non-Western ways of life. Some Westerners learned the languages, ate local food, enjoyed hospitality in the villages of their research, yet they came up with shocking interpretations of ways of life of their subjects of inquiry. Edward Evan Evans-Pritchard (1902–1973), an anthropologist who did field research among the Nuer in Sudan criticised missionary anthropology, rejecting its claim to accuracy even though missionaries spent a long time among the locals and learned their language. Evans-Pritchard argued:

> It is true that some missionaries were well-educated men and had learned to speak native languages with fluency, but speaking a language fluently is very different from understanding it, as I have often observed in converse between Europeans and Africans and Arabs. . . . For someone who has not made an intensive study of native institutions, habits and customs in the native's own milieu (that is, well away from administrative, missionary, and trading post) at best there can emerge a sort of middle dialect in which it is possible to communicate about matters of common experience and interest.[15]

Gross misrepresentations were made by Western travellers who spent very brief time among the locals. Take, for instance, the point Samuel Baker (1821–1893) made to Ethnological Society of London in 1866, about the people of Sudan and the Nile valley: "Without any exception, they are without a belief in a Supreme Being, neither have they any form of worship nor idolatry; nor is darkness of their minds enlightened by even a ray of superstition. This mind is as stagnant as the morass which forms its puny world".[16] Are there really people without religion anywhere in the world?

Such gross misrepresentation should make any student of religion very careful and self-conscious about claiming to understand other people's religion. This is why religious studies can at best, only claim to be an *appreciation* of what others believe and how they live according to their belief system. Religious studies help to remove the vail of ignorance that sometimes make people arrogant, proud, or believe in the superiority of their beliefs or themselves. A student of religious studies learns to be respectful and nonjudgemental about other people's religions to avoid making the mistakes of the scholars who spend two weeks or two months in an African or an Asian village, after which they became experts on Africa or Asia and write many books full of wrong things about African or Asian spirituality.

The point here is not that only those of a particular religion should write about their religion. For instance, that only Africans should write about African ways of life. It is good for those inside the religion to write about their religion, to give an insider's perceptive that is often not available to the most sympathetic student of religion. There is indeed no denying the fact that insiders have an advantage of understanding the gestures, signs, and the nuances of their group or people. Insiders can and do throw some light on the unspoken language, the "coded language", or the signs that outsiders often fail to notice, see, appreciate, or understand.[17] An outsider may sometimes notice the coded language, the gesture or sign, but fail to interpret, and instead interpret it completely wrong. For example, many missionaries learn and speak African languages fluently and about African ways of life, but they fail to understand the place of ancestors in the minds of Africans. Even when foreigners grasp what ancestors mean to Africans, they do not feel the sentiments that make Africans cherish their long-gone relatives. So, it remains to the African to write about Africans to give the insider's view, feelings, and meaning of ancestors.

Some scholars within religious studies and other related fields such as anthropology and sociology, argue that the insider's view is often not deep enough and sometimes not critical at all. They claim that there are so many things that the insider takes for granted in his or her religion or everyday life. There are so many things that the insider does without questioning why they are done or believed. In the case of African ways of life, for example, these may be some practises that Africans do, or beliefs that were handed down from ancestors. So, scholars against the insider view say the insider has unexamined beliefs and practises. Therefore, the accuracy of the insiders' report is subject to question, or at least suspicion because the insider leaves so many things untouched or unanswered. These scholars of religion claim that the knowledge of the locals, or the insiders is only partial and sometimes biased knowledge. To arrive at knowledge that is free of bias, not one sided, one needs to be objective, which means to be aware of, and not to be involved in the subject of one's inquiry.

According to this view, the true report about a particular group of people would be that of an outsider because he or she questions why people believe what they believe and do what they practise. Indeed, outsiders are often curious, sometimes too curious to know, so they ask many questions, some of them irrelevant and certainly stupid, but as we know, insiders do not always give outsiders deeper answers. Insiders' answers are often just enough to give the outsider some sense of a belief or a practise. Only in very few instances do insiders give outsiders deeper knowledge of their beliefs and practises.

The question of scientific objectivity in research became popular with the works of Max Weber (1864–1920), especially his *Methodology of the Social Sciences*.[18] He said objectivity demands a rejection of value judgements, therefore the need to be ethically neutral. Ethical neutrality makes research results universal in the sense that the findings or propositions can be tested by others and yield the same results. This is not possible without objectivity and avoidance of value judgements in scientific research. In *Theories in the Study of African Religion,* I have argued against objectivity because as humans, it is impossible not to be involved, in one way or another, with what we are studying.

> However, to what extent can the observer bracket personal existential and historical experience? If we take into account the inseparability of subject-world, is it possible to have a slate-clean mind to conduct a research without the mind affecting interpretation? Further, one wonders how far back can reduction really go before the investigator begins to treat psychology as fact and speculation as objectivity.[19]

My point is simply this: no person has a mind that is like a clean slate waiting to be written upon. We all come to a subject matter with some knowledge which influences the way we deal with, or interpret what we see or hear. What is needed when learning about other religions is an open mind and a realisation that one will always be an outsider and as such it will not be possible to know everything about the religion being explored, unless one joins that religion.

To conclude, religious studies are academic or intellectual approaches to religion. These approaches are about broadening one's knowledge of how people of various religions understand the world and their place in it. Religious studies are not about faith commitment or faith development. In fact, religious studies have nothing to do with faith matters or faith itself, but what people or particular religions consider ultimate meaning and reality, and how the ultimate organises their lives. Learning religion from this angle will not make one religious or have faith. The aim of religious studies is to help one to develop an appreciation of how other people understand the world, believe, and live in it. Religious studies teach students how to live as good citizens in our multi-religious or pluralistic world.

GLOSSARY

Cosmology	How one sees and interprets the world. A world view
Ethics	A branch of philosophy that deals with how people ought to live or conduct themselves in life. The rules of conduct.
Homage	Deep respect showing reverence and humbleness before someone or something of greater authority. In religion homage is respect and honour to God
Imam	A local clergy person, religious leader in Islam who conducts worship and prayers.
Rabbi	A religious leader, a clergy person in Judaism.
Revelation	A term about seeing or hearing something hidden. In religion revelation is about divine appearance, God's self disclosure, self-presentation, or showing in word, deed, or any other manifestation.
Ritual	An act with deep meaning, or representing something beyond itself. In religion it is an act of piety or holiness.
Sacred	Something set apart out of respect, reverence, or fear. Something holy.
Sacrifice	An act of giving oneself to God by offering God something as a form of giving thanks or honour to God.
Scripture	Holy writings of various religions.
Semitic	Something of, or about the people of Middle East. Both Arabs and Jews are Semites.
Spirituality	From the Latin word *spiritus*. Something about and beyond human physical being. A religious sense or a way an individual or a group of people connects to a power greater than themselves.
Theology	Talking about God. God talk.
Tradition	Something that is passed on or handed down because of its value or importance.
Transcendence	A theological word meaning beyond oneself and the world. God is said to be transcendent.
Wahhabi	An Islamic ultraconservative reform movement of Saudi Arabian origin stated in the eighteen century by Muhammad Ibn Abdul al-Wahhab (1703–1791). Al-Wahhab taught complete monotheism, or that the oneness of God should not be comprised in any way. Therefore, the Wahhabi seek to purify Islam by removing cultural elements and any innovations in the teaching and practise of Islam.

NOTES

1. Harvey Sindima, *Drums of Redemption: An Introduction to African Christianity* (Westport, NY: Greenwood Press, 1995), 56.

2. *Ibid*, 6.

3. *Ibid.*, 23–24.

4. Harvey Sindima, *Religious and Political Ethics in Africa: A Moral Inquiry*: Westport, NY: Greenwood Press, 1998), 145, 153, 157.

5. Harvey Sindima, *The Legacy of Scottish Missionaries in Malawi* (Lewiston, New York: Edwin Mellen Press, 1990), 107–111.

6. Simon Maimela, "The Concept of Israel", 15, 2 *Africa Theological Journal* (1986).

7. Maimela, "Theology and Politics in South Africa", *Chicago Theological Seminary Register* (Spring 1979): 11.

8. Allan Boesak, "Wholeness Through Liberation", *Church and Society* (May–June): 36.

9. Harvey J. Sindima, *Religious and Political Ethics in Africa: A Moral Inquiry* (Westport, CT: Greenwood Press, 1998), xii.

10. See Albert J. Raboteu, *Slave Religion: The Invisible Institution in the Antebellum South* (New York, NY: Oxford University Press, 1980).

11. F. Eboussi Boulaga describes the missionary method for Europeanising African an "uprooting and Alienating Praxis". See his book, *Christianity Without Fetishes: An African Critique and Recapture of Christianity* (Maryknoll, New York: Orbis Books, 1984), 19–24.

12. I have written about *umunthu* in many places, in books and articles. One article will do. See Harvey Sindima, "Bondedness, *Moyo* and *Umunthu* as Elements of Achewa Spirituality, Organising Logic and Principle of Life", *Ultimate Reality and Meaning: Interdisciplinary Studies in the Philosophy of Understanding* 14, 1 (March, 1991).

13. Emil Durkheim, *Elements of Religion* (London: Allen & Unwin, 1964).

14. Max Müller, *Introduction to the Science of Religion* (London 1873), 12.

15. Samuel W. Baker, "The Races of the Nile Basin", *Transactions of the Ethnological Society of London*, n.s. 5 (1867): 231.

16. Harvey Sindima, *Theories of Religion in the Study of African Religions* (forthcoming), 215.

2
What is Religion

THE SEARCH FOR A DEFINITION

Scholars of religion are not in agreement concerning the definition of their discipline. The problem is not because there are many religions in the world, but that religions are different in what they are in themselves, their character, and what they teach. For example, while many religions have a supreme being or a divinity, there is no deity in Buddhism. Some religions preach salvation or liberation in different forms: for Buddhism it is *nirvana*, or liberation, release, or refuge. *Nirvana* is release from lust, hate, or things that are between one's life and the true self; it is a release from all the forces upon one's life and who one really is. Other religions of salvation—Christianity, Hinduism, Islam, and Judaism—all understand salvation differently. Take, for example, the difference between Christianity and Hinduism. While for both religions salvation means being with God eternally, they differ on what form that will be. For Christianity it will be with a new body, a body raised from the dead as was the body of Jesus, the founder of the religion. For Hinduism it is through cycles of rebirth or incarnation. Christianity, Islam, and Judaism teach that time moves in a straight line towards the end when the one God in whom they believe will come to judge and reward each individual, but Hinduism says there is no end time; time is cyclical

On the other hand there is a set of different religions that might be called religions of structure whose focus is on sanctification or celebration of life as opposed to the idea of salvation. This does not mean that the religions of salvation do not sanctify life, rather that the mind of the faithful in these religions is on being saved, earning eternal life. Therefore, this earthly life is considered unimportant since the *real* life is yet to come. This is the life that will be given as a reward to the faithful. So the faithful in these religions long for the *real* life that will be given on the day of judgement, when the world will end. Such religions, Christianity and Islam among them, teach that the world will end. In contrast, religions of structure stress celebrating this life, seeing it as the beginning of a life that will never end, but not as a reward for faithfulness. In religions of structure there is no salvation or judgement day. "Religions of structure", says Evan Zuesse, "find fulfillment precisely in the norms and eternal relationships which structure all process and change in the world. . . . [religions of structure] rejoice in the sanctification of every day life and finds eternity in the midst of change".[1] In religions of structure there is no place that is not filled with life or spirit(s); no every day aspect of life that is not holy. The holy is infused in everything and every space in a seamless fabric of life which will never end. Time is cyclical, like the circle of the seasons: dry season following the rainy season, planting time and time for harvest; each year following the same order and back again the next year. Time is not moving towards the end. Religions of structure, life-affirming religions, include the religions of Africa, the original people in the Americas (north and south America), and the original people of Australia.

These religions are also different from the Semitic religions in their image of divinity. In Islam and Judaism God is one. They are *monotheistic* religions. Christianity too, is monotheistic for it teaches that God is *one being*, or a single entity with three "persons": Father, Son, and Holy Spirit. This doctrine, called the trinity, maintains that although there are three centres of consciousness, with individual identities, God is one because these "persons" are united in their works and will. Among the people of Africa, the natives of Australia, and of North and South America God is one with attendants, who are either themselves deities or spirits. Western scholars of religion, in spite of monotheism of Christianity, call the religions structure *polytheistic*, belief in many gods. Some scholars go further, calling religions of structure *pantheistic*, which is a belief that sees God in every thing.

Many African scholars have argued vigorously against referring to religions of structure as polytheistic. For example, Bolaji Idowu says the Yoruba (the majority of whom are in Nigeria) have what he calls "primitive monotheism" that the supreme deity is the "one essential factor which the life and belief of the Yoruba cohere and have sustenance".[2] In the book, *Olódùmarè: God in Yoruba Belief*, Idowu describes the creator as a supreme sovereign ruler, priest-king, beyond comparison, all-wise, all-knowing, all-seeing, ultimate controller of everything. He writes, "The name Olódùmaré has always carried with it the idea of One with whom man may enter into covenant or communion in any place and at any time, one who is supreme, superlatively great, incomparable, unsurpassable in majesty, excellent in attributes, stable, unchanging, constant, reliable".[3] Idowu insists on calling African religion monotheistic: "I conclude that the religion [Yoruba] can only be adequately described as monotheistic. I modify this 'monotheism' by the adjective 'diffused,' because here we have a monotheism in which there exist other powers which derive from Deity such being and authority that they can be treated, for practical purposes, almost as ends in themselves".[4] He maintains that this diffused monotheism is the bedrock of the structure and elements of African traditional religion. He discusses the many attributes and status of Olódùmaré (chapters five and six), his ministers and other lesser divinities who are autonomous, each with a local name, language, and a priesthood and a set of rituals (chapters seven through ten). Divinities are functionaries, ministers in the divine government for the ordering of nature and service to Olódùmaré. Although divinities are independent, they are united in Olódùmaré, the Supreme Being, from whom they derive. Below the divinities are intermediaries, spirits, and ancestors.

These examples show how difficult it is to have a definition that encompasses all religions. It is difficult to have a definition that describes, or explains the various religions because a definition must be precise in describing and explaining an appearance, an event, an act, a practise, or a thought. While a definition must be precise, it should not be too exact that other characteristics or behaviours of the event, act, or practise are lost. This is more true and needed in religion. Let us say one defines religion as belief in God. With that definition Buddhism is not a religion because there is no God in Buddhism. Well, how about defining religion based on what it does, its usefulness as Robertson Smith who says religion is "for the preservation and welfare of society"[5], or Emile Durkheim who defines religion as "a unified set of beliefs and practises relative to sacred things, that is to say, things set apart and forbidden . . . beliefs and practises which unite one single moral community called church, all those who adhere to them".[6] In their definition Smith and Durkheim make religion simply an organisation, or "a moral community" as Durkheim himself puts it. It was pointed out in chapter one that morality alone does not make for religion. Durkheim's understanding of religion is functional; it focuses on the function, what religion does, or its use for humans. Here is another functional definition by Milton Yinger, a sociologist, who writes, "Religion can be defined as beliefs and practises by means of which a group of people struggles with ultimate problems of human life". Yinger's definition could apply to any ideology, social or political, since the definition avoids any mention of the holy, supreme being, or transcendent and it focuses on the struggle to cope with the problems of life. It is true that religion helps people to struggle to deal with the problems of life, but people do so with faith, or thinking and believing in a power beyond themselves. Yinger's definition ignores that fact. The definition could fit magic because it is a way to deal with the struggles of life albeit that magic is performed for individual needs.

The reader must now be wondering whether a precise and all-inclusive definition is possible. The problem in defining religion is made much more difficult by the fact that definitions are influenced by the theory behind them. Durkheim's definition was obviously influenced by Robertson Smith who wrote before him. Durkheim as Smith, focuses on society, accordingly, his definition is based on sociological theory. Durkheim is known as the pioneer of sociology. The first definition that religion is belief in God, is a theological definition. Here is another definition influenced by theological thinking: "Religion is that which grows out of, and gives expression to, experience of the holy in its various aspects", says Rudolf Otto, a German theologian of the early twentieth century. In his book, *The Idea of the Holy*, Otto emphasises that the heart of all religion is the concept of the holy.[7] According to Otto, the holy is the core of religion: "There is no religion in which it does not live as the innermost core; and without it no religion would be worth the name", asserts Otto. "Holy" for Otto means something above moral and above reason; or preethical and nonrational. That is why he characterises the holy as the "Wholly Other", which means something completely different from anything else we consider moral or rational. This "Wholly Other" is *numinous* (from the Latin word for spirit, *numen*). An encounter with the numinous, which is mysterious, causes one to tremble or shudder (Otto uses the Lain word *tremendum*) giving one the experience of dread, awe, urgency, and majesty. Some scholars have described this dread as the sense of feeling something creepy or eerie. While the encounter with mysterious causes dread, it also causes fascination that draws people.

This is the sense of the holy that Otto is talking about. One would think that Otto's holy would cover Buddhism; it does not, and neither does it include religions of salvation where the holy is infused with everything and everywhere. The problem with Otto's definition is that it makes a sharp distinction between individuals and the object of holiness. Such a distinction is unacceptable in Buddhism whose teaching is to overcome duality of mind and body. Bliss in Buddhism is to abolish the mind-body duality through enlightenment.

Realising the problem of defining religion, Clifford Geertz, a cultural anthropologist, has suggested an inclusive definition which says: "Religion is (1) a system of symbols which acts (2) establish powerful, pervasive, and long-lasting moods in [people] by (3) formulating conceptions of a general order of existence and (4) clothing these conceptions with an aura of factuality that the moods and motivations seem uniquely realistic".[8] Note the absence of the holy which for most people is the heart of religion.

William P. Alston, a philosopher, has seen that it is difficult and almost impossible to give a precise definition of religion and has therefore suggested a list of things that make for religion.

1. Belief in supernatural beings (god).
2. A distinction between sacred and profane.
3. Ritual acts focused on sacred objects.
4. A moral code believed to be sanctioned by the gods.
5. Characteristically religious feelings (awe, sense of mystery, sense of guilt, adoration), which tend to be aroused in the presence of sacred objects and during the practise of ritual, and which are connected in idea with the gods.
6. Prayer and other forms of communication with gods.
7. A worldview, or a general picture of the world as a whole and the place of the individual therein. This picture contains some specification of an overall purpose or point of the world and an indication of how the individual fits into it.
8. A more or less total organisation of one's life based on the worldview.
9. A social group bound together by the above.[9]

There is another problem and this lies in the meaning of the word religion itself and what it includes. The word religion is from Latin *religio*. The original meaning and usage of *religio* was a careful performance of ritual responsibilities. Later, *religio* was used in Latin Christianity to distinguish true from false worship. By the Middle Ages, *religio* stopped being used and in its place came "the religious" and it was to distinguish the laity from those who had entered a monastery, the priesthood and other religious orders. After the medieval period, religion was used mostly to refer to the major Semitic religions and Hinduism and other faiths were dismissed as superstitions. It was the beginning of the academic study in the nineteenth century that included other beliefs and practises as religion. It is a known fact that nineteenth century English anthropologists studied other religions to prove that other religions were just like Christianity. In other words, Christianity was not superior.

In as much as nineteenth century English anthropologists tried to change the minds of their people to begin to think of other people's beliefs as religion they did not succeed. This was in part because some of the anthropologists themselves did not really believe that beliefs and practises of non-Europeans were religions on the same level as Christianity and Judaism although the anthropologists themselves were either agnostics, or simply did not care about religion. Long before the English anthropologists, the president of Portugal, Charles de Brosses (1709–1777) used the term *fetico* (charm) in his theory of religion to refer to the practise of endowing natural objects, such as trees, or some inanimate things with divine power. In 1760 he published a book with the title *Du culte des dieus fétiches ou Paralléle de l'ancienne religion de l'Egypte avec la religion actuelle de Nigritie* (The Cult of the Fetish Deities, or the Resemblance of the Ancient Egyptian Religion with the Religion of the Negro at Present). President de Brosses believed fetishism was the religion of West Africa because this was where Portuguese sailors had first seen the practise of *fetico*. As term fetishism became less used, magic and mystical became standard words for describing African beliefs and practises. The one who started on the term magic was Edward Tylor (1832–1917), who understood religion as "belief in Spiritual Beings".[10] Tylor maintained there were three ways of looking at the world: through science, magic, and religion. The first stage, magic, was a stage for whom he called people of the lower races, meaning non-Europeans. It was James Frazer (1854–1951) who made popular Tylor's idea of magic as the religion of non-Europeans. Frazer used Tylor's religion-magic separation to argue that religion is always preceded by magic.[11]

Evans-Pritchard joined the religion-magic debate in 1937 writing on the Azade in Sudan. He was the first anthropologist to write on the relation between religion and magic in Africa. Evans-Pritchard claims that among the Azande witchcraft permeates every aspect of society, their thinking and everyday life, forming a central part of their religious life. He claims a day does not pass without a discussion on witchcraft because all misfortunes, including death, are attributed to witchcraft, unless sorcery or moral infraction are involved. Evans-Pritchard declares that the concept of witchcraft "provides them [the Azande] with a natural philosophy by which the relation between men and unfortunate events are explained and a ready and stereotyped means of reacting to such events. Witchcraft beliefs also embrace a system of values which regulate human conduct".[12] Evans-Pritchard insists that witchcraft is not a reality for the Azande, but a theoretical paradigm of explanation. It is an inevitable conclusion from Zande description of witchcraft that it is not an objective reality. The physiological condition which is said to be the seat of witchcraft, and which I believe to be nothing more than food passing through the small intestine, is an objective condition, but the qualities they attribute to it and the rest of their beliefs about it are mystical. Witches, as Azande conceive them, cannot exist.[13]

What Evans-Pritchard's arguement comes down to, is that witchcraft for the Azande is a theory that explains why bad things happen to people. Evans-Pritchard further argues that since witchcraft explains all misfortunes, including death—things that concern people deeply—witchcraft is a branch of religion among the Azande.

Mary Douglas (1921–present) agrees with Evans-Pritchard that witchcraft is a branch of religion. She maintains that magic should be seen as a religious style.[14] However, it appears though that this "religious style" is only in, or unique to African religion and extended to religions of structure. This religious style has led many scholars to reduce African religion to magic or witchcraft thereby placing African religion lower than Christianity. Can religion be without some elements of magic? Some scholars have argued that what the priest or pastor does, can be compared to the work of a magician who casts a spell to compel the gods or spirits to do what he or she wants. On the other hand, a priest says a prayer and performs a ritual that may, or may not work depending on the will of the gods. Of course, the difference between the two is that the magician does not have a group of people, but a clientele, whereas the priest has a community, a congregation.

African life or religion has been a puzzle to non-African scholars of religion. The African world is difficult to understand because of its cosmology which gives rise to African beliefs and practises. Lucien Lévy-Bruhl (1857–1939), a French sociologist developed a theory that described the cosmology of non-Europeans. He called the theory mystical union. According to this theory, non-Westerners conceive their world as one unbroken circle where there is no subject-object separation, but also no separation between self and non-self, sacred and secular, natural and supernatural, because nature, people, and the unseen are inseparably involved in one another in a total community. Everything is mystical in non-European cultures, or as he put it, "The reality in which primitives move, is itself mystical. Not a being, not an object, not a natural phenomenon in their collective representations is what appears to us"[15] The result of this kind of worldview, is that the non-Western people have no principle of identity; nothing that tells them who they are by themselves. This mean, for example, that the African sees himself or herself only in relation to someone or something else. Identity is not from within, but outside.

Indeed, this is exactly what Father Placid Tempels (1906–1977), a Belgium missionary in Congo said, that the African

cannot conceive a man as an individual existing by himself, unrelated to the inanimate forces surrounding him. It is not sufficient to say he is a social being; he feels himself a vital force in actual intimate and permanent rapport with other forces—a vital force both influenced by and influencing them".[16]

This feeling of being surrounded by forces is the root of magic and part of African religion. According to Europeans then, African religion is nothing but magic.

Here the reader appreciates how difficult it is to define religion. Since the term religion is difficult to define, some scholars have suggested the term spirituality. William James (1842–1910), an American psychologist, may have been one of the early scholars to have used the term spirituality. He used spirituality to denote moving from a state of wrongness to a rightness by contacting some higher power. The same idea is noted in John Hick (1922–present), a contemporary philosopher of religion who understands spirituality to be a movement from a state of egotism, always thinking about oneself, to the state of caring, a selfless state. These two definitions show that spirituality is difficult to define. The first problem is in origin of the term. Spirituality derives from a Latin term, *spiritus. Spiritus* presupposes a sacred-profane separation; that there are unholy things, they are profane. This division of the world into holy and unholy, or sacred and profane, sacred or secular things, is not known in many places in the world where religion is life-affirming. In the African world, there is no place that is not filled with religion as John Mbiti (1931–) points out in his book, *African Philosophy and Religion.*

> Africans are notoriously religious . . . Religion permeates into all the departments of life so fully that it is not easy or possible always to isolate it. Wherever the African is, there is his religion: he carries it to the fields where he is sowing seeds or harvesting a new crop; he takes it with him to the beer party or to attend a funeral ceremony; and if he is educated, he takes religion with him to the examination room at school or in the university; if he is a politician, he takes it to the house of parliament.[17]

We hear the same comments from the first African anthropologist, Jomo Kenyatta (1893–1978), the first president of Kenya. Writing in *Facing Mt. Kenya,* he says the following very important comments on the role of religion in Gikuyu society:

> Gikuyu religion is integrated with the whole of Gikuyu life. Religion is a dramatis-ation of belief, and belief is a matter of social experience of the things that are most significant to human life. In Gikuyu life the earth is so visibly the mother of all things animate, and the generations are so closely linked by their common participation in the land, that agricultural ritual, and reverence for ancestral spirits, must naturally play the foremost part in religious ceremonial.[18]

For African scholars defining religion is difficult because there is no word for religion in African languages. Some African scholars prefer spirituality to religion, but that is because spirituality reminds Africans that the world is full of powers and beings beyond themselves. Spirituality seems to express an idea of a spiritual world. Africans who use spirituality ignore or they are not aware of the separation between holy and secular since all life is permeated with religion. Is the word religion then better? No, because it does not describe African life. Most of the words used for religion in African languages mean to worship, pay homage, to offer a sacrifice, or a libation. For example, in Chichewa (the national language of Malawi) the word *Chipembezo* is used to refer to religion. *Chipembezo* from the root *pembedza*, means to pacify or quieten (as in a putting child to bed), to worship, adore, or to pay homage. The question: "what is your religion?" is for the Achewa to ask "what is your worship?" The question does not make sense, because the word religion does not make sense in Chichewa.

Given these multitude of problems on defining religion, some scholars have decided that the word religion be replaced by faith tradition, or simply tradition. So we can speak of the Christian tradition, African tradition, Hindu tradition, Islamic tradition, Jewish tradition, and so forth. Instead of calling all these religions, they call them faith traditions, or faith communities. In this way all faith communities are included. The word tradition derives from the Latin *tradea* which means something handed down or passed on. While tradition seems a neutral term, it is not because most scholars in religion use the term to denote other religions other than Christianity, Islam and Judaism and Asian religions: Buddhism, Hinduism, Jainism, Shinto or Confucianism. In most books on religion, the religions of Africa, the first peoples of North and South America, and Australia always appears together, labeled as "traditional" or "indigenous religions", tucked away towards the end of the book, or sandwiched between Semitic and Asian religions. In addition, only a few pages are devoted to traditional religions. It is clear that the term tradition is reserved for non-Semitic and non-Asian religions, the "real religions".

Many African scholars like the term tradition, not because it puts African religion on the same level with non-African religions, but because it captures African life and belief system. However, they do not use the term alone as African tradition, rather, they prefer to use the term along with religion, as a kind of qualifier. African scholars speak of *African Traditional Religion* because to call it simply African tradition would mean it is unlike non-Semitic religions. Idowu was the first to put *traditional* before religion, so that the study of African religion could be called *Traditional African Religion*. Traditional is important to Idowu because it points to something that is current, living, and

> not only as a heritage from the past, but also that which people of today have made theirs by living it and practising it, that for them connects the past with the present and upon which they base the connection between now and eternity with that, spiritually, they hope for or fear.[19]

3
The Elements of Religion

There does not seem to be a definition for religion, at least a definition that would be inclusive enough in description or explanation for all religions. Since it seems impossible to define religion, may be the way to know the meaning of religion is to examine what makes religion. This is what Alston's nine characteristics of religion do. I want to attempt to cast the understanding of religion in the manner of Alston, but with a different order of ideas.

1. ULTIMATE REALITY AND MEANING

I usually teach beginners in the study of religion that religion is about the deepest human values beyond the grasp of reason. In other words, religion is not about specific data of consciousness, things people are aware of, but a matter of the value given to them. To say the data of religion is beyond reason, is not the same as to say it is irrational, but non-rational. Religion is not philosophy or science that it can be understood by the use of logical reasoning. The ways and rules of logic fail to grasp the datum of religion. That is why I say to upper-class students that religion is about ultimate reality and meaning. To both sets of students I teach that in religion people are about themselves, yet they feel held, led, or driven by some power beyond themselves, an ultimate reality that gives meaning to their life. In other words, religion is the organising and guiding principle of life. Religion orders life. Or, simply put, how people live, depends on what they believe as of the utmost value and importance in the world. In the following paragraphs I want to elaborate on the view of religion as about deepest human needs or ultimate reality and meaning. Upon what does this view of religion rest?

Most people will agree that religion is for humans and yet beyond humans. This "something beyond" transcends humans, a transcendent reality, so to speak, varies from one group of people to another, or from one religion to another, and it has different names. For some that reality may be something holy, a holy being, a god, but for others it may be a state of being or awareness such as enlightenment in Buddhism. It is to this reality that life is connected and derives its meaning. In other words, the transcendent reality tells people what is "real" or true value, thus meaningful in life. The transcendent reality becomes the "real" thing, the truth, to which life orients itself to fully realise itself. Accordingly, religion gets its identity and character from its transcendent reality, and people organise their life, and how they live in the world guided by the transcendent reality. The transcendent reality gives life, meaning, and purpose. The transcendent is both ultimate reality and meaning, the foundation of life. That is why people become what they believe, their ultimate reality. A Buddhist seeks enlightenment—the ultimate reality and meaning in Buddhism—and, therefore, plans his or her every day life to follow the path of enlightenment, the path of the Buddha. Likewise a Hindu calls himself or herself a devotee of a particular deity, the Lord Shiva, for example, and attempts to live according to Lord Shiva. Christians imitate Jesus in their life; Africans follow the tradition of the elders, as Jews keep the tradition of their elders found in the *Torah* (the law). In doing so, both Africans and Jews live the fullness of life as given by God.

2. THE SACRED

Ultimate reality is not an ideology, even though it has a transforming power and gives a perspective on life. Ultimate reality in religion is a holy power, or a holy state of being, that invites devotees to holy living. In February 2005, I visited Delhi, India, upon the invitation of His Holiness Baba Virsa Singh (d. 2007), founder Gobind Sadan Institute for Advanced Studies in Comparative Religion, to make a presentation at the Institute. During one of his sessions with his devotees and admirers, His Holiness talked to his devotees about ultimate reality. I want to paraphrase his views. He said: "An individual becomes his or her ultimate reality that to which one devotes one's life. A person of faith becomes holy and everything else around him or her becomes holy: his or her own shadow becomes holy, the shadow of the tree under which he or she stands becomes holy too, and even the tree itself becomes holy. Why? Because his or her life is transformed by the ultimate reality, to which his or her whole life is directed". It is this transcendent power, the transforming power of the ultimate reality that is the core of religion, and distinguishes religion from ideology. An ideology may indeed liberate individuals intellectually and physically, but what it will not do, is make individuals holy, that is, beyond themselves. The best humanistic ideology is about self-interest, individual or group, and not beyond human interest. Religion on the other hand, is always beyond humans even as it includes them. Religion is always beyond individuals and groups, it points them to a transcendent ultimate reality and meaning that is perceived and known by different names in various religions. There is no religion that does have the holy or the sacred understood in one way or the other, as the ultimate reality to which devotees are drawn.

3. MYTH

Every religion has an account of its origin and an account of the beginning of the world including the first human or humans. These accounts of the beginning are called sacred stories. They are stories about gods, the world, and people. The term for these sacred stories in religion is myth. Myth derives from the Greek *mythos*, which means story. Myth in religion does not mean fake stories, tall tales without any significance, or with vague reference to what might have happened at the beginning of time. Myth is a symbolic story outside time and space. These are stories about the origins of the universe and human beings. The White Buffalo Calf Woman myth of the Oglala Lakota of North America is an example of myth as a story outside time and space. The Oglala say *Ptehicalasan Win*, or the White Buffalo Calf Woman was the one who gave them the gift of the sacred pipe at a time when they were suffering because they had forgotten the importance of living in harmony. The woman appeared to two hunters and instructed them to make a special lodge in the village. The text day, she came bearing the people a gift of the sacred pipe, which is a religious symbol of the highest order among the Oglala as among many other groups of indigenous peoples of North America. Explaining the sacred pipe she said:

> The red stone bowl of the pipe was the earth. Carved in the stone was a buffalo calf, representing all the four-leggeds. The wooden stem symbolised all that grows on the earth. The twelve feathers stood for the Sported Eagle and all the winged creatures. She told them that when they prayed with the pipe, they would be praying with and for everything and everyone. The seven circles on the round stone, she said, were seven rites in which the pipe would be used. When she left, the woman said she would look back at the people in each of the four ages to come, and at the end she would return. As she walked away she turned into a buffalo, then into a white buffalo, and next a black buffalo, which bowed to each of the four directions and disappeared.[1]

Here is the history of the sacred pipe. Myth is a form of story that describes people's history, or what makes them who they are, and the nature of social organisation. Myth is a way of knowing, or a mode of knowledge about the foundations of life or creation. Myth carries with it a certain mystique, not mystery necessarily, but an aura, a depth difficult to penetrate, or something that arouses curiosity. That mystique can be seen in the founders of religion: Siddhartha Gautama (Buddhism), Moses (Judaism), Confucius (Confucianism), Lao Tzu (Daoism), Nataputta Vardhamana (Jainism), Jesus (Christianity), Muhammad (Islam), or Nanak (Sikhism). There is something, a mystique, about these holy people that arouses curiosity in us. How they lived, their lives of self-denial, the many hours they spent in prayer, and many other things that seem hidden from us, yet not completely.

Narrative

The most important part of myth is narrative or the telling of a story. Myth recounts stories of people, communities, or faith traditions in the distant past. Myths are told for their sacramental power that transforms their listeners so that the stories cease to be mere stories, but the stories of their own life. Listeners are transported back in time to the original event that established the ritual, the founding event. The story told at a Seder meal, the Jewish Passover, reminds Jews of the night they escaped from slavery in Egypt. The Christian Eucharist or Lord's Supper reminds Christians of the night on which Jesus was arrested and his subsequent trial and execution. Let us look at sections of these two events.

Seder. The setting for Jewish children to learn the history of their people begins with the story of the night of their escape from Egypt, the Passover meal. At the meal a Jewish boy, asks a set of ritual questions:

> Why does the night differ from the other nights? For on all other nights we eat either leavened or unleavened bread. Why on this night only unleavened bread?
>
> On all other nights we eat all kinds of herbs, why on this night only bitter herbs?
>
> On all other nights we need not dip our herbs even once, why on this night we must dip them twice?
>
> On all other nights we eat either sitting up or reclining, why on this night we all recline?

The people present at the Seder meal take turns in explaining each question, and in so doing all the questions are answered:

> The Passover sacrifice which our fathers used to eat at the time when the Holy Temple still stood—what was the reason for it? Because the Holy One blessed, blessed be he, passed over the houses of our fathers in Egypt.
>
> This *matzah* which we eat, what is the reason for it? Because the dough of our fathers had not yet leavened when the King over all kings, the Holy One, blessed be he, revealed himself to them and redeemed them.
>
> These bitter herbs we eat, what is the reason for them? Because the Egyptians made the lives of our forefathers bitter in Egypt.
>
> In every generation let each man look on himself as if he came forth out of Egypt.[2]

Compare this to the Christian ritual of the Eucharist or the Lord's Supper when a priest or a minister says the following words as the establishment of the holy meal (words based on 1 Corinthians 11:23–26; Luke 22:19–20):

> One the night on which our Lord was betrayed, he took bread. After he had blessed he broke it and saying, "take eat this is my body which is broken for you. Do this in remembrance of me". In the same manner, the cup after supper, saying, "This cup is a new covenant sealed in my blood, shed for the forgiveness of sins. Do this in remembrance of me".

Note how the two suppers both retell the story of the founding event of their respective rituals. Both stories are told not simply for their historical significance to the faith, but also to remind the faithful of their identity, or better what constitutes them and distinguishes them from any other people.

Myth as Structure of Reality

Myth describes the structure of ultimate reality and meaning that gives rise to beliefs and practises. A myth of giant Purusha, the first human (male) in the Rig-Veda, sacred poems and hymns in Hindu scripture, will help to illustrate this point that myth gives rise to beliefs and the structure of the social order. According to mythology in Hindu scriptures, the first man, Purusha, was sacrificed by the divinities. Here is what happened thereafter as recorded in Rig-Veda, 10.90: 11–14.

When they divided the man into how many parts did they apportion him? What do they call his mouth, his two arms, thighs, and feet?

His mouth became the Brahmin [priests]; his arms were made into Warrior, his thighs the People, and from his feet the servants were born.

The moon was born from his mind; from his eyes the sun was born. Indra [a warrior and storm divinity] and Agni [divinity of the sacrificial fire] came from his mouth, and from his vital breath the Wind was born.

From his navel the middle realm of space arose, from his head the sky evolved. From his two feet came the earth and the quarters of the sky from his ear. Thus they [gods] set the world in order.[3]

This is the foundation myth of the social organisation in Indian culture which is hierarchal in structure and runs as follows: priests, warriors, commoners, and servants. According to *Laws of Manu*, another scripture in Hinduism, *Purusha*, "the radiate one", each class has duties and responsibilities. Teaching, studying, offering sacrifices, generosity, and acceptance of gifts are prescribed for the priestly class. The duties and responsibilities of the warrior class are: protection of the people, generosity, patronage of sacrifice and study. Commerce and agriculture are for commoners, while "the Lord assigned only one activity to a servant: serving these (other) classes without resentment" (1,91).[4]

Cosmogony

Some myths are about the origins of the universe, the stories of the beginnings of the universe, the origins of life and the first humans—creation stories. Cosmogony gives an account of how the world came to be and its order. The word cosmogony is made up of two Greek words, *kosmos*, meaning world and the root of *gignestai* which means to be born. Cosmogony then is about the "birth" of the world. Most religions have a cosmogony as the foundation of their beliefs and practises. In order to truly know a religion, it is necessary to learn the cosmogony of the religion. Cosmogony answers the "big questions" of life such as: how did the world come into being? Why are we here? What is the meaning of life? Or, the questions whose answers adults would want to know, but silence children when they ask them: Where did God come from? Who created God? Cosmogony gives answers to these important and curiosity questions. Below are some cosmogonies. The first is a Shinto cosmogony that teaches the Japanese the beginnings of the five heavenly spirits or divinities and descent of the divinities *Izanagi* (*kami*-who-invites) and his spouse, *Izanami* (*kami*-who-is-invited) who begat the first humans.

Birth of the Kami

At the beginning of heaven and earth, there came into existence in the plan of Heaven and the Heavenly Centre Lord Kami, next the Kami of High Generative Force, and then the Kami of Divine Generative Force.

Next, when the earth was young, not yet solid, there developed something like reedshoots from which Male Kami of Excellent Reed Shoots and the Heavenly Eternal Standing Kami emerged.

The above five Kami are the heavenly Kami of special standing.

Then came into existence Earth Eternal Standing Kami, Kami of abundant Clouds Field, male and female Kami of Clay, male and female Kami of Post, male and female Kami of Great Door, Kami of complete surface and his spouse, Kami of awareness, *Izanagi* [*kami*-who-invites] and his spouse, *Izanami* (*kami*-who-is-invited).

The Oglala mythology as outlined by anthropologist and medical doctor James Walker goes as follows:

Before there was any other thing, or any time, *Inyan* was, and his spirit was *Wakan Tanka*. . . . *Inyan* was soft and shapeless but he had all powers. The powers were in his blood and his blood was blue. He longed for another that he might exercise his power upon it. There could be no other unless he could create it of which he must take from himself. If he did so he must impart his spirit to it and give it a portion of his blood. As much as of his blood would go from him, so much of his blood would go with it. . . . So he took from himself that he spread over and around himself in the shape of a great disk whose edge is where there is no beyond. He named the disk *Maka* and imparted to it a spirit which is *Maka-akan* (the Earth God).

To create *Maka* he took so much from himself that he opened all his veins and all his blood flowed from him and he shrunk and became hard and powerless. As his blood flowed it became waters and it is the waters. But the powers cannot abide in the waters so they separated themselves and became a being in the shape of a great blue dome whose edge is at but upon the edge of *Maka*. The powers are spirit and the blue dome, the sky, the Great Spirit *Skan*. *Inya, Maka* and the waters are the world and *Skan* is the sky above the world.[5]

In this mythology the story answers the great question of where did the earth come from? Myth gives the story of origins.

The *Qur'an*, Muslim's holy scriptures, has a very short creation of the first human from whom descended all people. From the Holy *Qur'an* (*Surah* 32:6–9) we read:

Such is He, the knower of all things, hidden and open, the Exalted and Merciful:
He who has made everything which He has created from the earth Most Good:
He began the creation of man with [nothing more] than clay.
And made his progeny from a quintessence of the nature of fluid despised;
But He fashioned him in due proportion, and breathed into him something of the
Spirit. And He gave you hearing and sight and feeling; little thanks do you give.

Some cosmogonies are very simple while others are complex. The Apache of
North America have a very simple cosmogony. The Apache say in the beginning
was only two divinities, Tepeu and Gucumatz (Feathered Serpent) who created the
world simply by thinking, for whatever they thought came into existence: they
thought Earth, and there it was; they thought mountains, and there were! So they
thought of everything else including trees and sky, but nothing they thought of could
praise them. They formed more advanced beings of clay, these too were a failure
for they fell apart when wet. Creatures made out of wood did not work either, they
just caused trouble on the earth. So the divinities decided to start all over again.
They sent a great flood to wipe out everything. In their second attempt, they had
help from Mountain Lion, Coyote, Parrot, and Crow when they fashioned four new
beings. These four beings carried out their functions well. These the ancestors of the
Quiché. In the beginning was only Tepeu and Gucumatz (Feathered Serpent).

Cosmogony gives the systematic fundamentals to understanding all the aspects
of thought and social organisation. Take, for example, the cosmology of the Dogon
in Mali. Their cosmology is not simply about the beginnings, a creation myth, a
cosmogony, it is a cosmology that informs social organisation and all industry and
activities in Dogon life: farming, weaving, pottery, and iron works. The work of
iron smiths and potters illustrate the connection between human activity and the
original divine activity as given by Dogon cosmology. Ogotemmêli, a Dogon elder,
explains to a European how the technique of weaving is part of Dogon cosmology.

Spinning is a day work and it is done by women. A woman spinning is the seventh
Nummo. The ginning-iron, like the smith's hammer, is a symbol of the celestial
granary, and thus is associated with seeds. The carding stick is like the rod with
which the smith sprinkled water on his fire to damp it down. The skin on which the
woman spins is the sun, for the first leather so used was that of the bellows of the
smithy, which had contained the solar fire. The twirling of the spindle is the
movement of the copper spiral which propels the sun, and is often represented by the
white lines decorating the middle of the spindle-wheel. The thread coming from the
woman's hand, which is wound round the spindle, is the gossamer down which the
world system came to earth from heaven. The spindle itself is the arrow which, with
the gossamer attached to it, pierced the vault of the sky. It is also the arrow buried
in the celestial granary.[6]

Cosmogony is about origins of life, but they are also the origin of evil and
suffering, or what theologians call the problem of theodocy. Some cosmogonies,
Dogon, for example, trace the problem of evil to creation itself, that it is imperfect,
or that the creator (or the creator's subordinates, other spiritual beings, or divinities)

is responsible. However, most cosmogonies trace the origin of evil and suffering to human beings because of doing something that separated them from their deity.

Cosmogony is about the origin of life, but also about the original state of people, the quest for immortality, and significant events in people's history. In Hebrew scriptures there is a myth concerning the loss of immortality. According to the myth, people were to live forever, but a snake made the first couple lose eternity.

> Now the serpent was the most cunning of all the wild animals that the Lord God had made. He said to the woman, "Did God really say, 'You can't eat from any tree in the garden'?" 2 The woman said to the serpent, "We may eat the fruit from the trees in the garden. 3 But about the fruit of the tree in the middle of the garden, God said, 'You must not eat it or touch it, or you will die'". 4 "No! You will not die", the serpent said to the woman. 5 "In fact, God knows that when you eat it your eyes will be opened and you will be like God, knowing good and evil". 6 Then the woman saw that the tree was good for food and delightful to look at, and that it was desirable for obtaining wisdom. So she took some of its fruit and ate; she also gave to her husband, with her, and he ate. 7 Then the eyes of both of them were opened, and they knew they were naked; so they sewed fig leaves together and made loincloths for themselves.

This story from Genesis 3:1–7 presents the snake as wiser than people, wise enough to mislead the first couple. The snake was considered clever among other Middle-East people, as the Sumerian *Epic of Gilgamesh* reveals. *Gilgamesh*, the hero of the epic engaged in a quest for immortality. The quest took him into the underworld where a god, Utnapishtim, told him a secret of life, "a plant in the river. Its thorns will prick your hands as a rose thorn pricks, but it will give you new life. He would find a plant of life that would make him live forever". *Gilgamesh* tied stones to his feet and dived into the river where "he saw the plant of rich rose colour and ambrosial shimmering in the water like a prism . . . he seized it, and it cut into his palm. He saw his blood flow in the water". Cutting the stones loose, *Gilgamesh* swam to the surface "calling out, I have it! I have it!" Out of the water, Urshanabi guided him to another shore and there they departed.

> Gilgamesh was alone again, but not with loneliness or the memory of death. He stopped to drink and rest beside a pool and soon undressed and let himself slip in the water quietly until he was refreshed, leaving the plant unguarded on the ground. A serpent had smelled its sweet fragrance and saw its chance to come from the water, and devoured the plant, shedding its skin as slough. When Gilgamesh came from the pool, his naked body glittering and refreshed, the plant was gone; the discarded skin of the serpent was all he saw. He sat Down on the ground, and wept.[7]

When one reads myths from one region interesting patterns about the region's sense of the ultimate and divine acts begin to emerge. An example drawn from the Middle-East will help in understanding regional spirituality. The Hebrew or Jewish and ancient Sumeria myth of the flood are very illuminating in this regard. The Hebrew account of the flood is given in Genesis 6:5–18.

5 When the Lord saw that man's wickedness was widespread on the earth and that every scheme his mind thought of was nothing but evil all the time, 6 the Lord regretted that He had made man on the earth, and He was grieved in His heart. 7 Then the Lord said, "I will wipe off the face of the earth: man, whom I created, together with the animals, creatures that crawl, and birds of the sky-for I regret that I made them". 8 Noah, however, found favour in the eyes of the Lord. . . . 14 "Make yourself an ark of gofer wood. Make rooms in the ark, and cover it with pitch inside and outside. 15 This is how you are to make it: The ark will be 450 feet long, 75 feet wide, and 45 feet high. 16 You are to make a roof, finishing [the sides of the ark] to within 18 inches [of the roof.] You are to put a door in the side of the ark. Make it with lower, middle, and upper [decks].

18 But I will establish my covenant with you, and you will enter the ark with your sons, your wife, and your sons' wives. 19 You are also to bring into the ark two of every living thing of all flesh, male and female, to keep them alive with you. 20 Two of everything—from the birds according to their kinds, from the livestock according to their kinds, and from every animal that crawls on the ground according to its kind—will come to you so that you can keep them alive. 21 Take with you every kind of food that is eaten; gather it as food for you and for them.

The text says the reason for the flood was the wickedness of the people, and the corrupt and violent earth. However, in the Sumerian *Epic of Gilgamesh*, excerpts of which are given below, say six divinities decide to cause the flood, but only two Mama and Anu are mentioned.[8] The epic goes back to third millennium before the common era (B.C.E.). We will look at Tablet 11, various columns. Gilgamesh is told to build an ark "One acre was its whole floorspace; ten dozen cubits the height each wall; ten dozen cubits its deck, square on each side". He entered the boat.

All I had I loaded into the boat:
All I had of silver I loaded,
All I had of gold I loaded,
All I had of the seed of all living creatures I loaded;
I made all my kin and family go onto the boat,
The animals of the fields, wild beasts of the fields, the children of all craftsmen I drove aboard.

Gilgemesh then says it rained heavily for six days and seven nights flooding all the earth. He describes the scarey nature of the wind, lightening, and the rain until it stopped.

I sent out a dove, letting it fly up. The dove went out and returned. It could see no place to stand, and turned around. I sent out a swallow, letting it fly up. The swallow went out and returned. It could see no place to stand, and turned around. I sent out a crow, letting it fly up. The crow went out and, seeing that the waters had receded, it ate, circled around, turned, and it did not come back.

Note here the similarity with the biblical account: the measurements are such that they will be able to contain all seeds, all living creatures including animals of the wild. However, unlike the biblical account Gilgamesh sends three birds: dove, swallow, crow. In the biblical account, Noah sends a raven once and a dove three times (Genesis 8:7–13). We do not have space to follow the whole flood story in both traditions, but here are some more similarities. When he gets of the boat Noah builds an alter and offers a sacrifice to God; we find the same in Gilgamesh. Utnapishtim makes offerings to the gods. "The lady of the god" great goddess, "Ishtar raises a fly ornament, a pendant made of lapis lazuli" as a sign never to forget the devastation of the flood. In Genesis 9:13–17 Yawhew, the Hebrew God, raises the rainbow a sign that he "will remember my covenant between me and you and every living creature of all flesh: water will never again become a deluge to destroy all flesh" (Genesis 9:16–17).

Not all religions have a cosmogony. Among them are Buddhism, Confucianism, and Jainism although they all have a world view. To use cosmogony as a fundamental element of religion, or as one of the things that make for religion, would exclude those religions that do not have, or reject stories of the origin. Jainism rejects cosmogony as mere speculation and urges followers to focus on freeing themselves from evil and suffering. The passage below, shows that Jainism considers cosmogony a speculation full of contradictions.

> Some foolish men declare the Creator made the world.
> The doctrine that the world was made is ill-advised . . . and should be rejected.
> How could God have made the world without any raw material?
> If you say that he made this first, and then the world, you are faced with endless regression.
> If you declare that this raw material arose naturally, you fall into another fallacy, for the whole universe might thus have been its own creator, and have arise equally naturally.
>
> If he is ever perfect and complete, how could the will to create arisen in him?
> If on the other hand, he is not perfect, he could no more create the world than a potter could.
> If out of love for living things and need of them he made the world, we did he not make creation blissful, free from misfortune.
> Good men should combat the believer in divine creation maddened by an evil doctrine.
> Know that the world is uncreated, as time itself is, without beginning and end.
> Uncreated and indestructible, it endures under the compulsion of its own nature.[9]

Jainism puts emphasis on the need to focus on saving one's soul from the continuous, endless cycle of rebirths because of one's deeds, *karma*. One should focus on doing good deeds to free oneself continuous reincarnations. Buddhism teaches the same too, and that is why the founder of the religion, Siddhartha Gautama, the Buddha, told his disciple Malunkyaputta that:

A holy life does not depend on the dogma that the world is eternal or ⌐
so forth. Whether or not these things obtain, there still remain the prⲟ⌐⌐⌐
old age, death, sorrow . . . all the grim facts of life—for their extinction in the present
life I am prescribing this *Dhamma* [teaching]. Accordingly, bear it in mind that these
questions which I have not elucidated . . . I have not elucidated purposely because
these profit not, nor have they anything to do with the fundamentals of holy life nor
do they tend towards Supreme Wisdom, the bliss of *Nibbana* [*Nirvana*].[10]

The advice of the Buddha is not to bother with questions of the origin of the
world because the answers may be not available. Further, that such questions are not
profitable to what one needs to deal with the realities of life and reaching eternal
bliss, nirvana.

Worldview

It is clear from Jainism and Buddhism that cosmogony excludes these two faiths,
among others, from religion. It is for this reason that I propose to consider
cosmology—how people understand the structure of the universe and its implications for their life—as an essential part of religion. There is a tendency to conflate
cosmology into cosmogony, but I want to separate the two, to have the former refer
to a worldview without reference to the origin of the universe or cosmogony.
Worldview is an overall perspective of the universe, or a point of view about the
world that derives from a particular orientation or interpretation. Worldview is what
we see in Buddhism, Jainism, or Confucians. In the worldview of these religions,
especially the first two, the world is full of evil and suffering, hence the need to live
a holy life to save oneself from the pain of rebirths because of bad *karma*. Holy life
is the way to reach eternal bliss. This world of suffering and bliss make the
worldview of these religions without reference to the origins of the universe.
Worldview is how Buddhists and Jains interpret the world. In other words,
worldview informs beliefs and how people ought to live. This is true to all religions
that the structure of the world informs their beliefs and practises.

Another example of a religion without a cosmogony, but with a worldview is
Confucianism. Although Confucianism makes some reference to the origin of the
world through the interaction of the forces of *Ying* and *Yang*, it is vague for a
cosmogony. There are no stories about the origin of human beings. Confucianism
has an ultimate reality, *Tian*, that regulates the world and moral order. What is
important in the worldview of Confucianism is moral order, or the doctrine of *li*,
which is the way of virtue and power consistent with the mandate of Heaven.
Confucianism considers human problems as the result of moral decay. On the other
hand, Confucianists believe education is the way to save human beings. Hsü Tzŭ,
one of the great interpreters of Confucianism, traces the problem of moral decay in
unrestrained pursuit of personal desire. He states:

Whence to the rules of decorum arise? From the fact that men are born with desires,
and when these desires are not satisfied, men are bound to pursue their satisfaction.

When the pursuit is carried on unrestrained and unlimited, there is bound to be contention. With contention comes chaos; with chaos dissolution. The ancient kings disliked chaos and set the necessary limits by codifying rules of decorum and righteousness.[11]

4. RITUALS

Closely related to myth is ritual. Actually, ritual is the other side of myth. William Young puts it better when he says: "If myths are stories outside time and space, which order the reality of those who accept them as true, then 'rituals' are those actions outside time and space that bring the power of myths of the people who practise them. . . . The source of ritual is myth. Rituals are often, one might say, myths enacted".[12] Ritual is the symbolic expression of communication with the ultimate reality, and it is an integral part of every religion. Writing on ritual from an African perspective, I said the following in another work:

Ritual can be defined as a way of expressing communion or solidarity with the living, the dead, the origin of life, deity, through word, action, or material means. People participate in this communion to find fulness of life. Ritual may also be understood as people's attempt to explain the mystery of life or the unexplainable. Ritual is about human life, cosmic origin, and destiny. This "explanation" of the incomprehensible does not exhaust nor completely reveal the mystery it seeks to "explain". There is always a dimension that is not fully comprehended, but the "explanation" given by ritual suffices for the time. Ritual is always "part" disclosure for the "whole" for the full view is never realised.[13]

Rituals, whether religious or not, are an effective form of communication with ultimate reality. In addition, rituals have the power to draw people together, or to serve as a means of redress, an appeal, or as a way of expressing thanks to the ultimate. The effectiveness of rituals lies in their ability to involve the whole person towards engaging ultimate reality. Livingston says:

Ritual is primordial and universal because it appeals to the whole person weaving together bodily gestures, speech, and senses—the sight of colours and shapes, the sounds of chants or mantras, the tactile feel of water and fabric and the smell of incense and the aroma of symbolic foods. Through its appeal to bodily movement, verbal chants and responses, and our multiple senses, ritual is symbolic in the most profound sense, for it "brings together" the mind, the body and the emotions and, at the same time, binds us to a community of shared values.[14]

Similarly, Zuesse notes:

Ritual itself is concerned first of all with ordering movements in space, and clearly the body is the foundation for all awareness. But ritual not only provides for classifications of bodily, social and cosmic space, it also seeks to interrelate these spheres in a harmonious and fruitful manner, so as to transform and renew the universe.[15]

Religious rituals have two dimensions: vertical and horizontal; towards ultimate reality and the social order, or people. Again, let us turn to Hsü Tzŭ, the Confucianism scholar-teacher, who explains the value of rituals.

It is through rites that Heaven and earth are harmonious. . . . He who holds to the rites is never confused in the midst of multifarious change; he who deviates therefrom is lost. Rites (*li*) rest on these three bases: Heaven and earth which are the source of life; the ancestors who are the source of the human race; sovereigns and teachers who are the source of government. If there were no heaven and earth, where would life come from? If there were no ancestors, where would the offspring come from? If there were no sovereigns and teachers, where would government come from? Should any of the three be missing, either there would be no people, or people would be without peace. Hence rites are to serve heaven and earth below, and to honour the ancestors and to elevate the sovereign and teachers. Here lies the threefold bases for rites.[16]

Hsü Tzŭ underscores the fact that in Confucianism rites are for the harmony of nature and social order. While rituals are informed by a worldview in Confucianism, they are rooted in cosmology in African religion. Christopher Ejuzi shows the relation between ritual and cosmology in *Ofo* ritual among the Igbo in Nigeria. Ejuzi says:

Ofo is intrinsically "bound up with the Igbo cosmology serving as a vital medium of communication between human beings and the supernatural order". *Ofo* is an equally important medium of communication between people, "because of its ability to relate the implications of the essential ideas which the symbol represents and imports to the traditional Igbo thought and life".[17]

First and foremost *Ofo* is a sacred stick of prayer.

Every morning in most of the major sub-cultural areas, the head of the family, lineage, etc. whether titled or not, generally brings out the lienage *Ofo* for the ritual act of traditional morning prayer. Kola-nut, alligator pepper, and *Nzu* are the items used for the exercise. If palm'wine is available, it is also utilised. . . . The name of the ritual is in fact *Igo Ofo Ututu*. The elder handles the kola-nut and utters the verses of his usually long prayer. He then strikes the *Ofo* on the ground, to seal his prayer. Finally, he sprays the *Ofo* profusely with chewed kola-nut and alligator pepper, and pours some libation of palm-wine on the *Ofo*. In the course of the day occasions might arise for the elder to pray special intentions or to invoke divine blessings on some persons. *Ofo* symbol is the principal object of prayer on all such instances, known as *Igo Ndu*.[18]

Liminal Rituals

There are different types of rituals: transitional or liminal from the Latin word *limen*, meaning threshold, seasonal, sacrificial, or healing. Life is full of rituals that moves one from one stage of life to another. Some rituals are light-hearted like graduations and weddings. Other rituals are very serious such as puberty. Rituals of liminality, or liminal rituals are those which mark the stages of life: birth, puberty, initiation (into womanhood pregnancy, manhood, eldership), death as in funeral rites. Rituals of liminality literary set a limit to one stage of life while leading the candidate through a threshold. African life is full of rituals from birth to death because rituals bring together everyday experiences to celebrate them as all religions of structure. Zuesse observes that:

> Religions of structure must necessarily be more complex than religions of salvation, since . . . the integration of the simple things of everyday life is far more complex and profound than any artificial narrowing of the spirit to exceptional experiences. The personal egoistic sphere, the social sphere, and the transcendental cosmic one must be all brought together. Religions of structure generally do this through ritual, and through the ritual type of instruction which emphasises the concrete and transforms it into a symbol.[19]

In religions of structure life is full of the rituals of liminality. Rituals of liminality are religious in nature, often connecting the candidate to the original event, the founding hero, or heroine or the first person to have undergone the ritual. The puberty ritual of Apache western United States of America demonstrates the religious nature of puberty ritual. The Apache are one of the many original peoples of North America. Like most indigenous people of North America, the Apache have puberty rituals for girls who have experienced their first sign of womanhood. The ritual called *na'i'es* or the Sunrise Ceremony is a four-day and nights grueling physical and spiritual exercise. The ceremony includes singing, dancing, enactments, running towards the four cardinal directions, participating and conducting sacred rituals, receiving spiritual power of White Painted Woman, giving blessings and "healing" their people in their role as women of the Apache nation.

The girls, covered with a sacred mixture of cornmeal and clay, reenact the myth of the primordial White Painted Woman, *Esdzanadehe*, who was instructed by the spirits to establish the puberty ritual of the Apache as well as their rites of womanhood. The White Painted Woman survived a flood in an abalone shell. While wandering the land after the water receded, she reached on a top of a mountain where she became pregnant by the sun, bearing a son, Killer of enemies. She became pregnant again, this time by the Rain, and bore another son, Son of Water. These two sons killed the Owl Man Giant, thus delivering their tribe from the terrorising giant. When her sons reported to her of the killing, she cried out in joy and triumph, the cry that is now repeated by a godmother of girl going through the ritual. When she became old, the White Painted Woman walked to the east where she met her younger self with whom she merged and became young again. So, she is born again in every generation of the Apachi.

Now compare the Apache White Painted woman puberty rite to *Chihamba: the White Spirit*, a girls' puberty ritual of the Ndembu in Zambia, as told by Victor Turner in *Drums of Affliction*. Turner writes:

> She has to lie there motionless for eight hours covered with a blanket, while women from near and far dance around singing and stumping. The site is known as the "dying-place" (*ifwilu*) or "place of suffering" (*chinung'u*), for it is there that she dies from childhood and enters the *passage* ritual which is aimed at making her a mature and fruitful woman. Birth and death are both represented by her attitude: it is the fetal position and the position in which corpses are buried.[20]

The initiate lies at the foot of the *mudyi* tree (*diplirrhyncus condylocarpon*), which when cut, exudes a white milky latex and the women informants of Turner told him that the *mudyi* meant breast milk and the maternal breast, but also a mother and her child, motherhood, the candidate's own matrilineal descent group, principle of matriliny, and Ndembu tribal customs.

In his study of rites of passage Arnold van Gennep (1873–1957), a Belgian anthropologist, has observed that liminal rituals have three phases: separation, transition, and incorporation. The first phase, separation, is the severance from the former life, a kind of death through ritual process. In both the White Painted Woman and *Chihamba* separation is physical for the initiates leave their homes and go away from the village to come back women of their nations. One dies to the old self to be reborn to a new being through the mortification or ordeal of ritual process, the transitional stage. This transitional stage is called the threshold, a moment of self confirmation. The new person born through stage two, is one who has gone through sacred ritual or sacred world, therefore has tools to use in the world. The ritual process, does, if it were, take one into the sacred world and back into this world.

Seasonal rituals

These are the rituals that mark the passing of the seasons: new harvest, a new moon, different festivals, new year, among them. Africa is full of festival rituals, one example of a festival ritual would be *incwala*, a Swazi agricultural rite that is performed annually and lasting four days, involving the royal clan with the king taking the centre stage.[21] Theodore Caster has observed that seasonal or festive rituals almost follow the same pattern:

> First come the rites of MORTIFICATION, symbolising the state of suspended animation which ensues at the end of the year, when one lease on life has been drawn to a close, but the next is not yet assured.
> Second comes rites of PURGATION, whereby the community seeks to rid itself of all noxiousness and contagion both physical and moral, and of all evil influences

which might impair the prosperity of the coming year and thereby threaten the desired renewal and vitality.

Third comes the rites of INVIGORATION, whereby the community attempts by its own concerted and regimented effort, to galvanse its moribund condition and to procure that new lease of life.

Last come rites of JUBILATION, which bespeak men's sense of relief when the new year has indeed begun and the continuance of their own lives . . . is thereby assured.[22]

Sacrificial rituals

Sacrifice is another word from Latin, *sacrificare*, which means "to make sacred". There are many types of sacrifices, some involving spilling of blood, slaughtering of an animal, others involving vegetables, fruits or agricultural products, or cultural products. Robertson Smith's theory of sacrifice is communion according to which a clan periodically expresses the unity of its members and their God by killing a totemic animal and eating its flesh raw in a religious feast. Through this rite, the people participate in social communion or solidarity between themselves and God because they share sacred food and friendship.

Sacrificial festivals are many in every religion, but usually there are some very important ones. Sacrifices have more or less the same characteristics and goals, that is, to remove pollution or defilement known as evil or sin. That is achieved by making amends or atonement to restore the broken moral order. Three moments are observed: (1) admission of guilt, or confession of breaking the moral order; (2) making the atonement by offering a sacrifice; and, (3) a promise to lead a moral or ethical life. Two examples for sacrificial rites will be drawn from Nuer (Sudan) sacrificial system and the Jewish sacrifice of atonement. The Nuer offer sacrifice when they feel they are at fault with God and that their actions or behaviour have caused divinity to be separated from them. The Nuer sacrifice an ox—connecting them to a personal sense of guilt for the wrongs committed, but at the same time express their desire for reconciliation for their wrong having been purged, expiated, cleansed, and expelled. The sacrificial animal is essentially a substitute for a person, the evil committed is transferred to it so that in its death that part may be eliminated and flow away with the ox's blood. The sacrifice is usually offered by an agnatic kinsman, or by a priest of the earth (*kuaar muon*).

Individual sacrifices on the other hand concern personal misfortune such as illness, infertility or disease. Sacrifices are essentially offered in connection with moral and spiritual crisis, and they are performed during the rainy season. The ceremony is dramatic, involving four acts: presentation, consecration, invocation, killing and immolation. In the first act, the sacrificial animal, usually an ox, is presented to the spirit; it is then consecrated by invocation by the priest, who with a spear in his hand, states the intention of the sacrifice and matters relating to it; the last act is killing and allowing the blood to ooze out for it belongs to the spirit while the participants eat the meat.[23]

The sacrifice of atonement is performed on the Jewish most holy day *kippurim* or *Yom Kippur*, held in the seven month, on the tenth day of the month in Jewish calender, or 15th. October in the Gregorian calender. The sacrifice is described in detail in the Hebrew Bible in Leviticus 16: 20–30.

> When he [Aaron the priest] has finished atoning for the holy place and the tent of meeting and the altar, he shall present the live goat. Then Aaron shall lay both his hands on the head of the live goat, and confess over it all the iniquities of the people of Israel, and their transgressions, all their sins, putting them on the head of the goat, and sending it away into the wildness by means of someone designated for the task. The goat shall bear on itself all their iniquities to a barren region; and the goat shall be set free.
>
> Then Aaron shall enter the tent of meeting; and shall take off the linen vestments that he put on when he went into the holy place, and shall leave them there. He shall bathe his body in water in a holy place, and put on his vestments; then he shall come out and offer his burnt offering and the burnt offering of the people, making atonement for himself and the people (Leviticus 16:20–23).

Note that the sins of the people are carried away from the people into the desert, thus leaving the community free of pollution. To complete the process of cleansing the community, the priest, Aaron, takes ritual a bath in a holy place. Take note again that substitution is the key idea in the Jewish sacrifice of atonement, both myth and rite represent the conversion of a situation of separation into a situation of reconciliation or of death into a situation of life.

Healing rituals

Health rituals are found in all religions. In Africa the most common of healing rituals is exorcism, or spirit possession. In many places ritual exorcisms include singing and dancing to the tom-tom beat of a drum, around the victim sitting at the centre, inside the circle.

5. SYMBOLS

Myths and rituals rely on symbols to express their meaning, because of their ability to communicate, or express that which is beyond concept or language. Symbols are not signs which lose their usefulness once they are used, passed, or their time is over. Symbols are universal or eternal while signs are temporary. Signs, like road signs, do not go beyond themselves. Once one passes a road sign, it is no longer needed for it is no longer useful. A road sign that shows that there is a narrow bridge ahead or a rail-crossing, it is no longer useful once one has gone beyond the bridge or the rail-crossing. Symbols on the other hand, they transcend time and space. This is much clearer with religious symbols: whether it is the crescent for Muslims, or the cross for Christians, the menorah for Jews. No matter how many times or places religious symbols are used, they do not lose their meaning within the faith community in which they stand. Symbols have a surplus of meaning, that is why no matter how many times they are used, they still retain their original meaning or what they stand for. This is what I wrote in *Drums of Redemption* concerning this aspect of symbols:

> What makes symbols inexhaustible is their double intentionality: they have literal (manifest) and latent meanings, and the latter is reached only through participation in the former. By participating in what is manifest, one is assimilated in that which is symbolised and is led by it beyond itself. This does not mean that through symbols one is able to see or to understand fully, because symbols reveal even as they disclose.[24]

Dealing with the subject of symbols in *Theories in the Study of African Religion* I have further stated that:

> Symbols represent structures of wholeness of people and nature. As structures, symbols are lived through networks of relations, institutions, and activities of daily living. Symbols regulate present activities as well as invoke the past in which they stand and the future to which people are bound. Stated differently, symbols invoke memories of the past while challenging people to the future. Or, more precisely, symbols have the ability to present the interplay of past, present, and future.[25]

Human life is full of symbols; humans depend on symbols to make sense and find meaning in the world. We would not be able to express ourselves without symbols. The world is full of symbols; every thing is a symbol: the language we speak; this page you are reading now is full of symbols, the letters are symbols and reading is interpreting the symbols written on a page. Mathematics and science are only possible through the use of symbols. Religion uses symbolic language. Religions of structure have a great number of symbols as their way of expressing ultimate reality or the sense of reality. Zuesse comments, "A different mode of concentration is evoked by such a thoroughgoing religion of structure to grasp transcendental truths, one must learn to enact the world differently. One sees every *thing* as a *symbol*".[26]

Religion is a very complex subject that defies definition because of two reasons: (1) the nature of religions itself, that religion is not homogeneous; (2) and that attempts to define religion are theory laden and theory-oriented. Further, that theory is influenced by culture, thus making any definition of religion culture based. People see things through the lens of their culture. Therefore, theory cannot escape culture. To be extravagant with words, we say religion can be taken as a theory of culture. I agree with those scholars of religion who argue that in order to have a fuller view of religion, it is important to look at the elements of religion: ultimate reality, the sacred, myth, rituals, and symbols. Noteworthy of these elements are myth and ritual. Each has different dimensions. The dimensions of myth are narrative, cosmogony, worldview. There are different types of rituals: liminal, seasonal, sacrficial and healing rituals. Any student of religion must examine these components to have a grasp of the nature of religion. This requires a lot of critical thinking: analysis, reflection, and synthesis.

GLOSSARY

Agni	Hindu God of fire, the messenger of the Gods. The one who accepts sacrifices.
Brahmin	The priest class of India.
Indra	Indian God of thunder, rain, and ruler of heaven
Kami	Spirits of divinities in Shinto, Japanese religion.
Karma	One's deeds that determine whether one will be reborn into a lower or higher levels of society or nature, or enter eternal bliss.
Liminality	Threshold. Used in connection with various rites of passage.
Mantras	Repeated words of praise or sayings.
Shiva	Hindu divinity, the third in the triad of Trimurti of divinities. Shiva is known as the destroyer of bad habits or evil,
Yom Kippur	Jewish ritual of sacrifice for purification for forgiveness.

NOTES

1. William A, Young, *The World's Religions: Worldviews and Contemporary Issues.* 2nd. ed. (Upper Saddle River, NJ: Pearson , Prentice Hall, 2005), 43.

2. Nahum N. Glazer, ed. *The Passover Haggada* (New York, NY: Schoken Books, 1953), 25 ff.

3. Wendy Doniger O'Flaherty, trans., *The Rig Veda* (London, Penguin Books, 1981), 31.

4. Wendy Doniger and Brian Smith, trans., *The Laws of Manu* (London Penguin Books, 1991), 13.

5. James R. Walker, *Lakota Belief and Ritual*, Raymond J. Demallie and Elaine A. Jahner, eds. (Lincoln, NB: University of Nebraska Press, 1991), 51–52.

6. Marcel Griaule, *Conversation with Ogotemmêli: An Introduction to Dogon Religious Ideas* (London: Oxford University Press, 1965), 71–72.

7. Herbert Mason, *Gilgamesh: A Verse Narrative* (New York, NY: Penguin Books, 1972), 84–87.

8. John Gardener and John Maier, trans. *Gilgamesh* (New York, NY: Vintage Books, 1985), 226–246.

9. Cited in W. Theodore de Barry, ed. *Sources of Indian Tradition,* Vol. I (New York, 1966), 76–78.

10. Kenneth Morgan, ed., *The Path of the Buddha* (New York, NY: 1956), 19.

11. Theodore de Barry, ed. *Sources of Indian Tradition* I (New York, 1966), 76–78.

12. William A. Young, *The World's Religions: World views and Contemporary Issues* 2nd. ed. (Upper Saddle River, NJ: Pearson/Prentice Hall, 2005), 17.

13. Harvey Sindima, *Drums of Redemption: An introduction to African Christianity.* Westport, CT: Praeger, 1994), 143.

14. James C. Livingston, *Anatomy of the Sacred: An Introduction to Religion*, 5th. ed. (Upper Saddle River, NJ: Pearson/Prentice Hall, 2005), 82.

15. Evan M. Zuesse, *Ritual Cosmos: The Sanctification of Life in African Religions* (Athens, Ohio: Ohio University Press, 1985), 9.

16. V. P. Mei, trans. in William T. Bary, ed. *Sources of Chinese Tradition* (New York, NY: Columbia University Press, 1960), 123,124.

17. Christopher I. Ejizu, *Ofo: Igbo Ritual Symbol* (Enugu, Nigeria: Fourth Dimension Publishers, 1986), 61.

18. *Ibid.*

19. Zuesse, *Ritual Cosmos*, 8.

20. Turner, *Drums of Affliction: A Study of religious Processes of the Ndembu of Zambia* (Oxford: Claredon, 1968), 17.

21. A great deal of discussion took place in the twentieth century concerning this Swazi festival. See Hilda Kuper, *An African Aristocracy* (London: Oxford University Press, 1947); B. A. Marvic, *The Swazi* (London: Cambridge University Press, 1940); D. Ziervogel, *Swazi Texts* (Pretoria: Van Shaik, 1957); T. O. Beidelman, "Swazi Royal Ritual", *Africa*, 32 (1966): 374–75.

22. Theodore Gaster, *Thespis: Ritual, Myth, and Dram in the Ancient Near East* (New York, 1961), 23.

23. Harvey J. Sindima, *Theories and Methods in the Study of African Religions* (forthcoming).

24. Harvey Sindima, *Drums of Redemption: An introduction to African Christianity*. Westport, CT: Praeger, 1994), 139.

25. Harvey J. Sindima, *Theories and Methods*, 243.

26. Zuesse, *Ritual Cosmos*, 8.

4
Celebration and Divination

TYPES OF RELIGIONS

Celebration or divination lies at the heart of every religion. That is to say, religion is at its highest in acts sanctification of life, when individuals seek ultimate reality to establish or renew contact. Acts of sanctification may involve prayer, praise (which may include music or chants), reciting and, or reading scripture, offerings, libation, sacrifice, and others rituals. Through these acts one encounters or recognises the ultimate. Becoming aware of, or being in the presence of the ultimate is what I am calling divination. Divination here does not mean a way of discerning, or knowing the future, but being aware of the divine, or being in the presence of, or being with, or simply, encountering the ultimate. The common word for what I am calling celebration or divination is worship. The reason I am using these terms is to be more inclusive, to cover both religions of salvation and religions of structure. In most religions of salvation there is a marked distinction between the holy or the divine and the profane. In such religions prayer, praise, offerings, etcetera, become ways of recognising, or experiencing the divine or the holy. I must point out, however, that celebration does not necessarily mean joyful, rather recognition of oneness with ultimate reality.

The worldview of religions of structure is that all the cosmos is infused with the divine, spirit or spirits, and everything else as related: spirits with humans as with nature. In such a world there are neither profane nor sacred things. Everything is a symbol that reveals the deep structures of relationships in the cosmos. Accordingly, the focus is put on celebrating life, the norms, and the bonds of deep and eternal relationships that structure all process of change in this world. Prayers, praises, rituals, and sacrifice become the means of celebrating life and the deep structures of relationship, process, and change in the cosmos. These acts are central to establishing harmony and reconciliation within the deep structures of relationships.

To say that the focal point in religions of structure is celebration life, is not to deny that the religions of salvation celebrate life, but to underscore the fact that for religions of structure this life and all its relationships are taken with utmost seriousness and importance. In religions of salvation there is a tendency to downplay the importance of earthly life, for the life that is to come. This life is seen as unredeemed, almost as against the divine or the ultimate. One wonders why God made this life in the first place. We find this in Hinduism, Buddhism, and Jainism where the human body is nothing, but *maya*, a vehicle of sin. In all these religions the focus is on developing a spirituality that will help one flee this evil life. Even Christianity whose second person in the divinity is believed to have become human, Jesus, there is a tendency to be a world-fleeing religion. Christianity is a religion of salvation as Otto describes it:

> Christianity . . . [is] in the first and truest sense a religion of redemption. Its characteristics are today salvation—over-abounding salvation, deliverance from and conquest of the "world" from existence in bondage to the world, and even from creaturehood as such, the overcoming of the remoteness of and enmity to God, redemption from servitude to sin and the guilt of sin, reconciliation and atonement, and, in consequence grace, and the doctrine of grace, the Spirit and the bestowal of the Spirit, and the new birth and the new creature[1].

Although this describes Christianity, Otto has here pointed out common elements of the religion of salvation. The main point being that humans are in bondage of this world, therefore the emphasis on other worldliness. In religions of structure there is neither sin nor eternal judgement, although grace is known and experienced in the gifts of life that God gives. God does indeed judge, but there is no eternal condemnation. Prayers, sacrificial rites are ways to atone and establish harmony within the deep structures of life and eternal relationships.

ACTS OF CELEBRATION AND DIVINATION

I am using the terms celebration and divination and not the usual term, worship, because the word worship is exclusive in the sense that it does not fully capture what goes on in religions of structure and also in non-theistic religions such as Buddhism. At any rate, let us define worship. I have done that in another book where I have said the following concerning the word worship:

> The English word worship derives from the Saxon *weorthscipe, worthship*. The word implies homage, the attitude and activity of recognising someone's worth, an exercise which always prompts honour, respect and reverence. Used in the context of religion, worship refers to activities, attitudes, or behaviour proper to God. Simply, worship means the adoration and praise of God.[2]

Worship also means religious service or homage, to make obeisance, to do reverence. Worship implies a humble submission to the will of God, or grateful acknowledgment of gracious initiative to those concerned.

Worship is essentially a Christian term for a direct translation does not seem to exist in many other languages, even in the Hebrew, the background of Christianity. The Hebrew word *abodah*, means to labour or to serve, or the service of God. Many African languages do not have an equivalent word for worship. "Instead", says Mbiti, "we find other words like 'to pray', 'to sacrifice', 'to perform ritual', 'to make an offering' and so on. These words describe actions which are directed towards God and spiritual beings".[3]

1. Prayer

While each religion has its own order of celebrating or divining, there are some elements common to all. The first common element is prayer. All religions take prayer as the channel to ultimate reality, or to God and to God's power. Prayer is a channel for expressing the deepest desires of the human heart or gratitude. Prayer is a way of invoking, celebrating life, seeking and divining the ultimate, interceding on behalf of others, and blessing. Prayer is fundamental in religions of salvation. A life of prayer is critical to salvation for salvation is impossible to a prayerless heart, for the ultimate never lives in a prayerless heart. For one to be transformed, or be enlightened one has to devote oneself to the life of prayer.

Prayers are said by anyone, any time and any where, and for a variety of reasons. Prayers are said in the morning, during the day, in the evening, or at night. We will begin our study of prayer by taking a look at some prayers in religions of structure, Oglala Lakota and African prayers. Of the utmost importance among the Oglala is holiness. So they pray at different occasions seeking holiness as in this prayer: "O you Grandmother, from whom all earthly things come, and O you Mother Earth, who bear and nourish fruit, behold us and listen: upon you there is a sacred path which we walk, thinking of the sacredness of all things".[4] That path of sacredness begins with self-purification in the sweat lodge in which both men and women may go to purify themselves. They pray throughout the ritual of purification of the sweat lodge. As the fire is set at the fireplace, all participants offer prayer such as the following:

> O Grandfather and Father Wakan-Tanka, maker of all that is, who has always been, behold me! And you, Grandmother and Mother Earth, You are Wakan and you have holy ears: hear me! We have come from You, we are part of You and we know that our bodied will return to you. . . . By purifying myself in this way, I wish to make myself worthy of You, O Wakan-Tanka, that my people may live![5]

In African religion, there are many people who pray in the morning such as the Igbo mentioned in the last chapter, the Abaluya in Kenya who "kneel facing east to pray to God, spitting and asking him to let the day dawn well, to pour upon his people his medicine of health, and to drive away evil divinity".[6] Among the Dinka in Sudan, the functions of Master of the Fishing Spear include saying prayers and invocations for the people, and saying prayers in cattle pen every evening.

Prayers can be said aloud or quietly as the Nuer in Sudan do. They are so conscious of the presence of *Kwoth nhial* (divinity) that they often say quiet prayers to the effect "*kwoth nhial* is present". The Nuer say they feel dumb and small like tiny ants before *Kwoth nhial*.[7] Being quiet is an expression of deference and honour.

Invocations

In African religion invocations are usually, but primarily during "pouring of libation. As he pours libation onto the ground the officiant addresses the Supreme Being, the divinity or the ancestor by name, attributes and praise appellations, and invites him to attend and accept the worship. In some cases a gong or rattle is sounded to create an atmosphere of silence".[8] The following is a Dinka invocation said by an uncle of a sick man calling upon the ancestors for healing.

> Repeat this son of my sister. [The nephew repeats every sentence after his uncle.] You of my father, I call upon you my child is ill and I do not want words of sickness and I do not want words of fever.
>
> And you of my father when you are called then you will help me and join yourself with my words. And I did not speak [in the past] that my children should become ill; that quarrel is an old matter. . . . And your prayer, and my prayer of the long distant past, prayer of my ancestors, you are spoken now.
>
> Meet together now, ee! It is that of my ancestor Guejok, it is not of the tongue only, it is that of Guejok, it is not of the tongue only.[9]

After the uncle finishes speaking, a master of the fishing-spear leads the invocation:

> Repeat, ee! You, Flesh of my father, you will not deceive me with lying words [you will not mislead me] and if you are called upon, you will quickly accept my speech. And you, O earth, if you are called [upon] you will help me also, and you Deng, divinity of my father, you will help me also if you are called. And you of my father, you will help. I have no great speech to make to you, what I have to say is ended and my [clan] half brother will carry you.[10]

Some prayers in African religion include various elements of prayer into one prayer. The following Igbo prayer includes invocations, confessions, intercessions or petitions, blessings, and curses.

> (*Invocation*)
> Chineke eat Kola.
> Chukwu Abiama take sweet chalk.
> Lord of heaven, greeting.
> Son, king of heaven greeting.
> Earth-Deity of Mnewi eat kola!
> Edo eat kola! Ancestors eat kola!
> Who brings kola, brings life!
> We are asking for life.
> Life of a man, life of a woman!
> Long life, and old age!
> You God eat whole! We eat pieces!

God come break this kola for us, for we have no hands
But the fire given to a child does not hurt it.

(*Confession*)
Forgive who speaks evil
Forgive who speaks good.
If there is offence, there would be no forgiveness.
But I did not kill any man,
Nor did I kill any woman.
I never removed any man's thing.
Nor abducted another's wife.

(*Petition*)
We ask for life.
Give us children, give us money.
Whatever man does, let him prosper by it.

(*Closing: Curses*)
Both who wish me good
And those who wish me evil.
What one plans for other,
So God plans for him.
Let a visitor not maltreat his host,
Nor host poison his guest.
Who pursues a fowl will fall.
Let both the kite and the eagle perch;
Whoever tells the other not to let his wing break.[11]

The prayer begins with invocations to the Supreme Being, Chukwu Abiam, other divinities before the ancestors are invoked. In the second paragraph the prayer goes into confession, from which it gets into petitions, closing with the last paragraph with blessings and curses. This prayer resembles Christian prayers with the exception of the curses. The standard Christian prayer which every Christian uses, or is familiar with is the Lord's Prayer which Jesus taught his followers to use whenever they prayed.

Our Father,
Who art in heaven,
Hallowed be your name
Your kingdom come.
Your will be done,
On earth as it is in heaven.
Give us this day, our daily bread.
Forgive us our trespasses,
As we have forgiven those who trespass against us.
Lead us not into temptation
But deliver us from evil.

For thine is the kingdom, the power, the glory,
Forever, Amen.

This is a Protestant version of the Lord's Prayer because it includes the doxology, or words of praise "the kingdom, the power, the glory". The Catholic version does not have the doxology which is believed to have been added by some early believers of the faith. The prayer begins with an invocation "Our Father" followed by words of praise, a petition for basic needs (daily bread), a confessions, an intercession, and a blessing or words of praise to God.

2. Poetry, Hymns, Songs, and Chants

The spirituality of Asia, moves devotees to rise very early in the morning to pray or recite prayers. Most of the prayers are sung, they are hymns or chants celebrating creation and divinity. There are chants to a particular divinity or in praise of a holy person such as Guru Nanak in Sikhism. Chants, just like hymns and songs help the faithful or devotees to focus on divinity. Poetry, hymns, songs, and chants lift the devotee up into holy adoration and praise while at the same time intensifying divination or the presence of the holy, or awareness of the ultimate. Devout Sikhs rise before dawn, take a bath and recite praises from *Japji Sahib*.

Sikhism

There is but one God whose name is true, the Creator, devoid of fear and enmity, immortal, inborn, self-existent; by the favour of the Guru.
REPEAT HIS NAME
The true one was in the beginning;
    The true one was in the primal age,
The true One is now also, O Nanak;
    The true One also shall be.
By thinking I cannot obtain a conception of Him, even though I think hundred of thousands of times.
Even though it be silent and I keep my attention firmly fixed on Him, I cannot preserve silence.
The hunger of the hungry for God subsides not though they obtain the load of the worlds.
If man should have thousands of devices, even one would not assist him in obtaining God.
How shall a human being become true before God?
How shall the veil of falsehood rent?
By walking, O Nanak, according to the will of the commands preordained.

Some Sikhs recite the words of praise and appellations of Guru Godind Singh Ji written in *Jaap Sahib*, which open as follows:

O Lord,
Thou art without any form, symbols, caste, class or lineage.
Non can describe Thy form, hue, garb, or shape.
Eternal and immutable,

Resplendent in thine own light,
Thy poet is without any limit
Thou art the Lord of all Indras.
And the king of all kings.
Sovereign of the three worlds,
Thou art ever proclaimed infinite by gods, men demons—
Nay even the blades of grass in forests.
Who can ever recite all the names!
Inspired by thy grace, I recite the names
relating to thy deeds.

Salutations to the Eternal,
Salutations to the Merciful
Salutations to Formless
Salutations to the Peerless.

Salutations to the Garbless
Salutations to the One beyond the scope of written word.
Salutations to the One beyond the scope of birth.[12]

Japji or simply *jaap* means to recite. *Ji* is a suffix indicating respect or honour. So *Japji* refers to the respected most important verses or *bani* of the *Guru Granth Sahib*, the holy book in Sikhism. The *Bani* was written by the founder of the religion Guru Nanak Dev, the first of the ten Gurus (teachers) of Sikhism. Therefore *Japji Sahib* is not simply a morning prayer or hymn of praise. It contains the teachings of Guru Nanak, thus the very essence of Sikh theology and philosophy. In the absence of the living human gurus, the scripture is the eternal teacher or instructor that is why Sikhs call their holy book *Guru Granth Sahib*, or simply the *Guru*. It is the embodiment of the first ten *gurus*.

Japji Sahib is about the wisdom of dealing with problems of everyday life family, participation in the affairs of world, living a selfless life, and living a spiritual life, especially a contemplative life. While focusing on wisdom concerning family and the world, *Japji Sahib* deals with deep theological issues such found in the first verse of *Japji Sahib*: "How can one be a person of 'the Truth?'" *Japji Sahib* consists of the four essential teachings of Sikhism: (1) *Bhakti* or *Simran* (devotional worship), (2) *hukam* (divine law or will that governs the universe and brings grace to human beings), (3) creation, and (4) the five plains or levels of spiritual ways by which one may come to God. Among the many themes in *Japji Sahib* are the names or attributes of God (the Holy Spirit, Perfect Purifier of corrupt humans), the love of God, generosity, true *yoga*, and ultimate punishment as verse 34 states, "We shall be judged according to our actions; the Lord is true; his court is just. . . . In his court the good will be separated from the bad".

The *Japji Sahib* has 73 sets of salutations and they are followed by 199 different praises. All these salutations are said at one sitting. Sikhs usually begin reciting prayers at three o'clock in the morning, but prayers can be said any time and anywhere. During the day, a devotee in Sikhism may be heard reciting *naam*, names of the holy to keep focused in one's meditation. At a Sikh community I visit in India, Gobind Sadan, one may begin one's prayer by chanting the following invocation: "*En Konka, Shata nam, we Guru*" (Holy one, you are one, Great Master and teacher).

Hinduism

Hymns and chants are central to Hinduism whose scriptures include poetry and hymns. Hinduism is a religion of hymns found in the four books of its sacred writings, the *Vedas*. These scriptures date back to the founding of the religion in the Hindus valley. The *Vedas* were written over a period of two thousand years from 1500 B.C.E. to 400 B.C.E. Hymns in the *Vedas* are found in the fourth book, the *Rig Veda*, which means the *Veda* of verses of praise. The verses of praise are dedicated to various divinities of the Indian pantheon of Gods, the most popular of whom is Indra, the God of thunder and rain, the ruler of the space between heaven and earth. About 500 hymns of the *Rig Veda* are dedicated to Indra. The other Gods in line of popularity in the *Rig Veda* are: *Agni*, the God of fire and sacrifice, to whom two thousand hymns dedicated; *Varuna* personified as *Rita*, is the all-seeing and all-knowing God, who punishes those who violate the cosmic order and forgive those who acknowledge their mistakes; then comes *Soma*, the Lord of the plants, *Yama*, God of the dead, *Vishnu*, the principal deity, and, *Rundra*, the God of destruction, who became the precursor of the Lord *Shiva*.

The hymns in the *Rig Veda* are not about spiritual immortality, rather about long life, much wealth, and good health. In the *Rig Veda* are hymns about creation. Here the power of *Indra* in creating the universe is celebrated in the hymns of creation. Let us learn more about *Indra* in the "Hymn of Creation" from *Rig Veda* 2:12

1. He who, just born, chief God of lofty spirit by power and might become the Gods' protector. Before whose breath through greatness of his valour the two worlds trembled, He, O people, is Indra.

2 He who fixed fast and firm the earth that staggered, and set at rest the agitated mountains, who measured out the air's wide middle region and gave the heaven support, He, people, is Indra.

3 Who slew the Dragon, freed the Seven Rivers, and drove the kine forth from the cave of Vala, Begat the fire between two stones, the spoiler in warriors' battle, He, O people, is Indra.

4 By whom this universe was made to tremble, who chased away the humbled brood of demons, Who, like a gambler gathering his winnings seized the foe's riches, He, O people, is Indra.

5 Of whom, the Terrible, they ask, Where is He? Or verily they say of him, He is not.

He sweeps away, like birds, the foe's possessions. Have faith in him, for He, O people, is Indra.

6 Stirrer to action of the poor and lowly, of a priest, of suppliant who sings his praises; Who, fair-faced, favours him who presses Soma with stones made ready, He, O people, is Indra.

7 He under whose supreme control are horses, all chariots, and the villages, and cattle; He who gave being to the Sun and Morning, who leads the waters, He, O people, is Indra.

8 To whom two armies cry in close encounters, both enemies, the stronger and the weaker; Whom two invoke upon one chariot mounted, each for himself, He, O ye people, is Indra.

9 Without whose help our people never conquer; whom, battling, they invoke to give them succour;

He of whom all this world is but the copy, who shakes things moveless, He, O people, is Indra.

10 He who hath smitten, ere they knew their danger, with his hurled weapon many grievous sinners; Who pardons not his boldness who provokes him, who slays the Dasyti, He, O people, is Indra.

11 He who discovered in the fortieth autumn Sambara as he dwelt among the mountains; Who slew the Dragon putting forth his vigour, the demon lying there, He, people, is Indra.

12 Who with seven guiding reins, the Bull, the Mighty, set free the Seven great Floods to flow at pleasure; Who, thunder-armed, rent Rauhina in pieces when scaling heaven, He, O ye people, is Indra.

13 Even the Heaven and Earth bow down before him, before his very breath the mountains tremble. Known as the Soma-drinker, armed with thunder, who wields the bolt, He, O ye people, is Indra.

14 Who aids with favour him who pours the Soma and him who brews it, sacrificer, singer. Whom prayer exalts, and pouring forth of Soma, and this, our gift, He, O ye people, Is Indra.

15 Thou verily art fierce and true who sendest strength to the man who brews and pours libation. So may we evermore, thy friends, O Indra, speak loudly to the synod with our heroes.

Note here early references to the reverence of cows as associated with *Indra*. One hymn (6:28), associates cows with *Indra* and their milk with *Soma*. Cows are sacred animals in India; they roam about everywhere freely even in city streets where drivers stop for them or drive around them. Here is the hymn of "Cows" in *Rig Veda*, 6:28

I. The Kine have come and brought good fortune: let them rest in the cow-pen and be happy near us. Here let them stay prolific, many-coloured, and yield through many morns their milk for Indra.

2 Indra aids him who offers sacrifice and gifts: he takes not what is his, and gives him more thereto. Increasing ever more and ever more his wealth, he makes the pious dwell within unbroken bounds.

3 These are ne'er lost, no robber ever injures them: no evil-minded foe attempts to harass them. The master of the Kine lives many a year with these, the Cows whereby he pours his gifts and serves the Gods.

4 The charger with his dusty brow o'ertakes them not, and never to the shambles do they take their way. These Cows, the cattle of the pious worshipper, roam over widespread pasture where no danger is.

5 To me the Cows seem Bhaga, they seem Indra, they seem a portion of the first-poured Soma. These present Cows, they, O ye Indra. I long for Indra with my heart and spirit.

6 O Cows, ye fatten e'en the worn and wasted, and make the unlovely beautiful to look on. Prosper my house, ye with auspicious voices. Your power is glorified in our assemblies.

7 Crop goodly pasturage and be prolific drink pure sweet water at good drinking places. Never be thief or sinful man your matter, and may the dart of Rudra still avoid you.

8 Now let this close admixture be close intermingled with these Cows,
Mixt with the Steer's prolific flow, and, Indra, with thy hero might.

Judaism

Torah, the Hebrew Bible, has twenty-four books, divided in three major sections, and arranged as follows: the Law, called *Torah*, the Prophets or *Niviim*, and the Writings or *Kesuvim* which includes books on poetry and history. Among the most popular of the books in *Kesuvim* (Psalms, Job, Proverbs, Daniel, Ezra-Nehemiah, Chronicles), is the book of Psalms, a book of poetry set to songs and hymns that were sung on celebrations and other moments of divination. The Psalms were part of a hymn book of Israel, which was used more popularly after the Jews returned from exile in Babylon, modern day Iraq. There are different types of hymns in the Psalms they include such topics: thanksgiving, creation, the kingship of Yahweh (God), future deliverance, and Psalms celebrating earthly kings. The hymns about thanksgiving are: 33, 103, 104, 113, 117, 134–136, 145–147.

1 Praise YHWH.
Praise, servants of YHWH,
praise the name of YHWH.
2 Blessed be the name of YHWH
from this time forward and forever!
3 From the rising of the sun to its setting
the name of YHWH should be praised!
4 YHWH is high above all nations,
and his glory above the heavens! (113:114)

Sacred hymns about creation in the Psalms are: 8, 19, 104, 139, 148.

1 The heavens are telling the glory of God; and the firmament proclaims his handiwork.
2 Day to day pours forth speech, and night to night declares knowledge.
3 There is no speech, nor are there words; their voice is not heard;
4 yet their voice goes out through all the earth, and their words to the end of the world. In the heavens he has set a tent for the sun,
5 which comes out like a bridegroom from his wedding canopy, and like a strong man runs its course with joy.
6 Its rising is from the end of the heavens, and its circuit to the end of them; and nothing is hid from its heat (Psalm 19:1–6).

Sacred hymns praising the kingship of Yahweh in the Psalms include: 47, 93, and 96–99). A few verses from Psalm 93 demonstrate the nature of this set of Psalms.

1 YHWH is king, he is majestically robed, YHWH is robed, he is clothed with strength. He has founded the world; it will never be moved.
2 Your throne was founded in the beginning, you are everlasting.
3 YHWH, the floods raised, the floods raised their voice, the floods lifted their roaring.
4 But more majestic than the thunder of powerful water, more majestic than sea waves, is YHWH, majestic on high (93:1–4).

The 50 Psalms also include hymns concerning present and future deliverance, or the kingdom of Yahweh whose seat will be on Mount Zion are: 46, 48, 76, 84, 87, 122); the royal Psalms celebrating earthly kings are: 2, 18, 20, 21, 45, 72, 89, 101, 110.

African Religion

Singing, clapping, drums, and dancing are common in many practises of celebration and divination in Africa. Across the continent, singing, clapping, and drums may be heard during moments of divination whether the occasion is performing sacrifices or rituals of liminality to express gratitude to God and calling upon the ancestors for their blessings. Some occasions for community prayers for healing include singing, clapping and drums as in the case of spirit possession. Spirit possession is a general term that includes a whole array of illnesses including, but not limited to depression, or some other mental health problems and psychosomatic diseases. A sick person sits the centre or lies inside a circle of singers who sing, clap, and dance clockwise, to the tom-tom beat of drummers who may be inside the circle with the possessed, or outside the circle. The dancers and onlookers sing songs and clap hands invoking divinity and calling upon the ancestors to rise and intercede on behalf of their troubled earthly family. Here the dynamic presence of the ancestors is enjoined and urged to mediate the people and divinity or the divine spirit, since the ancestors themselves live in the spirit world. Dancers and onlookers sing songs, clapping as they call upon all the living members of the family to harbour no evil feeling, and join the living in chasing away the evil spirit, and bring healing.

In Africa singing, clapping, and drums may also be heard during communion or remembrance meals with those recently or long gone. This practise has often been misunderstood and condemned as "ancestor worship" by Christian missionaries and their African successors and anthropologists. Therefore, anyone worthy the name Christian, should not have memorials meals. In fact, over zealous African Christians condemn anything having to do with ancestors as non- Christian. Africans *venerate* and not worship their ancestors in the same way Christians do not worship their saints although they invoke and celebrate them at various times and occasions.

3. Scripture

Not all religions have sacred books, but those that do, reading and sometimes interpreting scriptures becomes a very important moment in celebration ritual. Scriptures are, or contain the distilled essence of truth and knowledge that give rise to the theological and philosophical assertions of the religion. Scriptures keep intact the spiritual heritage of a religion. When read during celebration or divination, scriptures remind people of their sacred history and their relationship with divinity or divinities. Scriptures make real the moment of divination: people hear the divine word, the word that remains in them, to inspire, encourage, exalt, and to uplift them in their encounter divinity, or in their presence divinity. In many religions, reading the divine word is the most sacred moment and it occupies the central part of celebration and divination. A full discussion on the role of scriptures is given in the next chapter.

4. Creeds

The word creed, derives from the Latin *credo*, I believe. A creed is a statement of faith that expresses what one believes and professes. While declaring one's confession of belief, a creedal statement also reveals the worldview of the believer. A creed does not necessarily have to be religious, it can be belief in a nation as the creed the United States of America passed in 1918, written in 1917 by William Tyler Page (1868–1942). However, most often than not, creed refers to a religious declaration or statement of faith. Some religions have creeds while do not require anyone to believe in established doctrines or teachings about the religion. We will explore a few creedal statements from different religions.

Buddhism

Enduring patience is the highest austerity
nirvan is the highest condition—say the Buddhas.
For he who injures the other is not a true renouncer
He who causes harm is not a true ascetic.
Not to do any evil, to practise the good to purify one's mind:
This is the teaching of the Buddhas.

Not to speak against others, not to harm others and to restrain according to the rule.
Moderation in eating, secluded dwelling, and the practise of mental cultivation.
This is the teaching of the Buddahs.[13]

Judaism has no creed, but the *Shema* in Deuteronomy 6:4–9 certainly forms the bases of Judaism. : "Hear, O Israel: The Lord is our God, the Lord alone". The full text of the *Shema* is as follows:

Hear, O Israel: The Lord is our God, the Lord alone. 5You shall love the Lord your God with all your heart, and with all your soul, and with all your might. 6Keep these words that I am commanding you today in your heart. 7Recite them to your children and talk about them when you are at home and when you are away, when you lie down and when you rise. 8 Bind them as a sign on your hand, fix them as an emblem on your forehead, and write them on the doorposts of your house and on your gates.

Moses Maimonides, a Spanish Jew who lived in the 12th century, condensed the basic beliefs of Judaism into the following Statement of Faith. It is still followed by the traditional forms of Judaism.

Statement of Faith

10. I believe with perfect faith that the Creator, blessed be His Name, is the Creator and Guide of everything that has been created; He alone has made, does make, and will make all things.

11. I believe with perfect faith that the Creator, blessed be His Name, is One, and that there is no unity in any manner like unto His, and that He alone is our God, who was, and is, and will be.

12. I believe with perfect faith that the Creator, blessed be His Name, is not a body, and that He is free from all the properties of matter, and that He has not any form whatever.

13. I believe with perfect faith that the Creator, blessed be His Name, is the first and the last.

14. I believe with perfect faith that to the Creator, blessed be His Name, and to Him alone, it is right to pray, and that it is not right to pray to any being besides Him.

15. I believe with perfect faith that all the works of the prophets are true. I believe with perfect faith that the prophecy of Moses, our teacher, peace be unto him, was true, and that he was the chief of the prophets, both of those who preceded and of those who followed him.

16. I believe with perfect faith that the whole *Torah*, now in our possession, is the same that was given to Moses, our teacher, peace be unto him.

17. I believe with perfect faith that this *Torah* will not be changed, and that there will never be any other Law from the Creator, blessed be His name.

18. I believe with perfect faith that the Creator, blessed be His name, knows every deed of the children of men, and all their thoughts, as it is said. It is He that fashioned the hearts of them all, that gives heed to all their works.

For Thy salvation I hope, O Lord.

Islam

The *Aqidah* or Islamic creed is found in the words of the *Shadada* which every believer recites: *La ilaha il Allah, Muhammad -ur-Rasool-Allah* (None has the right to be worshipped, but Allah, Muhammad is the messenger of Allah).

1. I testify that the Creator of all the universe, including the stars, the planets, the sun, the moon, the heavens.

t none has the right to be worshipped but Allah Alone.

... . .estify that all the best of names and the most perfect qualities with which You have named or qualified Yourself in Your Book [i.e. the *Qur'an*] or as Your Prophet Muhammad [*saaws*] has named or qualified You, with his statement, I confirm that all those [names and qualifications] are for You without changing their meanings or neglecting them completely or giving resemblance to others.

In addition to the Five Pillars of Islam, Sunni Muslims also the Sixth article of faith. A Sunni Muslim must have belief in: *Allah* (in God); *Nabi* (all the prophets), *Kutub* (sacred books), *Mala'ika* (angels), *Qiyama* (the last judgement and eternal life), and *Qadar* (destiny or fate). Shia Muslims on the other hand, have what they call the roots of their branch of Islam: *Tawhid* (the unity or oneness of God) *Adalah* (the justice of God), *Nubuwwah* (the priesthood in particular the infallible prophets), *Imamah* (leaders as the custodians of the faith), *Qiyama* (the last judgement and eternal life).

5. Liturgy: The Manner of Celebration

The elements of celebration given above: prayer, poetry, hymns, songs, chants, scripture, and creeds make for celebration in which the devotee is raised to a higher level of awareness of presence of the divine. Not all of these elements of divination are done in public celebrations; they may also be performed in private or personal acts of divination. One of the distinctive marks of divination is the order in which each element of the celebratory act is performed, or how the manner of presenting oneself or a gathered community before God. There is an order in which divination flows and more so at occasions of public celebration. The flow of the order of public celebration is called liturgy, a Greek word (*leitourgia*) which originally meant a public duty or a service that citizens performed to the state. Liturgy may be used to describe any manner of proscribed form of ritual or celebration in any religion.

In Judaism the proscribed manner of divine celebration is Hebrew scriptures. The liturgy is given for private devotion and public divination carried out as a function of the priests. However, the building blocks of both private and public liturgy are the *Shema* and the *Amidah* prayers. The *Shema* is recited in its extended form as found in the following Hebrew scripture passages: Deuteronomy 6:4–9, 11:13–21, Numbers 15:37–41. The *Amidah* are the 18 blessings or *Shemoneh Esreih*, recited while standing (*amidah*) facing the *Aron Kodesh* (the ark containing the *Torah* scrolls). Before reciting the *Amidah*, Jews take three steps backward and three steps forward facing the *Aron Kodesh*.

In Islam, *Salat* is the liturgy. It proscribes the five daily prayers required of a Muslim: dawn, noon, afternoon, sunset, and night. Before *Salat*, a Muslim makes ablution, a ritual purification of washing hands up to the wrists, the right first and in between the fingers three times; rinsing the mouth and spitting out the water three times; rubbing the teeth with *miswak* (natural tooth brush) or with a finger; three times put water in the nostrils, pitch them with the left hand and breathe out the water; wash the face, arms, and in between the fingers three times; perform *masah*, that is, passing wet hands over the head and then washing the feet, toes up, ending with the little left toe, thus completing the ritual cleanliness. After which a Muslim recites the *Shahadah*. This ritual is according to the majority Sunni Muslims, but it is not radically different from Shia purification ritual. Shia Muslims consider wiping the feet with wet hands as sufficient in contrast to Sunnis who must wash their feet to complete the ablution. Further, the Shia do not clean inside their ears with a finger as part of the ritual of ablution.

Salat is recited facing the *Kaba*, or the "House of God" (*bayt Allah*) in Mecca. To recite *Salat* is to repeat a set of prayers in cycles called *raka*. Each *raka* has its own sequence of postures, recitations from the *Qur'an*, and special formulas. *Salat* may be said privately or in public as the communal *Jumuah* prayers on Friday.

The *Kaba* is a small building 13x9 metres inside room. There is nothing inside. Oral tradition has it that it was first built by Adam, followed by Ibrahim (Abraham), Ismail (Ishmael), and Muhammad himself.

The liturgy in Hinduism consists of *kirtan* (singing the names of God), *bhajan* (devotional songs), *puja* (offering items such as flowers, food, water and incense to God), *sastra* (reading from scriptures), *sanga* (associating with fellow devotees), and *prasadam* (sharing food offered to God).

An African Liturgy

Africa is geographically vast and so too, is the expanse of the practises and experiences of religious sensibilities. Yet, there are elements of divination and manners of practise of celebration that are common in all Africa. From the West Africa all the way to Kenya and Tanzania on the East coast, down to South Africa, one finds almost a standard liturgy of divination, with some manner variations: libation, invocation, offering, prayer, songs, sacrifices. To illustrate, I will turn to a public practise of divination in which I participated in 2005. Before I present the liturgy, here is a caveat. As a boy I grew up knowing African liturgy of divination from my father and from my paternal relatives. One evening, at the age of twelve, I was greatly distressed watching a filmstrip produced by the Malawi Ministry of Information that launched an assault on traditional religion. The filmstrip showed a local village gathering at a holy place, a huge rock at the foot of a hill. There, the people prayed, invoking the ancestors to hear their prayers and to plead on their behalf before God. After the prayers, they poured out a libation of beer and placed two large, perhaps twenty-five litre clay pots of beer at the foot of the rock as their offering to divinity through the ancestors. Once back at the village, two elderly men secretly turned around up to the hill and to the village shrine. There they drank the brew offering. The next day, they told everyone that the ancestors had received their offering for the pots were empty. *Mangwiro*, the title of the filmstrip, was a frontal onslaught on the religious sensibilities of the people.

In relating my early disappointment with the media presentation of traditional religion, I have mentioned some elements of African liturgy: invocation, prayers, libation. On 13th August, 2005, I participated in a liturgy for ground breaking or dedication of the ground for building. I will draw from the experience to illustrate the acts of celebration and divination in African liturgy.

1. Drums of invocation

After all three hundred or so people gathered were seated, the celebration and divination opened with the tom-tom beat of five drums of various sizes. As the drumming reached a crescendo, three elderly women, my paternal and maternal aunts, the most senior living members of their families and clans, slowly walked to the shrine erected for the occasion. Each of them walked beside and hand in hand with my three oldest nieces, symbolising continuity of family, clan, and lineage.

2. Libation and Invocation

The older women and their young attendants knelt at the shrine. As each of them knelt, the tempo and rhythm of the drums slowed down and finally died out as the last, youngest escort knelt down. A moment of silence followed. My paternal aunt, the oldest of the three, in a soft voice, invoked God, by first calling upon the ancestors (my paternal ancestors) to be present with us as we were gathered to seek God's blessing upon the ground to be set apart for construction of a building. Beginning by calling, by name, the recently departed, to the host of all ancestors in the spiritual world, and to the founding member of our family and clan, my paternal aunt asked that they all be present before us and God to join us in seeking divine blessings.

My oldest maternal aunt followed, invoking first her mother, my grandmother. My aunt proceeded to call upon maternal ancestors, beginning with the recently departed, the long gone, and the host of all those now in the spirit world with God. She called upon them to join us in imploring God to look favourably at our gathering and hear our prayers. The last invocation came from my youngest maternal aunt who invoked the ancestors to seek God's protection during construction of the building, for the honour and prosperity of generations, and blessings upon God. As the three women made their invocations, they poured a libation.

3. Offering

At the end of their invocation each of the women sprinkled flour at the altar as their offering to the ancestors. At celebrations, the offering is usually a food item, symbolising unity between the living, the living dead, and ancestors participating in a common communion meal. Just as in life the ancestors sat and ate with those living, so too, in death and on occasions of divination when their presence is sought.

4. Prayer

It then fell to me to pray, because I was the one who had called upon everyone physically present, the recently departed this life, all my paternal and maternal ancestors, to be present and to intercede on my behalf to God for blessings, to dedicate the ground and to construct a building. The prayer had to be offered with concrete and specific intention, which was, for God to consecrate the ground, protect everyone working at the site, to bless everyone to the honour of the family, ancestors and to the glory of God.

5. Dedication

The Master of Ceremony, a religious functionary, rose up. Using a freshly cut small branch of a tree, he invoked the name of God, and blessed the place by sprinkling water, taking a few steps towards each of the four cardinal directions (north, east, south and west). As he walked in each direction, he dipped the leaves of the branch into a small water container that an assistant was carrying in his hands, drawing the branch out of the container he sprinkled into the air and the ground in that direction and called divine presence and blessings.

6. Presentation

Most occasions of divination call for an offering or sacrifice to be presented. However, in a divination seeking divine blessings it was necessary that a presentation be made for every member of the clan and land to join in seeking divine favour. My oldest niece, carrying a basket full of newly harvested maize on her head, walked over to the Chief of the land, knelt before her, and offered the family's gift of the first fruits. This was a presentation to the ancestors of the land through her majesty, the Chief. The chief raised her hand over the basket, accepting the family gift to her and the people and the ancestors of the land. Then the youngest niece of my three nieces participating in the divination, also carried another basket full of newly harvested maize to the village headman of the area from which the maize had been harvested.

7. Song and Dance

A time of song and dance followed the presentation of gifts. There were songs of praise and thanksgiving, songs of reverence to God and sanctification of life. There were traditional dances of jubilation; dances of vigour and joy celebrating the might of the ancestors, dances and songs that made some of the high ranking invited guests in formal attire, jump in and join the dancers as the women's voices of ululation rose to a crescendo. During divination, festive occasions, and funerals Africans sing songs relevant to the occasion.

8. Restatement

Usually, it is the chief who leads in communal divination. All religious matters are under the aegis of the chief in most African societies. This is not because the chief is the beginning of the line, rather the opposite. The chief belongs to the line of the ancestors. The chief is the living ancestor. Since the chief belongs to the land of ancestors, he or she becomes the proper liaison between the world of the living and of the ancestors, between the "givers" and the "recipients" of blessings. On this occasion, however, the family matriarchs on both sides of my family led the invocation for it was the family that had called the gathering. It was, therefore, an imperative that her majesty, the chief be called upon to offer her blessings. Before her majesty spoke, two other individuals gave brief remarks that led up to asking the chief for her remarks and blessing. What the chief did, was in essence, restate the intent of the gathered community, namely, to dedicate the land and seek divine favour.

Sacrifice

If this were a divination for a sacrifice, the sacrificial animal would now be presented to the chief for a prayer of forgiveness and reconciliation with the ancestors and God. After the prayer the animal would have been slaughtered. Although this was not a divination for sacrifice, the day before, a large bull had been slaughtered by a village religious functionary who offered prayers as the bull's blood spilled out. The meet was cooked for celebration the following day. On the next day, after the chief's blessing the people had plenty to eat and drink. The first plate to be set was of the chief, and it had the choicest part of the cooked meat. She was given the best, not simply out of deference and reverence to her, but in her role as a liaison between the world of the living and of the ancestors. Moreover, as the living ancestor, she would share meal with all the ancestors by setting aside on the floor, for the ancestors, a piece of the meat and tiny portions of everything else on her plate for this was a communion meal. She would also pour few drops of her drink over the tiny food portions to share with the ancestors.

Here I have outlined the elements of the liturgy in traditional religion. Not all these elements are performed in every act of celebration and divination. The most common elements in many occasions are: invocation, libation, offering, prayer, song and dance, and sacrifice. Other elements may be added or dropped as the occasion for divination may dictate. Most of these elements are also followed in other religions, albeit with different orientation, emphasis, and language.

OCCASIONS FOR CELEBRATION AND DIVINATION

In any religious traditions there are numerous occasions for celebration and divination. The occasions may be personal and private, common and public, for specific reasons and activities: commemorations or anniversaries, a birth of a baby, death, marriage and other events of life. The personal private acts of celebration involve different things for different religions. Hindu acts of celebration, the *puja*, involves images (*murtis*), prayers (*mantras*) and diagrams of the universe (*yantras*). *Puja* may be done in private or with one's family at the family shrine in the home, offering divinities water, fruit, flowers, and incense. While they may have their prayers at the family shrine, Hindus attend the temple where a priest recites the *Vedas*, although technically any "twice-born" Hindu may read scriptures.

Religions of salvation have special days of celebration and divination, as well as high holy days, occasions of feasts and festivals. The three major Semitic religions have divided up the weekend: Friday is the day of celebration for Muslims; Saturday is for Jews, and Christians have Sunday. Some religions have more high holidays and festivals than others. Hinduism with 32 prescribed high holidays, is sometimes described as the religion of fasts, feasts, and festivals spread throughout the calender year. Islam has only nine festivals.

African Religion

There are no set regular times for elaborate celebration and divination among most African societies. However, in societies where people have family shrines, they have daily ritual prayers and, or sacrifices as we have already seen among the Igbo where the head of the household will rise in the morning and offer his prayer saying:

Good morning, *Chukwu* (God)
Good morning Ala (Arch-divinity)
Good morning, Ancestors
Take Kola, all.

On the east-cost, Abaluya men kneel early in the morning and pray:

O God, give me mercy upon your children that are suffering;
Bring riches to day as the sun rises
Bring all fortunes to me today.[14]

Many daily prayers are said all over Africa from different societies from shrines and homes. There are certain divinities in West Africa that have special days of divination, when there are several people. The Yoruba divinity of Buruku, for example, has every seventeenth day as a holy day. Concerning Buruku holy day, J, Omosade Awolalu and P. Adelumo Dopamu say:

On this day, worship takes place at the shrine in the open space, in front of the temple. The head-priestess and her assistant go there to offer sacrifices on behalf of themselves and other worshippers. Some senior members of the cult may also be present. Cold water, kola nut, palm oil, pawpaw, banana, porridge and bitter

kola are offered. The chief priestess or her delegate breaks the kola and prays to
the divinity for life and health, and for protection against their enemies.[15]

Religions of structure are religions of life; they celebrate life. Accordingly,
elaborate occasions for celebration are dictated by events in life. This does not
mean that in between events the people do not divine. In a world where everything
is fused with the spirits of divine presence, every act of life is preceded by some act
of recognition, a reverence to the ancestral spirits or divinity itself. One does not
begin hoeing in one's field without making the ancestor aware of one's presence in
the field; one does not undertake a journey, go fishing, gather firewood in the forest
without asking the ancestors to seek divinity's protection. One does not begin to eat
without first making offering of food (morsel) or pouring a libation to the ancestors;
individuals and groups will not take a sip of without first pouring out little, offering
a libation to the ancestors. No activity of life is beyond the purview of the ancestors
and divinity. So individuals are duty bound to show recognition, reverence, and
homage all the time to the host of ancestors that surround them and from whom they
descend. This is why the thesis that African religions or religions of structure are
utilitarian should be rejected because between the elaborate public acts of
divination, are numerous unnamed occasions of celebration and divination.

GLOSSARY

Chukwu	Igbo deity.
Jaap Sahib	Sikh morning prayer.
Kwoth nhial	Nuer Divinity.
Murtis	Images of the deities on the Hindu shrine
Nanak	Founder of Sikhism and the first of the ten great teachers, or *gurus* in Sikhism
Puja	Hindu ritual for remembering the ancestors and divinities.
Salat	Five obligatory daily prayers in Islam.
Shadada	Declaration of belief in God in Islam.
Shema	Jewish creed.
YHWH	Divinity in Judaism.

NOTES

1. Rudolf Otto, *The Idea of the Holy* (London, Oxford University Press, 1923), 164.

2. Harvey J. Sindima, *Reclaiming Christianity in the 21st. Century: Building A
Spiritual Powerhouse* (Blantyre, Malawi: Africa Academy Press 2007), 90.

3. Marla Powers, *Oglala Women: Myth, Ritual, and Reality* (Chicago, Ill: Chicago
University Press, 1986), 35.

4. Joseph Epes Brown, ed. *The Sacred Pipe. Black Elk's Account of the Seven of the
Oglala Sioux* (Norman, OK: University of Oklahoma, 1953), 33–34.

5. *Ibid*, 54.

6. John Mbiti, *African Religions and Philosophy*, 2nd. ed. (London, Heinemann, 1989), 61.

7. E. E. Evans-Pritchard, *The Nuer* (Oxford: Claredon Press, 1940), 12.

8. J. Omosade Awolalu and P. Adelumo Dopamu, *West African Traditional Religion* (Ibadan, Nigeria: Onibonoje Press, 1979), 128.

9. Godfrey Lienhardt, *Divinity and Experience: The Religion of the Dinka* (London: Oxford University Press, 1961), 220–21.

10. Godfrey Lienhardt, *Divinity and Experience: The Religion of the Dinka* (London: Oxford University Press, 1961), 239.

11. Emfie Ikenga Metuh, *God and Man in African Religion* (London: Geoffrey Chapman, 1981), 125–126.

12. Shri Surender Nath. *Jaap Sahib*. rev. ed. (New Dehli, India: Gobind Sadan Institute for Advanced Studies in Comparative Religion, 1996).

13. Jospeh M. Kitagawa, *The Religious Traditions of Asia* (New York, Macmillan, 1989), 49.

14. John Mbiti, *African Religions and Philosophy*. 2nd. ed. (Oxford: Heinemann, 1990), 62.

15. Awolalu, Omosade and P. Adelumo Dopamu. *West African Religion*. (Onibonoje Press, 1979), 126.

5
Scripture

In discussing poetry and hymns in the last chapter, we saw that the hymns of the religions of salvation were from sacred texts or scripture, the *Vedas, Torah,* and others. The word, scripture, derives from the Latin *scriptura,* meaning "a writing". Scriptures are recorded revelations or stories about how divinities made themselves known to their people. As such, scriptures are about the origins of life and the cosmos. So they establish the world-view of their devotees providing them a particular way of seeing and understanding the world, rules of conduct, and serve as a guide to everyday life. Initially, scriptures circulated as oral sacred stories that were passed on as oral tradition. The oral tradition was preferred even after the sacred stories were written. That is why in some religions, Hinduism, Sikhism, and Islam, for example, reciting scripture is of utter importance. In Hinduism scriptures are divided into that which is heard, *shruti* and that which is remembered *smriti.* It is noteworthy that the sacred writings of Islam, *Qur'an* signifies that which is recited.

INSPIRATION

A written text stands superior to the oral tradition from which it evolved. The written text is considered inspired and of divine origin. Hindus believe their scripture, the *Vedas,* have no beginning or end. They can be trusted because they are without errors or defects associated with human texts. The authority of the *Vedas* is believed to be eternal and absolute. Muslims too, believe the *Qur'an* was dictated by the head of angels, the Archangel Gabriel, who, in a piecemeal fashion spoke to Muhammad. The *Qur'an* is the very speech of God, dictated with heavenly language, heavenly inspired, perfect and without error. The *Qur'an* is God's miracle as the *Qur'an* itself says: "Truly it is the revelation of the Lord of all Being, brought down by the Faithful Spirit upon my heart, that you may be one of warners, in a clear, Arabic tongue" (26:193–195). The *Qur'an* with its 114 chapters or *suras* was the scripture that took the shortest time to reach canonisation, only 23 years after Muhammad's death.

The idea of divine inspiration of scripture is held by Christians. They believe that both the Hebrew scriptures which they call the Old Testament, along with a collection of Christian books known as the New Testament are inspired. Both the Old and New Testaments are inspired by God as the New Testament states: "All scripture is inspired by God and is useful for teaching, for reproof, for correction, and for training in righteousness, so that everyone who belongs to God may be proficient, equipped for every good work" (2 Timothy 3:16–17). Christians are not agreed on how to understand the idea of divine inspiration. At issue is whether scripture was divinely dictated, or what is known as mechanical inspiration, or that the inspiring Spirit gave the writers the freedom to express the word of God on their own. Mechanical inspiration implies that the writers were passive recipients of the word. To argue for non-mechanical inspiration is to maintain that the writers used their own experience, social, class, and cultural values to express the divine word. The question of inspiration raises another issue: the fallibility of scripture. How can scripture be believed when it was written by fallible human beings and contradictions are found within it? All the scriptures say they are without errors. Christians too, argue vigorously that the Bible with its 66 books is inerrant and infallible; it is simply perfect. In Christianity there are those who maintain the dogmatic position of the accuracy of the scripture since every *i* (ota) was dotted and every *t* crossed at the dictation of God. Some believe in the inerrancy of the Bible even if they do not believe in mechanical inspiration. These Christians maintain that although the books of the Bible were written by humans, the Bible is right when it claims that God guided the writing of scripture, in such a way that the result is an infallible book. Other Christians argue that inspiration does not suggest there is no room for humanness, fallibility, and incorrectness. In my forthcoming book, *I believe* I have said the following concerning the issue under discussion:

> There are human elements in the Bible and there are also inconsistencies, but *faith* perceives in all these human elements the echo of the voice of God. Faith accepts the Bible with all its human limitations knowing that even in revelation God's identity is concealed, and not given fully to human knowledge and reality. The biblical witness reveals God in ways people are able to know God. Our knowledge of God will always be partial for if God were to be fully understood, that God would be like human beings. How can people know God fully when they are not able to fully understand themselves and those around them?[16]

THE CANON

In most cases the oral traditions circulated for a very long time before they were committed to writing. The transition from oral tradition to writing took place to preserve the original message and in doing so to maintain the integrity and uniformity of the message. Once sacred traditions were committed to writing, they attained a privileged status and enjoyed authority that they did not have before. Their authority increased when at some point the leaders of the religion came to a consensus that the written text contained the norms of the faith and that it should become the authorised reading and training manual of the religion. So in a way writing closed the gate, so to speak, to additions to the message. The agreed upon text now became a canon, a Greek word *kanon*, meaning a measuring rode or a rule. When sacred writings were canonised, they became a norm, a measuring rod, or the rule of faith. Therefore, canon implies something obligatory, something bindingly established.

The process of reaching a consensus for sacred writings to be recognised as authoritative and the rule of faith is called canonisation. Canons grow over centuries as in Confucianism where it took a very long time for the *Si Shu*, the Four Books to be added to the *Wu Jing*, the Five classics. It was Chu Hsi (1130–1200 C.E.) who assembled them during the Sung dynasty. The *Vedas* took very long too, to be assembled as scriptures of Sanatana Dharma (The Eternal Religion), or Hinduism as it is known elsewhere. The Hebrew scripture, *Tanak* took centuries for the canon to be closed. The word *Tanak* is an acronym for the different types and groups of books that make Hebrew scriptures: *Torah* (books of Moses), *N'vi-im* (Prophets), and K'tuvim. *Tanak* has 39 books. The first five books of the Hebrew Bible, *Torah* also called the *Pentateuch* (from Greek *pente*, five, and *techos* book) were completed in 400 B.C.E. but the whole *Tanak* was not closed until 130 C.E. In *I Believe*, I have written how long it took to complete the canonisation of the Hebrew.

> The formation of the Hebrew canon, the Christian Old Testament, began during the time of the Persians, that is, in the 5th and 4th centuries (B.C.E.), when Israel was no longer an independent nation and had to find its identity in light of the revelation it had received. The first five books, the *Pentateuch*, seems to have been collected before the year 300 when the Samaritans (Jews of the Northern Kingdom) separated themselves and adopted the Pentateuch as their only scripture. From other historical sources *Sirach* 39:44 following, we learn that 100 years after the collection of the *Pentateuch*, the prophetic writings were collected and considered authoritative on matters of faith. The growth of the third section of the Hebrew Bible went on for some time so that in the time of Jesus there was no unanimity about the limits of the canon. The canonisation of the Hebrew Bible was not closed till a hundred years after Jesus. The decision to limit the number of authoritative books was done by a group a high council of rabbis during the 90s of the first century of the Common Era. This council of the rabbis that had settled in Jamnia after the fall of Jerusalem, assumed the spiritual responsibility of the people, and it was this group that decided which books went into the canon. The rabbis took Malachi as the last prophet although they also included Daniel which came much later than Malachi. The first complete Hebrew translation appeared in 130.[17]

The first books of the Christian scripture, called the Gospels, which are about the life and work of the founder of Christianity, Jesus of Nazareth, were probably completed writing around 95 C.E., Jesus himself having been crucified in 33 C.E. The complete canon of the twenty-seven books that make up Christian writings of the New Testament did not close until the middle of the third century. In his Easter pastoral letter in 367, Bishop Anathasius of Alexandria, Egypt listed twenty-seven books as canonical for the New Testament. In deciding the New Testament canon the church was guided by two criteria: apostolicity and ecumenicity or universality. Apostolicity referred to whether the author was an apostle or disciple of an apostle. This allowed the gospels of Mark and Luke to be included in the canon, but also the Letter to the Hebrews, on the general recognition at the time that Paul was its author. Ecumenicity referred to how widely the book was used and held in high esteem. Apostolicity was then about the first eye witnesses to the salvation event; those who heard and saw the event. In setting out the books of the New Testament, the early Christians presupposed the authority of the Old Testament, the Hebrew Bible. For the longest time, the term scripture in the early church was only reserved to the Hebrew Bible or the Old Testament, thereby emphasising the Jewish roots of Christianity.

Other Canonical Books

Religions of salvation have more than one set of sacred writings. There are some sacred writings that express the standard or the norm of the faith. Those standard books, or canonical books are taken as authoritative while others may be read for devotion or edification of faith. This is to say that sacred books do not have the same weight or value within the same religion. In Hinduism only the four *Vedas* (*Rig Veda, Sama, Yujur, Atharva*) or the *shruti* texts, are canonical. *Shruti* texts are of non-human origin, therefore, texts to be heard as opposed to *smriti* texts which are to be remembered. The *Vedas* have *Vac*, the eternal sacred and cosmic word or sound that brings into being the entire creation. In Islam, the *Qur'an* is the highest sacred book. After the canon of the *Qur'an* was closed, questions over the meaning of the *Qur'an* lead to the collection of the sayings of Prophet Muhammed which were collected and compiled as the *Hadith*, the second scripture: authoritative, normative, and canonised. The *Hadith* may provide guidance and promote devotional life.

The canonical book in Judaism is *Tanak* and the *Talmud* is extra-canonical sacred book. *Torah*, the written law, is from *Tanak*. The *Talmud* is a very important book in Jewish culture; it supports Jewish creativity and national life. *Talmud* is the summary of oral law that evolved over the centuries, developed by Jewish scholars who lived in Palestine and Babylon until the Middle ages. The importance of *Talmud* for Jewish culture lies in the fact that it contains thousands of years of Jewish wisdom, oral law, legends, philosophy, history, science, anecdotes and humour. *Talmud* has two main parts: (1) *Mishnah*, or the book of *Balakhah*, written in Hebrew and, (2) and a commentary on *Mishnah*, written in poor Aramaic-Hebrew.

In Christianity, the Bible is the canonical book while the apocrypha is considered the second canon or deuterocanonical (deutero means two or second). The deuterocanonical books or apocrypha are those books which have been left out of the official authorised version or canon. The Greek word, *apocrypha*, means "things hidden away", or books that are secret or esoteric in nature. Apocrypha books are excluded from the Protestant Bible. In some Bibles, Catholic and Greek Orthodox, apocrypha books are placed between the Old and New Testaments. There are many apocrypha books, but only Tobias, Judith, the Wisdom of Solomon, Baruch, and Maccabees are found in the Catholic Bible. Other apocrypha books: First Esdras, Second Esdras, Epistle of Jeremiah, Susanna, Bel and the Dragon, Prayer of Manasseh, Prayer of Azariah, and Laodiceans are excluded from the Catholic Bible.

THE USES Of SCRIPTURE

1. Public Celebration

Scriptures chronicle the history of a religion and are also considered authoritative in matters of faith, and good for guidance and instruction or training. As a guide to faith, scriptures are used for promoting devotional life of devotees, but also for propagating the faith. Sacred writings may be read, recited, or sung. In public celebrations and divination scriptures may become the object of focus, and thus easily be treated with almost magical powers than reverence. Devotees may believe that simply touching the sacred book, they may be blessed, or get healed of their disease, or die if there are not faithful and worthy devotees.

2. For Instruction

Since scripture is the basis of the teachings of the religion, doctrine, but also instruction, education, and training they require experts in interpreting them. These are the people who spend their time studying scriptures of their religion. These experts exegete (analyse) the text, puzzling over the meaning of the words, understanding their usage within the text, or the whole scripture to interpret the text in such a way as to let the word becomes alive to speak again as in its original context. These interpreters also known as exegetes or scribes are found in Buddhism, Judaism, and Islam. There are two types of interpreters in Islam: the *ulama* (the learned leaders) and the *fuquha* (jurists or men of insight).

3. Devotion and Meditation

One thing that strikes a visitor to Asia is the depth of the spirituality of the people no matter what religion. One quickly finds that the foundation of deep spirituality lies in their love of scripture which is meditated upon literally day and night in various holy places, temples, and public or family shrines. It is the book of books that people recite, imbibe, and embody in their daily life. Scriptures are treated with great care and reverence. I will draw from Sikhism to illustrate the role of scripture in devotion and meditation. The Sikh scripture is called *Guru Grath Sahib*, also called *Adi Granth*. Sikhs say the holy scriptures came at the end of the succession of the ten living *gurus* (teachers) in the line of Guru Nanak (1469–1539). After the line of the *gurus* the only teacher was their revealed teachings. In other words, the canonisation of *Grath Sahib* came after the end of *gurus* in the line of Guru Nanak. It is for this reason that Sikhs call their holy scriptures the *Guru*.

Guru Grath Sahib is always kept in the *Gurdwara*, the doorway to *Guru* (God). *Gurdwara* is the gateway through which God may be reached. *Gurdwara* is the Sikh house of prayer and public celebration and divination. At each *Gurdwara* is the Nishan Sahib, a triangular orange flag of Sikhs. Featured highly in each *Gurdwara* is *Guru Grath Sahib*. Three important things take place at each *Gurdwara*: *Kirtan*, the singing of hymns from the Guru Granth Sahib; *Katha* reading of the Guru Granth Sahib and explanations; the *Langar*, free community kitchen for all visitors of all religions.

Guru Grath Sahib is always placed in the main hall, *Darbar Sahib*. If the *Gurdwara* is not an elaborate temple, *Guru Grath Sahib* may be housed in a room situated in such a way that anyone entering the *Gurdwara* will face *Guru Grath Sahib*. The doors of the cabin or room remain open day and night. When one enters *Darbar Sahib* or the room, having taken off of shoes, and placed a covering over the head, one beholds uncommon holy reverence of scripture. There, on a stool rising a few centimetres (inches) from the floor, is a soft cushion with a bright red silk cover or some special clothes, placed on it is *Guru Grath Sahib* before which devotees prostrate or bow in holy reverence. The official reader sits on the other side of the stool cross-ledged, while an attendant stands, waving a fly-whisk of horsehair, fanning in veneration of the holy book. The official reader recites *Guru Grath Sahib* for a few hours and another comes. If *Guru Grath Sahib* is to be moved, the holy scripture is placed on the head indicating the exalted status of the holy book.

Guru Grath Sahib is the object of public celebration, for hymns are taken from it (as it has more than 5,000 *shabhads* or hymns, set to Indian classical music) and devotees read it. *Guru Grath Sahib* invokes the heart into holy adoration and raises one to a heightened perception of God in a moment of true divination.

INTERPRETATION OF SCRIPTURE

The Christian Canon

The challenge of every religion is to maintain the integrity of its scripture, thereby its teachings. Over the centuries, most of the divisions within the religions with scripture have been over differences in interpretation of scripture. The most well known break over the interpretation of scripture in Christianity was in 1517, when one evening a little known German priest by the name of Martin Luther (1483–1546), pinned at the door of the church in Wittenberg propositions or the famous Ninety-five Theses. Luther posted these propositions for a debate over the interpretation and meaning of scripture. Luther questioned the Catholic church's monopoly over interpretation of scripture and he claimed the church was in error as reflected by some of the teachings and practise of the church, which to Luther were unscriptural. Luther further questioned the role of the priest as a mediator between God and the people and also the church's belief that it was a custodian of the blessings of God to the people. Luther's position was that the individual has access to God directly, therefore should be able to read and interpret scripture in the light of scripture by the guidance of the Spirit of God. Luther's challenge to interpretation of scripture led to a major break in Western Christianity in what came to be called the Protestant Reformation which had as its catchwords: *sola scriptura* (scripture alone), *sola gratia* (grace alone), *sola fide* (faith alone).

The history of Biblical interpretation goes back to Origen of Alexandria (185–232), who is considered the first biblical scholar. Origen, explained his theory of Christian principles of biblical interpretation in his fourth book *De Principiis* (On First Principles). Of paramount importance to him was the realisation that all scripture is divinely inspired.[18] Origen developed his theory of interpretation in the *Hexapla*, his sixfold version of the Old Testament with the Hebrew text in one column, a Greek transliteration of the Hebrew in another, and then the four Greek translations of Aquila, Symmachus, the Septuagint, and Theodotion, all paralleled accordingly.

First, Origen maintained the unity of the Bible because it is divine in nature for it was divinely inspired and dictated by the Spirit of God. For Origen, there is nothing useless in scripture, since the Holy Spirit, as the author of the Bible, would not give human beings anything useless. The one God speaks throughout all scripture with one voice; therefore, there are no contradictions. The apparent contradictions within the text only reflect problems of human understanding rather than any real inconsistency in the divine word.[19] It is note worthy that Origen's view of inspiration of the scripture does not guarantee the accuracy of the historical and scientific information in the Bible. He makes this fact clear in his famous tract, *Contra Celsum* where he asserts, "We must say that an attempt to substantiate almost any story as historical fact, even if it is true, and to produce complete certainty about it, is one of the most difficult tasks and in some cases is impossible".[20] Explaining what seems to be apparent inconsistencies in the scripture Origen said:

> The divine wisdom has arranged for certain stumbling-blocks and interruptions of the historical sense to be found therein, by inserting in the midst a number of impossibilities and incongruities, in order that the very interruption of the narrative might as it were present a barrier to the reader and lead him to refuse to proceed along the pathway of the ordinary meaning: and so, by shutting us out and debarring us from that, might recall us to the beginning of another way, and might

thereby bring us, through the entrance of a narrow footpath, to a higher and loftier road and lay open the immense breadth of the divine wisdom.[21]

Origen demonstrates his exegetical practises even in expounding his exegetical theory. To make his practise clearer, Origen quotes Proverbs 22:20–21 in the Old Testament: "Have I not written for you thirty sayings of admonition and knowledge, to show you what is right and true, so that you may give a true answer to those who sent you?" Using these two verses Origen asserts his understanding of the three meanings of scripture: meaning of the letter, of the soul, and of the spirit.[22] The spiritual meaning of the text is of foremost importance for Origen. He comments, "For with regard to divine Scripture as a whole we are of the opinion that all of it has a spiritual sense".[23] Each text has "inner meaning" and this is the meaning that the Spirit intends to communicate. The inner meaning is arrived at "by comparing other Biblical texts containing similar terminology" so that it is the Spirit speaking in the auxiliary texts which teach us the meaning of the text in question.[24]

Biblical Hermeneutics

The issues of interpretation of scripture are complex, but they revolve around what is actually said, "the said", in the original context, who said it, and what it meant, or what it means now. One might see these as simply journalistic questions: who, what, when, to whom. However, matters of scripture go beyond journalism; they involve the meaning and application of the text in daily life and towards one's salvation. Biblical scholars, both Christian and Jewish, use a particular theory and method of understanding scripture known as hermeneutics, a word derived from Greek *hermeneutikos*, meaning the science of interpretation. This is the process of discovering the proper meaning of a text. To speak then of biblical hermeneutics is to refer to biblical exegesis, or analysis of a biblical text, or passage to discover its meaning. Most Christian biblical scholars engaged in biblical hermeneutics are encouraged by words found it scripture itself which say: "Be diligent to present yourself approved to God, a worker who does not need to be ashamed, rightly dividing the word of truth" (2 Timothy 2:15). The rules or principles governing biblical hermeneutics are:

1. Literary Analysis

Biblical hermeneutics begins by a serious study and analysis of a text. Hermeneutics is simply a theory of analysis of a literary text for correct interpretation. So in biblical hermeneutics one applies the rules for a literary analysis: (1) reading and re-reading the text with specific questions in mind; (2) understanding the basic ideas(s), names, and events; (3) taking note of basic concepts, or rules used in the text; (4) summarising in one's mind the thrust, major arguement, or thesis of the text.

2. Exegesis or Grammatical Analysis

Biblical exegesis involves examining words, phrases, passage(s) of a text. In order to make a proper exegesis, rules of grammar are applied to examine both words and structure of phrases and passages in a text. Of importance in exegesis, therefore, biblical hermeneutics is the knowledge of biblical languages, Hebrew, Greek, and to some extent Aramaic, a Hebrew derivative used in portions of the books of Ezra and Daniel in the Hebrew Bible.

3. Historical Analysis

Biblical hermeneutics answers the question "when", by making historical analysis. Historical analysis is not simply about the date something was said or happened; it is more inclusive or wholistic. Historical analysis looks at what was going on at the time of the writing the text and the impact, or lack thereof, of those events on the text. Historical analysis includes the current values, beliefs, social, and material facts that influenced the writer. It is at this stage of historical analysis that a biblical interpreter examines the cultural, economic, social, and the political climate from which the text arose.

4. Contextual Analysis

Biblical hermeneutics is a discipline or an exercise to limit one's preconceptions from influencing the meaning of a text. Biblical hermeneutics forces the interpreter to focus on the bible itself and not to import ideas to give meaning to a biblical text. So, a biblical interpreter analyses a text within its own context: words within a sentence; a sentence within a paragraph; a paragraph within a chapter, and chapters within the whole bible.

5. Theological Analysis

Biblical hermeneutics originated from theological hermeneutics. The principles of biblical hermeneutics given above apply to both Christian and Jewish biblical hermeneutics for there is a substantial overlap of their faith materials since they share the Hebrew scriptures. However, both Christian and Jewish scholars have to keep in mind that they arise out of different religions, therefore different theological orientation.

BUDDHIST CANON

No religion faces an enormous challenge to interpretation of scripture as Buddhism which in its two and one half millennium has covered all of Asia. From Sri Lanka, the country of its origin, Buddhism is to be found in Tibet, central Asia, China, Korea, Japan, Thailand, Cambodia, Vietnam, Burma, Nepal, and south Asia.[25] The result of such aggressive missionary activity has been a production of volumes of sacred writings, as each community of faith has tried to understand and apply the religion within its own context. So there are different canons with the most common being: the *Pali* (the Indian canon) with three baskets (divisions), *Vinaya Pitaka* (Basket of Discipline), *Sutta Pitaka,* (Basket of Discourses), and *Abhidhamma Pitaka* (Basket of Scholasticism); The Chinese canon *Ta-ts'ang-ching*

(Great Scripture-Store); the Tibetan canon *Bka'-'gyur (Kanjur)* (Translation of Buddha-word) and *Bstan-'gyur (Tenjur)* (Translation of Teachings). There are also canons in Korean, Mongolian, and Japanese.

Having scripture is not what the founder of the religion, the Buddha wanted. He did not write scripture, neither did he encourage his followers to do so. The Buddha did not want scripture for fear that people would depend upon it, or that scripture would limit or hinder people on their inward journey towards enlightenment. When asked by his disciple Ananda who would lead and guide his followers after his death, implying having scripture perhaps, Buddha is reported to have replied: "henceforth be ye lamps unto yourselves, and be ye refuge unto yourselves, seek no other refuge, let *dharma* be your lamp and refuge". During his fifty years of teaching the Buddha did not use one method or example lest his followers consider it a way to enlightenment. After his death in 483, a council of 500 monks called upon Ananda to recite all the discourses of the Buddha's teaching. The first division of these became the *Sutra* literature which now constitutes the official Theravada or *Pali* canon, later called *Tripitaka*. The second division of Buddhist sacred literature, *Vinayapitaka*, came from a report of monks on monastic life tradition. Later, a third division, *Abhiharmapitaka*, was added. The *Pali* oral tradition was committed to writing in 29 B.C.E., 400 years later. *Sutra Pitaka* has many subdivisions and it contains more than 10,000 sutras.

In addition to the *Pali* canon of Theravada Buddhism, there are also canons from its two other branches, Mahayana (Large Vehicle) and *Vajrayana* (Diamond Vehicle), Tantric or Esoteric. Each of these schools has its own vast body of *sutra*. The most influential of the Mahayana *sutra* is *Prajnaparamita* (the Perfection of Wisdom), developed more than a thousand years beginning around 200 B.C.E. The main theme of *Prajnaparamita* is *sumyata*, the doctrine of emptiness or the nonsubstantiality of all things. *Vajrayana* or Tantric Buddhism is influential in Tibet where it developed its own body of sacred literature. Beyond the holy writings of these three different schools of Buddhism there are numerous books of sacred literature including most popular ones as *Dharmapada*.

Buddhist Hermeneutics

All these canonical texts are considered authoritative because they satisfy the principle of authenticity in that they are consistent with the teaching, *Dharma,* of the Buddha. How do Buddhist scholars interpret such a diverse body of canonical text? Buddhist hermeneutics is guided by four principles:

1. *Dharma* is a criterion (the refuge), not person (*pudgala*).
2. *Artha* (meaning) is a criterion, not letter (*vyaññjana*).
3. A *sūtra* of definitive meaning (*nītārtha*) is a criterion, not one of provisional meaning (*neyārtha*).
4. Direct knowing or intuition (*jññāna*) is a criterion, not discursive knowing (*vijññāna*).

The first principle of Buddhist hermeneutics repeats what the Buddha himself advised his assistant and attendant Ananda: it is the teaching and not the person that is important. Here, the historical Siddhāartha Gautama, the Buddha is not important, but the "*dharma*" that is the lamp and refuge of the believer. The *dharma* is important because it leads the individual to enlightenment. The second principle explains the meaning of *dharma*, of which there are two dimensions: the external, the literal text, and the internal, the "personal realisation", much like the spiritual meaning in Christian interpretation of scripture. The two dimensions are united for the external is the teaching *dharma* while the internal *dharma* is its ultimate, or realised dimension. Buddhism teaches that the external *dharma*, the literal text, has value for it is "the word of the Buddha" for it leads to true understanding, or insight into spiritual truth. However, sometimes the letter must be given up for the spirit, for ultimately all means and support must be let go to realise enlightenment.

How does one get to a definitive *dharma* or meaning of the text? This is the question answered by the third principle in Buddhist hermeneutics. The issue about *direct* and *indirect* meaning of a *sutra* is about the freedom of the three Buddhist traditions: Theravada, Mahayana, Tantra. Whether a given text is definitive or interpretable, depends on the views expressed in that text from the perspectives of each of the traditions. Texts are spoken of as belonging to this or that "vehicle" (*yāna*), and this *yāna*-system is compounded by a discourse that refers not simply to the texts as such, but to attitudes through which the texts are practised. Each tradition has a hierarchy of teachings.

The fourth principle summarised as knowing or intuition (jñāna) and not discursive knowing (vijñāna).

The interpretive process begins by determining the authenticity of a sacred text and then proceeds to the recognition that it is the *dharma* and not the person, Gautma the Buddha, that is primary. One must then master the *letter* of the sacred text before one can rightly discern its meaning. Next, one must recognise the great diversity of texts and their teaching and how each can be viewed as a useful and valuable step on the path to enlightenment.[26]

ORAL TRADITION AS SCRIPTURE

In the study of religions scripture has always been taken as the measure of religious consciousness. Religions with scriptures are believed to have evolved to a higher level of divine or ultimate consciousness, while religions without scriptures remain at the elementary level of human development. Scripture then serves as a dividing line that separates higher religions from the so called preliterate religions and culture. For the longest period, religious studies in the West focused on inquiry into higher religions, the real religions. The lack of scripture made scholars in religious studies dismiss, ignore, or simply not take seriously religions of structure.

This prejudice is in the roots of religious studies. The discipline developed from Christian theology. Religious studies were taught as part of Christian theology or missiology. The bias of Christian theology towards other beliefs was taken lock and barrel into religious studies. Christianity proclaims it has the highest and more accurate knowledge of God. Christianity also recognises a higher, but not correct knowledge of God in Judaism because of its belief in one God, monotheism, having scripture. However, Christianity believes it stands much higher over Judaism, because it has the fullest special revelation in the divinity of its founder, Jesus of Nazareth. The doctrine of revelation in Christian theology is about God's self-disclosure, or God's manifestation to the people. The doctrine of revelation in Christian theology separates Christianity from other religions, but also divides religions into higher and lower level religions. Religions without scripture are believed to have only general revelation, while those with scripture have a special revelation. However, Christian theology maintains, not all religions with scripture are on the same level; neither are they true religions. As far as Christianity is concerned, there is only one true religion, which has a good will to Judaism from which Christianity itself developed. Although Islam has scripture, it is completely rejected by Christianity along with other religions with scripture. Some of those scriptures are much older than both Judaism and Christianity. It was not until the nineteenth century that scholars with no or little commitment to Christianity, started doing research on the so called polytheistic or lower religions. Hinduism fared much better in religious studies than all the religions with the so called general revelation. These religions had been labeled superstitions, and as such they were not worth learning about or scholarly attention. The reason Hinduism was favoured was because some European scholars studying linguistics such as Max Müller, maintained that the sophistication of Sanskrit showed that European languages must have developed from Sanskrit. Therefore, in studying Hinduism Europeans were actually exploring their own history.

Some early missionaries to the non-western world, started inquiring into the religious beliefs of the locals for the purpose of evangelising them. The only reason for studying other religions in Christianity and the missionary enterprise was evangelism, that is, to study particular religions with the intention of developing a strategy for converting the people. Converting others to Christianity is a divine imperative for Christians, because Christian theology maintains that it has the perfect understanding of God through its special revelation, Jesus. Christians believe there is no other way of knowing and being with God, but through Jesus who said: "I am the way, and the truth, and the life. No one comes to the Father except through me". While the view of having full revelation is specifically Christian, Western society as a whole, along with some non-Western Christian, Jewish, and Muslim scholars everywhere, view other religions as less than real religion, or lacking in the true facts of religion because they do not have scriptures.

It is wrong to dismiss or exclude religions of structure from academic and scholarly inquiry for what they do not have. Should not academic interest alone, arouse curiosity enough to spark a desire to inquiry into the unknown? For while there are no scriptures in those religions, there are oral traditions that mediate the people, or give the people the substance of life. Those mediations, or the substance of life between individuals and societies, are "oral scripture", if scripture is not understood simply as a written text, but as that which reveals the ultimate and mediates life. It must not be forgotten that scripture as a written text rose from scripture as an oral text. When scripture is simply a written text, it becomes an ideology of class, a dividing line that separates individuals and societies from one another. As an ideology, scripture makes people believe they have the right knowledge, therefore, the proper way of knowing God and the right manner of living in the world. Consequently, those who believe they have the truth, or a corner on the truth, so to speak, develop an air of superiority and arrogance which mitigates against life together in the world. This is the ideology that poisoned Eastern and Western minds, more so the latter, into dismissing religions of structure as mere superstitions. Scripture divided religions into higher and lower religions, with scripture being on the higher side. A book is not scripture unless and until it becomes the living substance of the people that mediates them.

DRUM AS TEXT

In looking at text or scripture as that which mediates the sacred, we turn to the drum which in Africa is a sacred text even as it is used in social occasions. The power of the drum among Africans was recognised even by both colonialists and missionaries. For the latter, the drum was an instrument of the devil that called people to their pre-Christian past. For colonialists, the drum was an instrument of resistence to colonial power. There are different types of drums in Africa and made for different purposes, social or ritual. The drum is a fundamental institution in Africa with the power to organise life and mediate the sacred. The talking drum in particular, is held as a sacred text, the word of God, the spirits, and the ancestors. Georges Niangoran-Bouah has written a poem about the drum as a sacred text:

Contemporary drum
Of founding ancestors,
Messenger coming
from the beginning of time.

Drum, wherever you are
And whatever your state,
Drum word,
Memory of Ancients,
We implore you, speak,
Talk to us in the African way
Of immemorial times,
Speak, speak to us
Of deep Africa
Of true Africa![27]

Talking about the sacred role of the drum, drumlogist Niangoran-Bouah writes:

Thus, some societies have books while others have drums. In fact, drums and books play the same role and have the same significance for their respective societies. For the Akan of the Gulf of Guinea, a drum text becomes the standard version of a historical event, of a personality, of an institution, and of fundamental beliefs preserved in the collective memory of the people. . . . For the Akan, the drummed documentation is serious; it is sacred and respected by the whole population. This is the reason that it is the preferred method of communication with gods, the spirits, and the ancestors. . . . Among the Akan in Cote d'Ivoire and Ghana, the drum defines its origin itself by saying:

God in creating the world
Has suffered to create.
What did he create?
He created the Drum.
Divine Drum,
Wherever you are
In nature
We call upon you,
Come.[28]

To an outsider the African drum may be just beat and rhythm, but to the locals, the beat is communication with God, divinities, ancestors during important occasions in the life of the people. Niangoran-Bouah has observed that: *"The texts of a talking drum are as reliable as those of the written word.* The texts are authentic (not manipulated), conventional (know and accepted by the sages, scholars, and drummers of the country), first hand (conceived by the founding ancestors or by a target group of the pre-colonial history), and, finally, signed (each drummer signs the documents which he disseminates by his name and genealogy)".[29] Looking at the role of the drum among the Akan, Niangoran-Bouah tells us to be open to the idea of a sacred text as only that which is written for there are others ways by which sacred stories are meditated. Thus, Niangoran-Bouah concludes:

It is customary when talking of the religious thoughts of the ancient people of the Middle East to refer to the Bible or the *Qur'an*. In the same ways the Akan refer themselves to the talking drum in order to quote any discourse related to the sacred. Bible, *Qur'an*, and Drum have the same vocation; these are fundamental sacred "books" venerated by their respected peoples. They are monuments of the human spirit because they are timeless. The drum is a tool and an appropriate instrument of knowledge which for a time was considered as not being accessible to the universe of African traditional beliefs. The discourse of the drum, unchangeable and conventional, is not a discourse of an isolated wise man, but a real ideology of several thousand years which the memory of a whole people preserves with piety from generation to generation.[30]

RELIGIONS AND THEIR CANONS

Religion	Scriptures
Therevada Buddhism	*Pali Tripitaka*. The Three Baskets 29 B. C. E.
Mahayana Buddhism	*Prajnaparamita* (Perfection of Wisdom)
Tibetan (Tantric) Buddhism	*Bka'-'gyur*, Kanjyur (Translated Word), *Bstan-'gyur*, Tenjyur (Transmitted Word). *Dhammapada* (Way of Truth), common to all Buddhists
Christianity	*Holy Bible* (different number of books: Catholics 73, Protestant 66, Orthodox 73).
Confucianism	*Si Shu* or the "Four Books"; the *Wu Jing*, the "Five Classics" (from 1130 C.E.).
Hinduism (Sanatana Dharma)	*Vedas* (from 2,500 B.C.E.)
Islam	*Qur'an* (from 632 C.E.)
Jainism	*Jain Agamas* (1500 C.E.)
Judaism	*Tanak* 400 B.C.E.
Shito	No revealed canon, but ancestral accounts: *Kokiji* (Record of Ancient Matters). *Shoku Nikongi* (Continuing Chronicles of Japan). *Rokkokushi* (Six National Histories).
Sikhism	*Guru Granth Sahib* (1604 C.E.)
Taoism	*Taozang* comprised of the *Sandong* (Three Grottoes 400 B.C.E.) and the *Sifu* (Four Supplements 500 B.C.E.)
Zoroastrianism	*Zend Avesta* (from 1000 B.C.E.)

GLOSSARY

Ananda	Buddha's cousin and follower.
Canon	Authorised writings.
Grath Sahib	Sikh sacred writings.
Hermeneutics	A theory of interpretation.
Inspiration	
Divine	Directly receiving divine revelation.
Mechanical	The view that God dictated the writing of Bible.
Meditation	mental control and the development of concen-tration, leading to calmness.
Pali	The earliest known scriptures of Buddhism written in the Pali language around the 1st century B.C.E.
Sumyata	Buddhist doctrine of emptiness.
Sūtra	Canonical scriptures of the words of Buddha.
Tanak	Sacred writings of Judaism.
Tantric	Tibetan Buddhism.
Torah	The first five books of the Hebrew Bible.
Vedas	Sacred writings of Hinduism.

NOTES

1. Harvey J. Sindima, *I Believe: Creeds, Confessions, and Statements from the First to the Twenty-first Century* (forthcoming), 3.

2. *Ibid.*, 18.

3. Origen, *On First Principles* IV.I.

4. *Ibid.*, IV.I.7; IV.II.9.

5. Origen, *Contra Celsum* I.42, trans. Henry Chadwick (Cambridge: Cambridge University Press, 1965), 39.

6. Origen, *On First Principles*, IV.II.9, 286.

7. *Ibid.*, IV.II.4.

8. *Ibid.*, IV.III.5. Compare Origen, *Homilies on Genesis*1.14.

9. Quoted in C. Jenkins, ed., "Origen on I Corinthians", *Journal of Theological Studies* (Old Series) 9 (1908):137.

10. In this section I am drawing from James Livingston, *Anatomy of the Sacred: An Introduction to Religion*. 5th. ed. (Upper Saddle River, NJ: Pearson, 2005), 122–127.

11. Livingston, *Anatomy of the Sacred*, 126.

12. Georges Niangoran-Bouah, "The Talking drum: A Traditional African Instrument of Liturgy and Mediation with the Sacred", *African Traditional Religions in Contemporary Society*. Jacob K. Olupona (New York, NY: Paragon, 1991), 82.

13. Niangoran-Bouah, "The Talking drum", 83, 84.

14. *Ibid.*, 87.

15. *Ibid.*, 92.

6
Religious Functionaries

In every religion there are certain individuals who by appointment of the spirit or divinity become custodians and interpreters of the religion. Religious functionaries exercise and enjoy enormous power and authority among their people whether they rise to their office through a divine call, or call by the ancestors, by appointment of the people, through training, acquired skills, ordination, heredity, possession of the spirit, dreams, or personal desire. Their power and authority come from their being set apart, sacred, or holy. Rudolph Otto explains:

> The point is this that the "holy man" or the "prophet" is from the outset, as regards the experience of his devotees, something more than a mere man (*philos anthropos*). He is the being of wonder and mystery, who somehow or other is left to belong to the higher order of things, to the *numen* itself. It is not that he himself who teaches such, but that he is experienced as such.[1]

Otto here articulates clearly the nature and office of holy people especially when he says they are people "of wonder and mystery . . . [who] belong to the higher order of things, to the *numen* itself". In every religion and society holy people are certainly viewed as belonging to higher order of things, whether they are priests, prophets, or seers. Some societies, especially those practising religions of structure, also place mediums, diviners, shamans, rain makers, and others in the category of people "of wonder mystery . . . who belong to the higher of order of things". Also included in this category may be traditional leaders such as kings, queens, and chiefs because they too, at times preside over certain ritual practises, or invoking the ancestors and interceding before God on behalf of their people. All these religious figures engage in ministrations of religious rites, interpretation of scripture, healing, communication with the spirit world, or meeting the religious needs of their community.

RELIGIONS AND THEIR FUNCTIONARIES

Religious functionaries are found in every religion although the function, scope, and depth of their office may vary from religion to religion. Let us look at the offices of some religious functionaries. It is not necessary to list the office and nature of religious functionaries in all religious. A few will suffice.

Buddhism

The religious functionaries in Buddhism are monks and nuns who commit themselves to a monastic way of life. Monks and nuns in Buddhism are not ordained to become priests. There are no priests in Buddhism. These men and women train for a very long time, most of the time beginning at an early age and lasting as long as seventeen years to become monks and nuns. Even after they have had so much training, they still continue studying their canon to various degrees. There are monks and nuns, but no ordained religious functionaries in Buddhism.

Hinduism

Traditionally, priests (*pundits*) in Hinduism have come from one caste, the *Brahmana* community. However, since the caste system was outlawed in India in 1949, a few non-Brahmins have entered the Hindu priesthood. Priests are usually paid professional holy men and extremely few women in some Hindu traditions. Priests are highly trained professionals employed to lead *puja*, to do temple services and to conduct rites: naming of a child ten or eleven days after birth; perform initiation rites (*Upanayana*) for boys to manhood at between eight and twelve years of age; perform *Vivaha* (weddings) and lead in *Antyes ti* (funeral rites, cremation), and *Tarpan* (men's veneration of the ancestors with the offerings of water and sesame seeds).

The office and roles of *Pundits* arise out of the *Vedas* which give four main classes of *Rtvijas* or priestly classes:

1. Although there is no hierarchical ranking of priests, the *Brahman*, come on top because of their great learning of the *Vedas,* required to have oversight of sacrifices, ensuring that there were no mistakes. The priestly functions are based on the *Atharvaveda* (the *Veda* of magic spells).

2. After the *Brahman* in responsibilities is the chief priest, *Hotar,* who presides over sacrifices. His office is associated with the *Rigveda*, the holiest of the *Vedas*, with 1028 hymns to various divinities.

3. The temple priest for divination (worship) is the *Udgatar*, the priest of music who works on hymns for the *Hotar*. The office of the *Udgatar* arises from the *Samaveda,* the third *Veda*, known as the book of hymns and chants.

4. From the *Yajurveda Veda*, the *Veda* of liturgy, rituals, and sacrifices, is the fourth priesthood, the *Adhvaryu*, who carry out the actual sacrifice (*adhvara*).

Islam

There are no ordained religious functionaries in Islam. The *Imams* or *Maulvis* (religious leaders) who lead their communities do receive variable amounts of training. However, in the absence of an *Imam*, any knowledgeable person from the *Jama'ah* (congregation) can lead in the Friday prayers, *Jumu'ah*. Some Muslims become highly educated scholars of the *Qur'an*, the *ulama* (the learned) and the *fuquha* (jurists or men of insight). The regular functionaries may have a combination of knowledge of the *Qur'an* and practical experience.

Sikhism

Like Buddhism and Islam, there are no ordained priests and there is no monastic life in Sikhism. Some *gurdwaras* may have a *granthi*, the keeper and the reader of the Sikh scripture, *Guru Granth Sahib*. During the celebration and divination, and at other times, the *granthi* sits on the *rakht* (platform) behind the *Guru Granth Sahib*. A *granthi* may be a man or a woman. *Granthi* may be a paid position in larger *gurdwaras* or temples. There is no special training for a *granthi*. In some *gurdwaras*, the *Kirtani* and other musicians may also be employed at larger temples to assist in leading celebrations and other occasions.

Judaism

There are a number of functionaries in Judaism. The highest religious functionary in Judaism is a *rabbi*, a person well trained in *halakhah* (Jewish law) and tradition to be a teacher and an instructor of the community in matters pertaining *halakhah* and to lead in celebration of God. A *rabbi* is a teacher of the community in matters of faith as well as social conduct. A *rabbi* is not only highly trained, but he also receives *semicha*, rabbinical ordination. A *rabbi* is paid position.

Chazzan. Every Jewish congregation has a *chazzan* (a cantor), the person who conducts the liturgical and musical part of holy celebration. A *chazzan* leads the congregation in prayer and songs. No special educational qualifications are necessary for a *Chazzan*. However, the person must have a thorough knowledge of the liturgy, the prayers and melodies. A *Chazzan* may be a paid position.

A *gabbai* is a lay person who volunteers to perform various duties in connection with *Torah* readings at religious services.

Rebbe. There are different types of Judaism, but may be surmarised as two: Orthodox and Progressive. In the Orthodox community there is the office of *Rebbe*, who is the spiritual leader, master to be more precise, for he is *Tzaddik*, the "righteous one". A *Rebbe* is not a rabbi, but the individual of this inherited office has the final word among Orthodox Jews.

Kohein or *Kohanim* (plural) are the descendants of Aaron, the brother of Moses, the founder of Judaism. The traditional role of *Kohanim* was in animal sacrifices and temple rituals. Most of their work today is done by rabbis. However, *Kohanim* are given the first opportunity to recite a blessing *aliyah*, over the *Torah* in the Shabat liturgy. In addition, *Kohanim* are required to bless the congregation at certain times of the year.

Levi: A *Levi* is descendant of the tribe by the same name whose responsibilities were connected with the temple. Just like the *Kohanim*, they too, lost much of the functions of their office after the destruction of the temple in 70 C.E. In the *Shabat* liturgy, a *Levi* gets the second opportunity to recite *aliyah* over the *Torah* reading.

Without going into details let us take a quick look at the types of Judaism. The two types of Judaism mentioned above, Orthodox and Progressive, have further types within themselves. Orthodox Judaism includes Hasidim (Hasidic Jews) and Haredim, also called Ultra-Orthodox, a term which Haredim themselves consider pejorative. Orthodox Judaism is the traditional Judaism with its emphasis on *halakhah*. Orthodox Judaism teaches and insists that the *Torah* and the Talmud are the actual inspired words of God. Thus, they must be definitive in matters of faith and applied in all aspects of life. Jacob Neusner, a contemporary leading Jewish scholar, describes Orthodox Judaism as follows:

> Orthodox Judaism is that Judaic system that mediates between the received Judaism of the dual *Torah* and the requirements of living a life integrated in modern circumstances. Orthodoxy maintains the world view of the received *Torah*, constantly citing its sayings and adhering with only trivial variations to the bulk of its norms for everyday life. At the same time Orthodox holds that Jews adhering to the dual *Torah* may wear clothing that non Jews wear and do not have to wear distinctively Jewish clothing: may live within a common economy and not practise distinctively Jewish professions. . . . The difference between orthodoxy and the system of the dual *Torah* was expressed in social policy: integration, however circumscribed, versus the total separation of the holy people.[2]

Haredim believe they maintain an unbroken chain of teachings and practises from the time of Moses when he received *Torah* on Mount Sinai to the present. This self-understanding necessitates a segregated lifestyle from larger society in lifestyle and dress. The men distinguish themselves from larger society by their looks, a beard, dark coloured suits, large-breamed hats, and frock coats. The women wear in modest dresses and skirts with head covering. Both men and women dress just like eighteenth and nineteenth century Europeans.

The Progressive (Liberal Judaism) accepts scripture as the word of God, but that it was written by humans. Therefore, it demands interpretation to distinguish between divine and elements in the canonical scriptures. Reform Judaism takes seriously the freedom or autonomy of the individual to interpret and to decide to subscribe to a particular teaching. The Reformed point of view concerning Jewish law, *Halakhah*, is that it "is not unalterable, divine law, timeless and unchanging, but a human historically conditioned body of tradition which evolves in response to social needs and historical circumstances", says Philips Alexander. His point is informed by J. Z. Lauterbach, a Reformed rabbinic expert who writes:

In instituting these changes, we are merely doing the same thing which our ancient teachers did. The *Halakhah*, as the complex of laws, forms and customs, is not something fixed or permanent. Its very name, *Halakhah*, suggests movement and progress. There has always been an older and newer *Halakhah*. From its very beginning the *Halakhah* was constantly changing and developing. Ours is the youngest *Halakhah*, representing its latest development, but it is still the living stream of *Halakhah*. We also have a complex of laws, forms and customs, whereby we regulate our religious life, our *Halakhah*.[3]

Reformed Judaism developed in the nineteenth century. Alexander explains what led to the rise of Reformed Judaism in Germany.

The nationalism and exclusivism of traditional Judaism, particularly the "Zionism" of the prayer book, was something of an embarrassment. Exclusivism conflicted with the universalistic notions of the Age of Reason, and now that Jews were being granted equal citizenship it was surely inconsistent for them to continue praying for the restoration of their own Jewish State, for a return to Zion. The Reform movement arose in an attempt to strip Judaism of what as anachronisms, and to reshape it in a such a way that it would continue to command the respect and allegiance of modern "westernized" educated Jews.[4]

Reconstructionist Judaism , an American Jewish movement, came into being in the twentieth century through the efforts of Rabbi Mordecai M. Kaplan (1881–1983). Reconstructionists differ very much from all other types of Judaism: they do not share the idea of choseness of the Jews, they reject exclusive monopoly on the truth; and they maintain that Judaism is a spiritual path for seeking ultimate meaning in life. God is meaning or the source of meaning. Kaplan's own book, *Judaism as a Civilization: Toward a Reconstruction of American Jewish Life*, published in 1934, shows that Kaplan's focus was to incorporate American ideals of equality and democracy. Even much more different from other modern Jewish movements, was that Kaplan emphasised or took as a priority was that Judaism is a civilisation not a religion.[5]

MONASTICISM

One of the common characteristics among religious functionaries in the religions of salvation is the rejection of this world to seek a higher spiritual life. These functionaries renounce the world and deny bodily pleasures to seek the ultimate or God. The preferred lifestyle for most otherworldly functionaries is monastic life. Monasticism is from Greek: *monachos*, meaning a solitary person. The functionaries who lead a monastic life are called monks (*monachos*) or *brothers* (male), and *nuns or sisters* (female). Monks and nuns are found in many religions of salvation: Buddhism, Christianity (in particular within the Catholic and Orthodox traditions), Hinduism, Jainism, and to a lesser extent, Islam. The aims and goals of monastic life are more or less the same across religions: to reach a higher level of religious consciousness, or a deeper spirituality by renouncing the world, including family, denying self bodily pleasures, and seeking and maintaining personal integrity expressed in various ways among the religions. In some religions monks and nuns do not seek this path all for themselves, but also to be of use to their communities: helping individuals deal with the problems of life by offering a helping hand, serving the community, or counselling. In Asian religions monks and nuns teach followers non-attachment to worldly conditions: happiness, pleasure, pain, or loss. Monks and nuns also instruct followers how to deal with trials and suffering, as in illness and death. Lastly, and even more important, is that monks and nuns assist in religious functions, they are custodians of the religion, or those who preserve the teachings and practises of their religion. Let us now see how monks and nuns satisfy the three objectives of monastic life: seeking higher personal spirituality, service to the community, and preserving the teachings of their religion.

Buddhist Monasticism

The *Sangha* (community or assembly), the order Buddhist monastic life, has been part of Buddhism as long as the religion has existed. The *Sangha* was established by Gautama, the Buddha himself more than 2,500 years ago. The Buddha put in high regard monastic life believing it was a higher form of living and as a way to preserve the teaching, now called Buddhism. A monastic life is for anyone who desires, but must be no less than eight years of age. Anyone willing to become a monk or nun must shave off all the hair as a symbolic act of one's renunciation of the worldly life. Then the candidate puts on a robe appropriate to the monastic tradition being entered. The candidate is now called a novice. A novice has a preceptor, a senior monk, and the candidate is ordained to the novitiate by the abbot, head of the monastery. The responsibility of the preceptor and an instructor is to guide the novice through the period of monastic training. After training, the novice receives *upasampada*, a higher ordination as a monk (*bhikkhu*) or a nun (*bhikkuni*). To become a *bhikkhu* or *bhikkuni* the candidate must be at least twenty years of age or older. These steps apply to both monks and nuns who are required to live as *Samaneras* (novices) for a longer period of time, typically five years.

Samaneras observe the Ten Precepts, but are not responsible for living by the full set of monastic rules. The Ten Precepts by which *Samaneras* live by are:

1. To abstain from harming or taking life.
2. To abstain from taking what is not given.
3. To abstain from any sexual contact.
4. To abstain from false speech.
5. To abstain from the use of intoxicants.
6. To abstain from taking food after midday.

7. To abstain from dancing, singing, music or any kind of entertainment.
8. To abstain from the use of garlands, perfumes, unguents and adornments.
9. To abstain from using luxurious seats.
10. To abstain from accepting and holding money.

The life of *Samaneras* involves doing the following:
1. Study, either in groups or individually;
2. Perform assigned tasks for the maintenance of the monastic institution;
3. Meditate three times a day;
4. Participate in collective observances like the recitation of the disciplinary code on new moon and full moon days;
5. Performance of religious services for the lay community.

Christian Monasticism

The history of monastic life in Christianity is traced to Egypt in the persons of Anthony (251–356) and Pachomius (292–348). Anthony, born in Koma, 200 miles up the Nile near the city in Memphis. Anthony was inspired by the words of Jesus in the Gospel According to Matthew 19:21, "If you wish to be perfect, go, sell your possessions, and give the money to the poor, and you will have treasure in heaven; then come, follow me". Writing on the origins of monastic life, I said the following in *Drums of Redemption*:

> Anthony sold the three hundred-acre family farm, deposited some money for the care of his sister, and the rest he gave away. He started living an ascetic life. He did this for fifteen years before he decided to go and live alone in the desert where there would be nothing to take his attention away from religious devotion. Anthony lived there for twenty years, during which he attracted some followers whom he instructed until his death in 356.[6]

Anthony introduced non-communal monastic life. It was Pachomius, an ex-service military man. He converted to Christianity in 313 and learned about monastic life from a monk by the name of Palemon who said to him, "Many have come hither from disgust with the world, and no perseverance. Remember, my son, my food consists of only bread and salt; I drink no wine, take no oil, spend half the night awake, singing Psalms and meditating on Scriptures, and sometimes pass the whole night without sleep".[7] Anthony persevered and one night an angel said to him, "Stay here and build a monastery and many will come to you in order to be monks". He built a monastery and within a short time he had nine cloisters with monks ranging from three to seven hundred. This was the beginning of community monastic life in Christianity. By the time of his death in 346, Pachomius had organised 3,000 communities of monks and nuns in the Thebaid area in Egypt.

Monasticism is not practised in all the branches of Christianity, but among Catholics, Orthodox, and Anglicans whose monastic membership has been experiencing a deep decline since the 1960s. Catholic and Anglican monasticism does not necessarily mean living in a monastery, but in a community being an example of faith to followers. While some Catholic and Anglican monks and nuns may live a cloistered life, many work with people in church related institutions such as schools, hospital, orphanages, and others.

Catholic Monastic Process

Monasticism in Christianity is a lay vocation. Although monks and nuns help in the ministration of the church, they are not members of the clergy. Monks and nuns live in a community (a monastery) with the permission of, and under the rule of an abbot or abbess, a head of the community. The focus of monastic life in Christianity is on an ideal called the religious life, also called the state of perfection. A person aspiring monastic life is known as a postulant (from *postulare*, to ask). So the aspirant is viewed as making a request for admission to enter monastic life. The aspirant is allowed to stay at a monastery without taking monastic vows. After a period of examination, the candidate is admitted as a novice. As a novice the aspirant professes the first vows after at least one year of the novitiate. The first vows are temporary and have to be renewed for the novitiate may last at least three years and as long as five. Through these vows, the novice joins the order as a temporary brother or sister as Catholic monks and nuns call each other. After passing through several vows of various lengths, the temporary brother or sister pronounces the last vows and joins the order as its permanent member. In the last vows to brotherhood or sisterhood the candidate takes the vows of poverty, chastity, obedience.

Eastern Monks and Nuns

The Eastern Orthodox monasticism is a life contemplation and prayer away from the world. The focus of Orthodox monasticism is the same as in Orthodox Christianity, namely, perfection and penance. This idea is expressed clearly in the *Philokalia* (a Greek term meaning the Love of Good Things) a collection of texts by masters of the Eastern Orthodox. A quote from *Philokalia*, Volume 2:355 could easily be thought to come from some of the monastic religions of Asia:

> When the intellect has been perfected, it unites wholly with God and is illumined by divine light, and the most hidden mysteries are revealed to it. Then it truly learns where wisdom and power lie. . . . While it is still fighting against the passions it cannot as yet enjoy these things. . . . But once the battle is over and it is found worthy of spiritual gifts, then it becomes wholly luminous, powerfully energised by grace and rooted in the contemplation of spiritual realities. A person in whom this happens is not attached to the things of this world, but has passed from death to life.

Orthodox monks are ordained clergy, but Orthodox bishops are only chosen from the celibate clergy, but widowers, who have accepted monastic vows, may also be chosen. The monastic process in the Easter Orthodox tradition is long and much involving. It has four steps. First, is a postulant who requests membership into an order and is permitted to stay for three months without taking monastic vows after which he or she become a novice, the rank of obedience. At the monastery the novice is under the direction of a spiritual father or mother. During the three months, or however the duration may be of being a postulant, the candidate is given a tunic and belt, a portion of the monk or nun clothing called a habit. This portion of monastic clothing serves to express the determination to live monastic life of self-denial or asceticism, depending on the approval of the abbot (abbess).

The first step may last as long as two years, or shortened depending on the judgement of the abbot or abbess. The second stage comes when the head of the monastery believes the novice is prepared to answer questions from the bishop. The novice makes solemn vows and receives the habit, an outer piece of clothing, with wide sleeves and down to the ankles. Along with it, the novice receives a head cover with a veil. The individual is not yet committed to monastic life at this stage.

It is at the third stage that a person pledges to remain in monastic life forever, in obedience to the leaders and head of the monastic community. The person takes in public the final vows of Stability, Obedience, Poverty and Chastity. After making these vows the person receives the tonsure (shaving of the hair), the candidate is vested with the *paraman* and small *mandyas* which are new added to the habit. The new monk or nun receives a new name at rising to the title and office of monk or nun.

The fourth and last stage, comes after an undefined time of perseverance a monk receives the great habit (*koukoulion*) and becomes *megaloschemos* (Greek *megas*, great and *schema*, habit), in the Greek Orthodox, or in Russian, *skhmnik*. Only a few monks reach this final rank of the monastic order of the great schema. It requires the most strict observance of ideals of monastic life which includes a life of total seclusion in perpetual prayer and contemplation. At this stage a new name is given along with a new monastic insignia, the great schema, is worn. The new insignia is embroidered with the cross which the monk is to take up daily in following Christ. The same representation figures on the hood, a thimble-shaped *kamelos*. The colour of the robes of monks in the Orthodox Church is black, symbolising the second baptism.

Ethiopian Monastic Community (Nefru geddam)

Christian monasticism has its roots in Africa and it is only proper that we take a look at African monastic life. We will now look at Ethiopian monastic life, which is in many ways like Egyptian monasticism since the Ethiopian church was placed under the church in Egypt by a precept inserted in Canon 36 of pseudo-Canon of Nicaea.[8] Christianity has been in Ethiopia from the first century C.E., and the Ethiopian Church has existed since the fourth century. Since then, Ethiopia has been a stronghold of Christianity in Africa with more than 29 million believers, 400,000 priests, and 40 archbishops. Accordingly, it has many monasteries than the Coptic

Church in Egypt, one thousand monasteries. Like the early monasteries in Egypt, traditionally Ethiopian monasteries are villages of fifty to five hundred monks. Most of these monastery villages are on mountains or cliffs because many of their founders were hermits living in mountain caves. Each monastery has two heads, the administrative head, or the chief, *Abbe Minet* or *mähir* (teacher) who is elected by the monks of his monastery for life or until he desires to leave the position. The *Abbe Minet* may live in the village or a short distance away. The *Abbe Minet's* deputy is the *Afe Memhir* whose responsibility is to keep the general discipline of the community, and he has the authority to judge and to punish disobedient monks. The *Afe Mämhir* is the deputy administrator of *Nefru geddam*. The second head of the monastery village in the spiritual head called the *Komas*. Unlike *Abbe Minet*, the *Komas* is appointed by the bishop as his representative. The *Komas* is often a senior monk with outstanding life of piety.

Practically anyone who desires to become a monk can do so in the Ethiopian monastic tradition: young or old, educated or illiterate, or windowed. Each monastery has a reading school (*nebab Bet*) to which young aspirants, including boys, may attend for one or two years and may return to their villages if they do not want to continue. Those who continue enter the Liturgy school (*Qidane Bet*) after three years are sent to the bishop to be ordained deacons and are thus able to assist in the holy liturgy. At this first stage in monastic life, the individual has a *kedet*, girdle or belt. After a few more years of being a deacon, and when he has proven himself fit for monastic life, senior monks examine the deacon for reading and knowledge of the holy scriptures. A deacon may take the examination as many times until he passes. After passing the examinations, the deacon may choose to return to his home and serve as a deacon before ordination by a bishop to secular priesthood. Those who decide to remain and become monks, have a long interview with the *Abbe Minet*, during which the deacon is discouraged from taking monastic vows. When the candidate demonstrates the desire, willingness, and resolve to become a monk, the *Abbe Minet* asks: "Are you prepared to serve God as a monk, according to the ancient traditions governing the monk's conduct?" To which the deacon replies, "Yes, I am".

Ethiopian monks are graduates of the monastery training who have gone beyond the Liturgy school (*Qidane Bet*). They have also been in the *Qene Bet*, the Poetry School, to study sophisticated poetry based on scripture. They have also attended the *Metsehaf Bet*, Literature school, memorising the comments of the Early Church Fathers in the *Amdemta* Commentaries. Not all the commentaries are memorised for it takes 40 years to do so. In addition to graduates of the monasteries, laymen and widowers are also welcome to monastic life. A few weeks after their interview with the *Abbe Minet*, a profession ceremony is held in a church, usually on a Feast day. The candidate wrapped in palm leaves, the funeral dress of the poor, monks sing a funeral requiem to signify his death to the world. Monks sing the requiem for candidate lying on the floor. When he rises up, the *Komas* places on his head a cotton skull cap (*qob*) which he must always wear as the sign of his profession. The candidate is given a new name. Then for 40 days the new monk usually confines himself to his hut, in imitation of Christ in the wilderness, to prepare for his future life. About a year after the profession, graduates from the monastery go to the local bishop to be ordained a priest. Monks with less education and widowers are not ordained to the priesthood.

There are no orders in Ethiopian monastic life. Monks may spend all their lives in one monastery or they may go elsewhere and they will be welcome. However, the most revered monastic life in Ethiopia is the hermitage, which is considered the highest life on earth. Close to one tenth of the monks in every monastery practise hermetic life, spending all their time alone in prayer without getting out of their dwelling. Some come out only for the Holy Liturgy on Sunday and Feast days. Food is brought to them by an assigned monk. While some hermits live within the monastery compound, few hide away in a cave, but may be visited. These monks who live in isolation are called *bahtawiyan*

Hindu Monks

Hinduism has a rich tradition of monastic life whose monasteries are known as *Ashrams*. Hindu monks, called *Sadhus*, are in most traditions recognised by their saffron robes. Monastic life in Hinduism is supported by the *Vedas* and other scriptures. There are different practises of monastic life in Hinduism. There are monks who live in secluded caves in distant forests; wandering as homeless mendicants; or itinerant monks who take pilgrimages to holy sanctuaries of Hinduism. Then there are also monks who live with fellow monks in *ashrama, adheenam* or *matha* of their *satguru*. These monks may live in these places without having taken formal vows. When they decide to renounce the world, they join the order of *sannyasa,* and they wear saffron robes and carry a *Kamandalu*, a water vessel symbolising self-contained life, freedom from worldly needs, constant *sadhana* and *tapas,* and the oath to seek God everywhere. *Sannyasa* is not for young people, nonetheless, young, unmarried men may qualify for renunciation, called *sannyasa dîîksha,* which may be conferred by any legitimate *sannyasin* or a *satguru* (a senior *guru*). Young men who enter monastic training before the age of twenty-five and meet other qualifications, may generally after a minimum of twelve years of preparation and training take the *sannyasin's* lifetime vows, called holy orders of *sannyasa.*

A Hindu monk is called a *Sadhu*, the one who practises *yoga* and takes vows of renunciation which forbid him from:
1. owning personal property apart from a bowl, a cup, two sets of clothing and medical aides such as eyeglasses;
2. having any contact with, looking at, thinking of or even being in the presence of women;
3. eating for pleasure;
4. possessing or even touching money or valuables in any way, shape or form;
5. maintaining personal relationships.

Jain Monastic Life

There are two branches of Jainism with slightly different practises of monastic life: *Shvetambara* monks who wear thin white robes and *Digambara* monks who reject all worldly possessions in order to live a totally ascetic life. Since they do not have any possessions whatsoever, they live without clothes and go "skyclad", which refers to their being naked. However, *Digambara* nuns wear simple white clothes. By their nakedness *Digambara Sadhus* (monks) and *Sadhvis* (nuns) express their complete detachment from the world which makes them beyond feelings such as modesty and shame. *Digambara* monks have only two possessions: a peacock feather broom and a water gourd. The feather broom is for sweeping their path so that they do not accidently step on insects and kill them. This is part of fulfilling the teaching of non-violence. They also believe that women are unable to obtain *moksha*, eternal liberation. There are more than 6,000 Jain *Sadhvis*, but less than a hundred of these belong to *Digambara* monastic life.

The monastic life of Jain *Sadhus* (monks) and *Sadhvis* (nuns) is austere. Like Hindu monks, they live away from their families and wander from one place to another on foot, and without shoes. They are not allowed to live in one place for a long time. In fact, monks and nuns are expected to be homeless, shave their heads and beg for food, but cannot accept food that is cooked for them. They usually live in groups of five or six and the most senior monk among them delivers a lecture every morning. During the day, the monks study scripture and meditate on it three times. On their short stays in one place, they do not participate in social or political matters.

The doctrine and vow of *ahimsa*, the principle of nonviolence to any living thing, are of paramount importance to all Jains. To fulfill this vow, some monks and nuns do not eat vegetables, but only fruit, nuts and milk. It is also because of *ahimsa*, that some Jain *Sadhus* and *Sadhvis* wear masks over their mouth and nose to avoid inadvertently harming insects or microbes by inhaling them. It is also because of *ahimsa* that *Digambara* monks go around sweeping their path with a peacock feather broom. Jain *Sadhus* and *Sadhvis* take the Five Great Vows:

1. Non-violence (*ahimsa*). This vow is about never cause harm or violence to any living being including even the tiniest creatures.
2. Truth (*satya*). Never to lie.
3. Non-stealing (*asteya*). Never to take or use anything without the permission of the owner. They will not take anything from anywhere.
4. Celibacy (*brahmachanga*). Never touch a member of the opposite sex regardless of their age.
5. Non-possessiveness (*aparigraha*). Never to possess anything and do not have any attachment for things except their daily needs.

At the end of their renouncing the world, they vow:

O Lord *Arihant*! I will not commit the sins of violence, express falsehood, steal and enjoy sensual pleasures, or be possessive, by speech, thought or deed; nor will I assist or order anyone to commit these sins. I will not approve or endorse anyone committing such sins. Oh Lord! I hereby take a sacred and solemn vow that throughout my life, I will follow these five major vows and strictly follow the code of conduct laid out for a *sadhu* and a *sadhvi*.

CELIBACY

Another common practise among most religions of salvation is celibacy. In Buddhism, Christianity, Hinduism, and Jainism celibacy is a virtue of the highest order for it is the complete denial of pleasure, thus of self for the sake achieving self-realisation and highest spiritual development and enlightenment. Religions of salvation are united in overcoming desire and pleasure. Since sexual desire is viewed the ultimate of all desires, denying oneself this desire, is a sign of complete self-control. Therefore, it is treated as an essential aspect of spiritual development. It is for this reason that celibacy is an important feature of the spirituality of religions of salvation. Hindus consider celibacy (*brahmacharya*) as an important virtue and an essential aspect of spiritual life. So do Buddhists, two traditions of Christianity, Jains and members of other religions in Asia. All these religions consider celibacy as ideal for realising a higher level spirituality for it frees one from strong attachment and self-indulgence that sexual desire demands. Celibacy frees one from thinking and talking about, and let alone actualising sexual desire. Without celibacy, one remains bound to this world where attachment, desire, and indulgence prevent overcoming body and mind (false-self) on its journey to the self (true-self, *Atman*) or realising the divine.

Even Judaism, a religion that does not embrace celibacy, did have celibacy in the early decades of the first century of the Common Era through a movement called the Essenes. This was a very small group, numbering four thousand by the time of Jesus. They lived in communes in the desert where they had retreated to maintain the purity of Jewish culture and religion by strict observance of the Law as given by Moses. They considered Temple and general observance of the Law in society impure. So they retreated to the desert where they lived waiting for the Messiah who would overthrow Roman rule and establish a new covenant and kingdom with them as the true Israel.

Hindu Celibacy

Celibacy has always been the highest ideal for spiritual life in the 5000-year-old Hindu religion. To this day, orthodox Hindus abstinence from sex and getting married as ideal. This should not be understood as abhorring marriage. On the contrary, marriage is a very important and necessary stage in a Hindu's life. Marriage is one of four stages, *asrama*, of development of spiritual life in

Hinduism. In Upanishads, there is an overwhelming tendency to glorify the status of a householder. The reason Orthodox Hindus consider celibacy a high virtue is because through celibacy one is able to convert *retas* (sexual energy) into *tejas* (spiritual energy). Hindus maintain that sexual energy not controlled is dissipated, but through the discipline and practise of celibacy that energy is channeled up the spine to activate *chakras*, centres of spiritual energy. Ancient Hindus firmly believed that observation of celibacy was very essential to reach the world of *Brahmans*.

The four stages ideal spiritual life in Hinduism, represent four developmental behavioural stages of ideal human growth. In ancient Hinduism and still today, the life of a young Hindu is to devote himself or herself to the life of the mind or study. This stage begins at around ten, when one learns the *Vedas* and other scriptures from a master who is celibate. The master teaches the young person scriptures as well as the discipline of celibacy. The young person at this stage is known as the *brahmacharya* (celibate). This period of rigorous training in scriptures and understanding and maintaining celibacy lasts twelve years. The period of learning is followed by the stage of *garhasthya*, the active life of marriage and family. Not all choose to marry; a *brahmacharya* may decide to continue as monks and remain celibate for life. Please note that while celibacy is viewed as ideal for spiritual life, Hinduism equally respects both paths celibate and married life.

Some of those who get married, usually continue to put in high regard the ideal for spiritual life and commitment. In the third of life *asrama*, those often leave active life, to become *vanaprastha*, partial hermits in the forests to learn detachment from material life, in preparation for the fourth stage of *sanyasin*. In the beginning of the third stage, *vanaprastha* married couples may live together in the forest or mountains, but as celibates. The third stage is essentially a return to celibate life, freeing onself of worldly possessions and family duties. The two may not go into the forest or mountains right away, but may decide to travel together visiting places of pilgrimage. Later, however, the wife returns home. *Vanaprastha*, lasts from fifty to seventy-five years.

The last stage is *sanyasa*, a life of complete detachment which the individual lives a life of solitude, having renounced all emotional and material ties to the world: family, friends, and all material possessions. *Sanyasin* are mostly men, but I have met women *sanyasin* in a home courtyard. A *sanyasin*, one spends time in meditation and is committed to the purity of mind. As emotionally detached, a *sanyasin* is indifferent to sensual pleasures; he does not hate or dislike anything or anyone, he neither loves anything or anyone. A *sanyasin* is free from desires, egoism, lust, anger, greed, and pride. A *sanyasin* is a wanderer; he depends on charity for food. He has no religion nor nation. A *Sanyasin* is the individual who has attained perfection of the human spirit and body by mastering control over all feelings and state of being.

Christian Celibacy

Christian celibacy is voluntary for monks and nuns, but involuntary for all desiring to be priests in the Catholic church. Eastern Orthodox does not impose celibacy on its priests. In defining celibacy the Catholic Encyclopedia says: "Celibacy is the renunciation of marriage implicitly or explicitly made, for the more perfect observance of chastity, by all those who receive the Sacrament of Orders in any of the higher grades". Priests are bound by to celibacy by 1983 Code of Canon law, Canon 277 paragraph one which states:

> Clerics are obliged to observe perfect and perpetual continence for the sake of the Kingdom of heaven, and are therefore bound to celibacy. Celibacy is a special gift of God by which sacred ministers can more easily remain close to Christ with an undivided heart, and can dedicate themselves more freely to the service of God and their neighbour.

Paragraph 2 of the same Canon cautions clergy against associating with individuals who might cause them to break their vow of celibacy: "Clerics are to behave with due prudence in relation to persons whose company can be a danger to their obligation of preserving continence or can lead to scandal of the faithful". Beyond Canon law, there are three devotional assertions of celibacy: (1) celibacy is a symbol for living for the kingdom of God; (2) celibacy is recognition of the calling; (3) celibacy is a witness to action of the spirit that draws humans to prayer and devotion.

The practise of celibacy differs from one Christian tradition to the other. Orthodox Churches do not require celibacy for what are called minor clerics: Subdeacons, deacons, and priests. If they remarry, they cannot be promoted to higher office, and if they marry for the third time, or proven guilty of having a sexual relationship with any other person, they are no longer allowed to exercise the functions of their office. In the Russian Church, the candidate for any clerical office must be either already married, or formally declared his intention of remaining celibate. Eastern Orthodox Churches follow the general principle of married clerics before taking their vows to any clerical office. While minor clerics may marry in the Orthodox tradition, bishops are selected only from celibate clerics. If a married priest is selected for the office of bishop, he must not live with his wife. They are not divorced, but they must not live together. She may join monastic life and become a nun.[9]

For Catholics or the Latin Church as Orthodox call it, celibacy is involuntary for clerics. Scriptural support for involuntary celibacy in Christianity is not there and it is very thin for celibacy itself. The often quoted verses on celibacy are: Matthew 19.11–12; 1 Corinthians 7: 26–35. Matthew 19:12, 19. Celibacy is all right if it assumed freely for the "sake of the kingdom of heaven". However, Jesus himself made it clear that "not all can accept this teaching" (Matthew 19.11–12). By which he meant that celibacy is not for everyone and should not be forced on anyone. In the second reference 1 Corinthians 7: 26–35, the writer, Paul of Tarsus, stresses celibacy as a more perfect state for service to God. He says that especially 7:32–34 which says:

> I want you to be free from anxieties. The unmarried man is anxious about the affairs of the Lord, how to please the Lord; but the married man is anxious about the affairs of the world, how to please his wife, and his interests are divided. And the unmarried woman and the virgin are anxious about the affairs of the Lord, so that they may be holy in body and spirit; but the married woman is anxious about the affairs of the world, how to please her husband.

Paul neither condemns nor undervalues marriage, and, once again, celibacy is for those who feel free to do so for the service of God. In spite of the absence of scriptural mandate for celibacy, the Catholic church tends to value virginity as a much higher level of sanctity.

THE DEVELOPMENT OF CHRISTIAN CELIBACY

Without overwhelming support, or rather with thin biblical support for celibacy as necessary condition for service of God, the issue of celibacy has been a matter of debate within Christianity from the first century of the Common Era. First there was the Paul whom we have already cited above. Over the years, many other individual church leaders followed Paul in elevating celibacy and equating it with a higher spiritual status good for the service of God. It will be too far afield for us to give the full development of celibacy in Christianity, but few highlights will be given here.

The first serious push for the whole Christian tradition to make celibacy official came from Spain at the Council of Elvira, Spain, in 306. Decree 33 of the Council said: "Bishops, presbyters, deacons, and others with a position in the ministry are to abstain completely from sexual intercourse with their wives and from the procreation of children. If anyone disobeys, he shall be removed from the clerical office". The Council did not ask clerics to divorce their wives, but only not to sleep with them. This decree does not seem to have been put into practise in the whole Christian tradition for we see it being a topic of discussion at the first gathering of bishops from the Christian world in 325 at Nicaea (the city of Nice, in Bithynia). This gathering known as the First Ecumenical (worldwide) Council was attended by 318 bishops most of them were from the east with only five from the Western church, namely churches west of Egypt in communion with Rome, the old capital of the Roman empire. The churches in the east were those from Egypt, through Palestine, Syria to all those in communion with Constantinople, *Nova Roma* (new Rome, today's Istanbul in Turkey) as it was called. At the first Council of Nicaea, a Spanish bishop Ossius, of Cordoba, pushed the Council to decree celibacy as a requirement for ordination throughout the universal church, but Egyptian bishop

Paphnutios, protested that such a rule would be difficult and imprudent and that celibacy should be a matter of vocation and personal choice.[10] After its deliberations, the Council decreed in Canon 3 that: "The great Synod has stringently forbidden any bishop, presbyter, deacon, or any one of the clergy whatever, to have a subintroducta dwelling with him, except only a mother, or sister, or aunt, or such persons only as are beyond all suspicion".

It is difficult to explain subintroducta, but it appears to refer to women who were neither wives nor concubines, rather women who would be introduced into the house to live with the priest on the pretext of a spiritual relationship of some kind, a disciple, for example. The canon does not expressively say a cleric should live with his wife, for a wife would not be introduced into the house as a spiritual partner or soul mate. The fact that the canon did not prohibit clerical marriage is seen by the fact that although the majority who voted for it was from the east, there being only five bishops from Western church, they continued to allow married clerics after the Council. While the Western Church interpreted the canon as prohibition to married clerics, the east did not take it that way. For at an earlier council, the Council of Ancyra in 314, the Eastern church allowed its clergy to continue living with their wives, and allowed deacons to marry if they had previously sought permission from the bishop to marry. Canon 10 of Council of Ancyra in 314 stated:

> They who have been made deacons, declaring when they were ordained that they must marry, because they were not able to abide so, and who afterwards have married, shall continue in their ministry, because it was conceded to them by the bishop. But if any were silent on this matter, undertaking at their ordination to abide as they were, and afterwards proceeded to marriage, these shall cease from the diaconate.

This position was repeated in canons of the Council of Constantinople in 692, also known as the Council of Trullo. Canon 13 of the Council makes it clear that celibacy was not what the First Ecumenical Council of Nicae intended for all clerics. Canon 13 of the Council of Trullo reads:

> Since we know it to be handed down as a rule of the Roman Church that those who are deemed worthy to be advanced to the diaconate or presbyterate should promise no longer to cohabit with their wives, we, preserving the ancient rule and apostolic perfection and order, will that the lawful marriages of men who are in holy orders be from this time forward firm, by no means dissolving their union with their wives nor depriving them of their mutual intercourse at a convenient time. Wherefore, if anyone shall have been found worthy to be ordained subdeacon, or deacon, or presbyter, he is by no means to be prohibited from admittance to such a rank, even if he shall live with a lawful wife. Nor shall it be demanded of him at the time of his ordination that he promise to abstain from lawful intercourse with his wife: lest we should affect injuriously marriage constituted by God and blessed by his presence, as the Gospel saith: "What God hath joined together let no man put asunder".

Celibate Priesthood in the Catholic Church

Over the centuries the Western Church has continued to argue in favour of celibate priesthood. Several popes have made decrees on celibacy. The first was Pope Damascus I (pope from 366–384), who in his 384 letter wrote that only a celibate cleric could properly advise widows and virgins, certain scriptural texts require celibacy and drew several references of scripture: Romans 8:9, 13:14; 1Corinthians 7:7, 29. Pope Damascus was followed in this position by popes Siricius (385), Innocent I (404), and Leo I (458) and many more. The current situation in Catholic celibacy was decreed by the Council of Trent. During its Twenty-fourth Session, the council decreed Canon 9 which states:

> If any one saith, that clerics constituted in sacred orders, or Regulars, who have solemnly professed chastity, are able to contract marriage, and that being contracted it is valid, notwithstanding the ecclesiastical law, or vow; and that the contrary is nothing else than to condemn marriage; and, that all who do not feel that they have the gift of chastity, even though they have made a vow thereof, may contract marriage; let him be anathema: seeing that God refuses not that gift to those who ask for it rightly, neither does He suffer us to be tempted above that which we are able.

Canon 10 of the Council of Trent also affirmed and elevated virginity and celibacy decreeing: "If any one saith, that the marriage state is to be placed above the state of virginity, or of celibacy, and that it is not better and more blessed to remain in virginity, or in celibacy, than to be united in matrimony; let him be anathema".

The decree of Trent has guided the Catholic church over the centuries. However, in 1951, Pope Pius XII allowed a married Lutheran pastor in Germany to be ordained a catholic priest. In 1966, Pope Paul VI gave celibacy dispensations (exception to the rule). On 24 June 1967, the pope issued a Papal Encyclical (a circular letter to bishops and all Catholic churches) called *Sacerdotalis Caelibatus* (Latin for Clerical Celibacy) in which he explained the reasons for the dispensations or special considering married men to become priests.[11] The first reason he cited was the lack of biblical authority. The pope wrote:

> The first seems to come from the most authoritative source, the New Testament which preserves the teaching of Christ and the Apostles. It does not openly demand celibacy of sacred ministers but proposes it rather as a free act of obedience to a special vocation or to a special spiritual gift. (Matthew 19: 11–12). Jesus Himself did not make it a prerequisite in His choice of the Twelve, nor did the Apostles for those who presided over the first Christian communities (Timothy 3:2–5; Titus 1:5–6).

The Pope wrote that in the writings of the early church leaders, often called Church Fathers, the emphasis was on chastity in marriage than celibacy. Moreover, circumstances were different. He wrote:

In patristic texts we more frequently find exhortations to the clergy to abstain from marital relations rather than to observe celibacy; and the reasons justifying the perfect chastity of the Church's ministers seem often to be based on an overly pessimistic view of man's earthly condition or on a certain notion of the purity necessary for contact with sacred things. In addition, it is said that the old arguements no longer are in harmony with the different social and cultural milieus in which the Church today, through her priests, is called upon to work.

Having given five other objections, in section 14 of the encyclical, Pope Paul VI affirmed clerical celibacy to continue. The dispensations were frozen in 1978 by Pope John Paul II only to unfreeze them in 1980 when married Anglican (or Episcopalian) as they are called in the United States of America) pastors were ordained as catholic priests in the United States of America. The dispensations were given to Anglican priests in Canada and England in 1994.

RELIGIONS OF STRUCTURE

Religious functionaries are many and varied in religions of structure. Religious leaders have multiple duties in religions of structure. They perform rituals, but also healing, counselling in addition to many others religious function as their societies expect of them. At the same time, however, religions of structure avoid wielding religious power and authority into one person all the time every time. So while an elder may perform a boy's ritual of coming of age, it is not always who he will be a medicine man. While a woman may be a diviner, she may not be an exorcist of spirit possession. The role of religious functionaries in religions of structure is complex. In order to develop a better understanding of the variety of offices, roles, and function, we will again turn to African religion which covers the terrain of religious functionaries.

In presenting an African liturgy chapter five, the reader will have noticed that among Achewa, acts of celebration and divination are not the exclusive prerogatives of religious functionaries, although the chief, very often than not, is responsible for religious matters. The main qualification to lead in a liturgy is age, the most advanced in age, the one at the end of the line of the living and at the border of the land of the ancestors. Gender too, does not prohibit anyone for participating in celebration and divination. Gender is certainly not a major problem in matrilineal societies such as among the Achewa, but it is in patriarchy. There is no question that colonisation worked hard to prevent women from certain functions in society. More than a generation after colonialism, matrilineal societies are still fighting colonised minds.

In the length and breath of Africa, are to be found various religious functionaries: priests, prophets, diviners, medicine people, mediums, herbalists, magicians. Here are the titles and roles of the functionaries in African religion.

Priests

Religious functionaries are the custodians of religion, especially priests whose responsibilities may include, but not exclusively performing religious activities such as praying for the people, offering sacrifices, leading in ritual process, speaking on behalf of divinity, protecting the religious emblems and other sacred objects, preserving religious knowledge of the people, taking care of the shrine. Priests may be the head of a family, clan, chief or king. One may be apprenticeship for the priesthood. Priesthood may be hereditary, being passed on from father to son. Others may become a priest after being possessed by the spirit or ancestral spirits.

Prophets

In Africa prophets belong to the line of priests, seers, diviners or even healers. They may offer sacrifices. Their functions run across those other related offices. When they speak, it is under the possession of Spirit, it is divine-human speech, but prophets may also be possessed by a different spirit, a spirit of the air as among Nuer in Sudan. A prophet is a charismatic leader, who is not trained, but appointed by the spirit. A prophet does not use his charismatic power to get a following, but to serve the community. The office of the prophet seems to be limited in appearance in African societies.

Diviners

The office of diviners in Africa falls under the rubric of medicine people which includes healers, herbalists, and magicians. Diviners are people blessed with an extra or a second vision for they are able to "see" the future using their instrument of divination such as cowries, kola, or other different types of nuts or pebble stones. Some divination practises are complicated such as the West African system based on 256 derivative figures, reached at by manipulating sixteen palm nuts, or by casting, tossing a chain, or string of eight half pods. How the diviner works these numbers to predict, or tell the future is the art and secret of the diviner.

Diviners are also able to read minds and situations, identify natural and supernatural causes of disease. Diviners are usually appointed by the spirit. They see a vision in which they are told to become diviners. Some may attach themselves to a diviner to learn the art. Those are usually diviners who interpret the future by use of divinatory instruments. These are the interpreters of omens. This other type of diviner does not use any type of divinatory equipment to tell the future. This type receives messages from beyond for mostly individuals. These types of diviners are usually called mediums in the sense that they relay messages to people.

Mediums

The role of mediums is to act channels through which the living and the dead communicate; to link the dead and the living and for the living to receive messages from beyond the grave. Mediums are normal people who act when possessed by a spirit. A medium may work with a diviner to diagnose illness and prescribe a cure.

Healers

It has been stated over and again that religions of salvation are about sanctification of life and are thus concerned with well-being or the totality of life. This means there is nothing that is outside, or beyond the realm of religion. So health, healing, and the manipulation of forces are all concerns of religion. The word *medicine* covers many areas of expertise in Africa, ranging from diagnosing diseased states, disease prevention, pharmacology, and herbalism. Disease prevention includes good living conditions, but also inoculations and warding off negative forces whether those forces cause diseased mental states such as depression, unexplainable behaviour, bad spells or curses. So in Africa there is good medicine that is curative medicine and bad medicine, magic. All these are religious functionaries because they all operate within the realm of spirits and the supernatural. No respectable traditional healer dispenses a prescription without a spiritual explanation, chant, and, or exercise.

Anthropologists and missionaries have often lumped together traditional healers, magicians, and sorcerers as witch doctors. The term witch doctor is not only pejorative, but it lies in what Africans call European (Western) "primitivism". Europeans or Westerners use "primitive" to distinguish themselves from those "others", the objective others, not like them and lower than them. Even when primitive is defended as referring to primal, original, first, or earlier it still carries a negative connotation. There are Africans who use the term witch doctor because of the colonisation of the African mind. Witch doctor implies "bad medicine", or practising magic and superstition. Indeed sometimes the traditional healer may not make a proper diagnosis and prescribe a poor concoction, but it is not different from a Western doctor who reaches a cure by experience, trial and error. African Christians and educated Africans also use some pejorative, negative labels to indicate how distant they are from traditional African beliefs and practises. In some southern African societies the word *ng'anga* (a person of horns) is used, implying a person who practises bad medicine, most often a cheat, a superstitious and backward person. In traditional societies they did not have bottles so all medicines were stored in animal horns, *nyanga*, or gourds. The fact that the traditional healers store their prescriptions in animal horns and gourds, and also use gourds or some other traditional listening device for heart beat or the flow of the blood in the veins, does not make his or her diagnostic procedure and treatment bad medicine or magic.

The stethoscope plays the same role in Western medicine. Since the last quarter of the twentieth century traditional healers have insisted on being called African doctors.

Traditional healers are all not involved in what Africans call bad medicine. They deal in curative medicine using their knowledge of disease etiology, plants, and spiritual forces to induce healing. Traditional healers concern themselves with pharmacology of health. They understand health as wholeness of social, spiritual, mental, and physical soundness. Therefore, the cause of illness has to be investigated in areas more than biological, in one's total life because the way one lives and relates to others, nature, and God affects health. Everybody knows how bad relations with others lead to stress, anxiety, and depression. Traditional healers are not interested in curing diseased parts of the body, or diseased states, but the whole person. Therefore, treatment is given a holistic approach. In an unpublished essay on African medicine titled "African Religion and Medicine", I have written:

> African medicine takes seriously the fact that people are not just a collection of physiological tissues and cells with blood flowing in and through them. Africans understand that physical pain is not just because of a malfunction of tissues or cells caused by a lack of certain necessary chemical substances in the body. There may be some chemical imbalances or a malfunction of tissues and cells in the body, but that is half the story. There is always an outside, call it "mysterious" or spiritual cause or effect. The traditional healer investigates the total human condition of the patient: the environment, social, spiritual, mental and physical states. . . . To the African, it is not enough to correct chemical imbalances, but to know *why* they went wrong in the first place. Why the particular individual, and at that given time?[12]

Good treatment to Africans is establishing the harmony or totality of the human, that is, the unity of the body, mind, spirit, the environment, and God. As part of treatment, traditional healers sometimes prescribe a religious ritual as a way of re-establishing harmonious relation between creation and divinity. In African society disease may be the result of breaking natural (physical), moral or spiritual "laws". The "power" of a healer is not determined by the number of efficacious herbs he or she knows, but the magnitude of the healer's understanding of natural laws. It is for this reason that diagnosis includes investigation into both physical and spiritual wholeness of the patient. Accordingly, treatment also includes religious symbolism and rites. Maurice Iwu sums up the art of healing in African society in the following words:

> The African healer therefore questions strongly any form of treatment that focuses only on organic diseased state and ignores the spiritual side of the illness. . . . If a sick person is given a leaf infusion to drink, he [she] drinks it believing not only in the organic properties of the plant, but also in the magical or spiritual force imbibed by nature in all living things and also the role of the ancestors, spirits and gods in the healing process. . . . The art of healing is part of African religion, there is a peculiar unity of religion and life that is characteristically African. Healing in

Africa is concerned with the restoration or preservation of human vitality, wholeness and continuity. It is a religious act, perhaps superseded only by the rituals or birth, puberty, marriage and death.[13]

Concerning the methods of diagnosis in traditional medicine, Adeoye Lambo has said that although traditional medicine may not approach cause and effect in a "scientific" notion, its results are not based on flagrant theories and fantasies. Lambo contends that traditional diagnostic methods yield a high degree of probability, the best that can be expected in an investigation of a socio-psychological data. "If we examine the process of diagnosis of diseases in these traditional societies, we may be able to rid ourselves of many misinterpretations. The inferences of the traditional healers may not have the cast-iron rigour of a microbiological demonstration, but they register certain important features of the objective situation".[14]

Magicians and Sorcerers

Good medicine is not only curative, but it prevents disease and harm from evil or bad spells. This is to say good medicine works in the physical and spiritual or mystical realms. To prevent disease or harm from the spiritual or mystical realms, good medicine may tap into other life forces. A traditional healer may perform or prescribe a preventive ritual, a chant, invocation, or an act for restoration to health. Such a ritual, chant, etcetera, reveals the power of the word to invoke intense feelings or desire for well-being, such as the word of a beloved invokes the intense feelings of love or desire. Invoking this unseen and undefinable force is often referred to as magic, a word that carries a negative connotation, as referring to something of evil nature, something to harm someone. Africans distinguish between good and bad magic. Good magic is good medicine. Non-Africans may have doubt and suspicion about the idea of invoking or tapping into unseen force for desired ends or good magic, John Mbiti, one of the early leading African theologians, enumerates examples from various sources showing magic being good medicine. However, I am drawn to Mbiti's own experiences on the topic in his book, *African Religions and Philosophy*. He tells of his discovery of the truth about good magic when he was a schoolboy. Locusts came to his land. His elderly relative and neighbour "burnt a 'medicine' in his field, to keep away the locusts. Within a few hours the locusts had eaten up virtually everything green including crops, trees and grass, and then flown off in their large swarms". While everyone was grieving about the tragedy, word went around that crops in his neighbour's field were left untouched because he had burnt medicine to protect them. "I went there to see it for myself", says Mbiti, "and sure enough his crops remained intact" while of the other people next to him had been destroyed.[15]

The second example of good magic is about Mbiti's boyhood friend who had a quarrel with an elderly man. The elderly man started sending snakes to Mbiti's friend house, and twice they had gone into the children, but were killed before biting the children. Mbiti's his friend.

> decided to do something. . . . When he went home to the country for Christmas he consulted a specialist medicine man, who instructed him on what ritual to follow in order to destroy the snakes which were threatening the life of his family. Mr. M. killed a cock and followed the instruction of the medicine-man. The next morning seven snakes were gathered at the door of the house where he had poured out the blood from the cock. He was then able to kill them all without danger; and since then his wife and children have had no more snakes coming to the house.[16]

These are examples of good magic and good medicine. The distinction between good and bad medicine, or between healers and magicians, is that the latter work with supernatural forces for personal ends. A client of a magician who practises bad medicine, may have health concerns, but the client seeks the magician to manipulate, or tap into spiritual forces for negative ends on someone else. Magic has mostly an evil intent; to harm some, or at least to prevent, or stop someone from inflicting harm of on the individual. A higher stage of magic is sorcery which is an antisocial use of spiritual forces and powers for evil intent. No one likes a magician except the one with evil feelings towards someone or others. Generally, a sorcerer is feared and hated because he or she may cause bodily harm, or destroy property, or disrupt the well being of individuals.

Elders

Being older brings honour to anyone who is so blessed as reach old age. In some society admission into eldership is regarded with high respect so that marked by a ritual ceremony of liminality. Kenyatta, who himself was an elder, writing in *Facing Mount Kenya*, details one such ritual of liminality which among the Gikuyu takes place at the candidate's own home. After several ritual acts one elder standing on behalf of fellow elders blesses the candidate:

> Immediately one of the elders takes the beer and fills a drinking horn with it. He stands facing Kere–Nyanga (Mount Kenya), and calls upon Ngai (God) to give them [the candidate and his wife] peace, wisdom and prosperity and to bless the candidate and his homestead. The rest of the elders lift up their staffs (*methegi*), and answer in chorus, saying: "Peace, peace, beseech Ngai, peace be with us, peace". After this the candidate is invested with his staff of office (*mothegi*) and a bunch of sacred leaves (*mayaathi*).[17]

Elders are respected very much in Africa because they are considered as living encyclopedias, full of wisdom and knowledge gathered throughout their life. Elders play a very important role in ritual process in many almost every society whether they have chiefs or not. Having participated in many rituals in their lifetime, elders have deep knowledge and understanding of ritual procedures. Elders know by heart the prayers and all the fine details of ritual process. Naturally, it falls upon them to lead and conduct religious functions. Elders lead or perform religious activities as individuals or as a group. Kenyatta gives an example of an elder acting alone as a religious functionary invoking God to bless a new home.

> You, the Great Elder, who dwells on the Kere-Nyanga [Mount Kenya], your blessing allows homestead to spread. Your anger destroys homesteads. We beseech You, and in this we are in harmony with the spirits of our ancestors: we ask You to guard this homestead and let it spread. Let the women, herd, and flock be prolific. (Chorus) Peace, praise or beseech ye, Ngai (God), peace be with you.[18]

The role of an elder as a religious functionary falls on the oldest in a family and village who leads, conducts, and, or presides over the family's or village's rituals.

Kings, Queens, and Chiefs

While rulers may be found in almost every village in Africa that cannot be said of kings, queens, and chiefs, but where they are found their office is held in high honour, respect, and sometimes with a holy reverence. In some societies these traditional rulers are regarded as having some spiritual connection. Therefore, their office is taken as sacred. Even where traditional rulers have no divine connection, they are still considered as having spiritual powers because they serve as liaisons between the world of the living, the ancestors and the spiritual world. It is for this reason that traditional rulers are also religious functionaries by the virtue of their office. Traditional rulers offer prayers and sacrifices, pour libations, and conduct many private and public rituals on behalf of their people.

Native Americans

The Lakota

Not all the religious functionaries within African religion are present in other religions of structure. Nonetheless, there are offices and duties that are common such as diviners, mediums (shamans), medicine men, and the elders. These offices are to be found among the religions indigenous peoples of the Americas, Asia, and Australia and elsewhere in the southern hemisphere. Religious functionaries play many roles among Native Americans just as among Africans. Among the Lakota, there are elders, medicine men, holy men, and magicians. The elders are respected among Native Americans because they are the store house of wisdom and knowledge, but also the very embodiment of virtue. Wisdom of the elders is received with reverence and respect because it is practical knowledge gained through experience and the blessing of age. So the elders play an active role in guiding and instructing the younger generation(s) in ritual practises and the virtues that have kept intact their society. The elders are practically guardians of the land, for they know the eternal wisdom or what is needed for a harmonious relationship among the living, with ancestor and the Great Spirit. For example, Lakota elders know what is forbidden *tehila* (taboo) to secure the favour if *Wakan Tanka* (a spirit). Likewise, the elders make it clear to all Lakotas that before anyone does anything of importance they should strengthen their life with *Inipi* (vapour bath) in an *Ini ti* (sweat lodge). Elders instruct individuals in making preparations for receiving their *Hable* (a vision or supernatural power), or for their greatest ceremony of Sun Dance.

Elders among Native Americans may also be medicine men, *wicasa wakan* (a holy man or a shaman). By their religious office and calling, these individuals play a very important role in ritual practise or healing with medicines or through powers from beyond as does the holy man of whom Elder George Sword said:

> The holy man is the most potent in treating the sick. He cans speak with the Great Mystery and they will help him. He does not treat the sick with medicines. He has a ceremonial bag. It is called *wopiye* in Lakota. This does not have medicines in it. It has a mystery in it and this mystery makes the bag very potent. The holy man invokes his ceremonial bundle or bag. It may be like a bag or it may be like a bundle. Or it may be anything that is revealed to him in a vision. This bag is prepared with much ceremony by other holy men and the thing in it is made by holy ceremony. It may represent the Bear or the Buffalo, or the *wakan* of the sky, or anything. Then it is like part of himself. It is like his ghost only it has more power than a man's ghost has. . . . The bag is called *wasicum*. A holy man does not give medicine unless he is a medicine man also. . . . A holy man may be a magician also. A holy man is more potent than a medicine man or magician. He can cause his ceremonial bag to overcome the medicines and the charms of others.[19]

The office of a magician among Native Americans is similar to that of Africans. According to Elder Sword, a magician makes the sick well as well make one ill. "He treats the sick secretly and no one knows what he does. He makes charms and philters and he may make very deadly portions. He is in league with the great evil one".[20]

The healer that Native Americans often go to for treatment is the medicine man called *pejuta wicasa* among the Lakota. The medicine man cures diseases caused by the *wakan* (mysterious) or by the mysterious-like (*wakanla*). A medicine man heals not only with medicines, but also a drum and rattles to please the *wakan* and a song. Thus, a medicine man must know medicines and various songs appropriate for each illness. It is to be seen here that the function of the medicine man is prescribing cures also and contacting the *wakan* on behalf of the sick. This makes a medicine man also a religious functionary. This means that medicine has no potency unless it has the power of the *wakan*. Therefore, healing is a religious function.

> All of the medicine men fast once a year, usual during warm weather, until a satisfactory vision is achieved. . . . One may understandably wonder at such a

severe exercise, but the Lakotas believe that medicine learn from each new vision; that is, they acquire more power. . . . An absorbing trait in the Lakota religious pattern is the conception that the medicine man possesses various spirits revealed in the visions. It follows, therefore, that the more spirits owned by the medicine man, the more powerful his ceremonials actions will be. A corollary to this is found un the belief that the spirits or objects possessed and used by him, the more dangerous he is to his family, and society at large. Thus, despite the employment of the words "has" or "uses" in English or Lakota, the medicine is dangerous business. Religion to the Lakotas is a dangerous business. What is benevolent can due to many causes, even if the medicine man himself is of good will.[21]

Shamanism

A shaman is a very important among medicine men and as religious function-ary. A shaman governs or oversees all the ceremonies of the Lakota. Accordingly, a shaman must know *iye wakan* (holy language) and *hanbloglaka* (spirit language) in addition to knowing all the laws and customs of the Lakota, that he may change or prohibit if it is the will of *Wakan Tanka* who governs everything and makes his wishes known through a vision or a shaman.

The term shaman has its roots in northern Asia, among the Siberia Tungus (Evenks), for whom the word means "the one who knows". The word entered the English language through Russian. In English the term has been popularised mostly by anthropologists and historians of religion such Mirce Eliade.[22] From the last third of the twentieth century, the word shamanism has been used by scholars wanting to get away from European primitivism, the pejorative witch doctor. Shamanism covers a wide range of religious experiences. Some scholars consider shamans as functionaries of a religion called shamanism, which they define as a technique of ecstasy. It is not clear why an experience, or a temporary state, ecstatic trance in this case, would be called religion. A shaman is a man or woman, who through some drug or any other means of inducement falls into a trance and communicates with the spirit world. A shaman may experience spirit possession, but often the shaman is conscious of moving beyond the physical world. While conscious, the shaman is at the same time without control of self. It is a dream state while being conscious, having a vision while being aware of one's surrounding. During the trance, a shaman may feel very strong and some shamans are said to accomplish impossible feats.

At the end of the experience the shaman is tired and relieved, yet satisfied. This sounds contradictory, but it is an experience beyond explanation. The shaman becomes satisfied because he or she brings messages, explanations, or healing from the spiritual world, or the world of the ancestors. A shaman in an ecstasy trance may accompany a soul to the other world, or receive prophetic messages from there. A shaman may experience an overwhelming presence of God while in a trance. Therefore, shamanism may be considered as a mystic union with other world or God. Thus, a shaman's mystic union may be described by Otto's *mysterium tredum* that brings dread. Here we see that a shaman may be a religious functionary who serves as a priest, prophet, seer, visionary, magician, or a medicine man or woman who heals those with shamanic possession and other illnesses.

Shamanism is a religious office that few choose to enter. Often those who appoint themselves shamans have little respect and are considered less effective as a religious functionary. Shamanism is inherited; one is initiated and trained as a shaman. A shaman with great respect is the one who receives a divine appointment, or the one who receives the powers of the office shamanism after taking a vision journey. Often the call comes after suffering some personal crisis: spiritual, mental, or physical. Whatever the crisis that leads them to their call, individuals are never the same after a shamanic trance. The vision they see is so powerful that it changes them, giving them an extraordinary clarity of mission and goal.

Trances or visions are very integral part of original people of indigenous communities of North America. In almost every community, visions or vision quest is part of their rituals of adulthood, or seeking clarity of direction in life, or a goal itself or what they call "cry for a vision". Those crying for a vision spend anywhere from two to four days alone in the forest, without eating or drinking, in addition to some strenuous physical exercises, until they see a vision. One elder of the Oglala Sioux, Black Elk, pointed out "Vision Quest is an experience of deeper understanding of Nature and Spirit". While "crying for a vision" is ritualistic, there are visions that are spontaneous like the Great Vision of Black Elk. Such visions are known as "power visions". Elder Black Elk related his own experience of a spontaneous "power vision". He received the vision as went up a sacred mountain of his ancestors to pray. As he ascended the mountain he heard "voices singing as the wind blew the leaves". At the top of the mountain he saw a large circle made of stones with a cross inside.

> I knew from my teachings that this represented the circle of life and the four directions. I sat down by the edge of this circle to pray. I thought this is only a symbol of the universe. "True", a very soft voice said. "Look and you will see the Centre of the Universe. Look at every created thing". As I looked around I saw that every created thing had a thread of smoke or light going from it. The voice whispered, "This cord that every created thing has is what connects it to the Creator. Without this cord it would not exist". As I watched I saw that all these threads, coming from everything, went to the centre of the circle where the four directions were one place (the centre of the cross). I saw that all these threads were tied together or joined here at this spot. The voice spoke again, "This is the Centre of the Universe. The place where all things join together and all things become one. The place where everything begins and ends. The place inside everything created". That's when I understood that all of creation, the seen and the unseen, was all related. The voice spoke one last time, "Yes, now you know the Centre of the Universe".[23]

Elder Black Elk was not a shaman, but the vision quest he received, he was like a shaman, "told to share with all who may be interested". Shamans see visions not for themselves, except the first, but the rest are for their community. A shaman is a needed religious functionary in a society because he or she is the mediator, a liaison between the world of the living and the beyond. A shaman is a person who brings spiritual and physical healing, but also tells the future, leads sacrifice rituals, and serves as the guide of souls, called a psychopomps from the *psuchopompos*. Shamans are diviners and interpreter of dreams and they are also said to have the ability to control the weather.

GLOSSARY

Abbot	A head of a monastic community or monastery, appointed by a bishop or elected by the members of the community.
Ashram	A monastery, hermitage, place of retreat for Hindu monks. In the past Ashrams were located in the forests ro mountains, away from people.
Asramas	Stages in life in Hinduism: *Brahmacharya* (student), *Grihastha* (householder), *Vanaprastha* (forestdweller or hermit), and Sannyasa (ascetic).
Atma(n)	the essential Divinity, or light of consciousness, in each individual; the Self as eternal super conscious spirit; or simply spiritual essence.
Bishop	A high ordained religious functionary in Christianity with oversight over priests, monks and nuns in a given church jurisdiction. A bishop must be ordained by at least three other bishops.
Brahman	The supreme single cosmic reality; divinity.
Garhasthya	A householder (in Hindu asmaras system) maintaining a family and engaged in a profession.
Mandyas	Or mantia. A long full-flowing processional gown in Eastern Orthodox Church worn only in the church.
Philokalia	A book of Christian monastic writings.
Sadhana	A spiritual practise that turns the mind from the world to the spiritual truths.
Sadhu	Someone who practises spiritual discipline and virtuous values; a *sannyasi* or wandering mendicant.
Sannyasi	one who has renounced the world by taking the *sannyasa* vows.
Tapas	Extreme measures of discipline on the physical, mental and intellectual levels that include yoga postures and consistent concentration and thought to a divine ideal.
Vanaprastha	A Hindu person living in the forest as a hermit after partially giving up material desires.

NOTES

1. Rudolph Otto. *The Idea of the Holy*, 158.

2. Jacob Neusner, *The Death and Birth of Judaism* (New York, NY: Basic Books, 1987), 116.

3. J. Z. Lauterbach quoted by Philip S. Alexander, ed. *Textual Sources for the Study of Judaism* (Chicago, ILL: Chicago University Press, 1984), p. 39.

4. *Ibid.*, 37–38.

5. Mordecai Kaplan's, *Judaism as a Civilisation: Toward a Reconstruction of American Jewish Life* (New York, NY: Jewish Publication Society of America published, 1994).

6. Harvey J. Sindima, *Drums of Redemption*, 20.

7. *Ibid.*, 21.

8. I dedicated the whole of chapter 2 in *Drums of Redemption* to the origin and the life of the Ethiopian Church. I discuss Canon Law on page 37.

9. Nicon D. Patrinacos. "Celibacy", *Dictionary of Greek Orthodoxy* (Pleasantville, NY: Hellenic Heritage Publications, 1987), 76.

10. Stephen Heid, *Celibacy In The Early Church: The Beginnings Of A Discipline Of Obligatory Continence For Clerics In East And West* (San Francisco, CA: Ignatius Press), 2000.

11. Pope Paul VI. *Sacerdotalis Caelibatus*. 24 June 1967. par. 5.

12. Harvey J. Sindima, "African Religion and Medicine". Unpublished Essay, 6.

13. Maurice M. Iwu, *African Ethenomedicine* (Enugu, Nigeria: SNAAP, 1986), 20.

14. Adeoye T. Lambo, "Traditional African Cultures and Western Medicine", *Medicine and Culture*, F. N. L. Poynter, ed. (London: Wellcome Institute of History of Medicine, 1969), 209.

15. John Mbiti. *African Religions and Philosophy*, 189–90.

16. *Ibid.*, 191.

17. Jomo Kenyatta, *Facing Mount Kenya* (New York, NY: Vintage books, 1965), 195.

18. *Ibid.*, 70.

19. James R. Walker, *Lakota Belief and Ritual*, Raymond J. DeMallie and Elaone A. Jahner, eds. (Lincoln, NB: University of Nebraska Press, 1991), 92.

20. *Ibid.*, 92.

21. Stephen R. Feraca, *Wakinyan: Lakota Religious in the Twentieth Century* (Lincoln, NB: University of Nebraska Press, 1998), 27.

22. Mircea Eliade. *Shamanism: Archaic Techniques of Ecstasy*. Original 1907. (London, England: Arkana, 1989), xxiii.

23. (Nicholas) and John G. Nehardt. *Black Elk Speaks: Being the Life Story of a Hly Man of Oglala Sioux*. New York, NY: William Morrow (Pocket Books ed., 1932), 17–39.

7
Magic, Sorcery, and Witchcraft

Magic, sorcery, and witchcraft have been of great academic interest and debate since the nineteenth century. While many people believe religion is far superior to magic, a closer look reveals the situations to be more complex. Both religion and magic are systems of beliefs with their own worldviews, attendant manner, and life style. Of interest among academics has been what magic and sorcery really are in themselves, and the reality of witchcraft, that is, whether witchcraft exists. To ask whether these three exist, begs the question whether religion exists since religion and the other three entities operate in the realm of the mysterious or spiritual. The question whether something is real, is difficult to answer. For it has to be clarified what is meant by "exist": does exist mean real or actual in the metaphysical manner, or in the empirical, observable, demonstrable sense? Real does not mean the same thing always: time is real, but it cannot be empirically demonstrated; quarks (the basic building blocks of matter) are real, but their presence can only be known by colour and flavour. Real then can mean physical, that is, empirical, but real can also mean metaphysical.

Magic, sorcery, and witchcraft became subjects of academic interest as Europeans travelled to other societies and cultures. Having entered the age of science under the auspices of Christianity, Europeans looked at magic, sorcery, and witchcraft as elementary stages of human or social development that Europeans had already passed. Victorian anthropologists and their society believed magic and witchcraft to be an infantile stage of human development on the way to the highest level of human cognition manifested in science. Magic, sorcery, and witchcraft were signs of backwardness, the infamous European "primitivism". However, magic, sorcery, and witchcraft, as all European "Primitivisms", provided scholars opportunities for tracing the journey of human development, or explained to Europeans the process of development and change. For disenchanted or agnostic British scholars, primitivism provided an opportunity to demonstrate that magic was a precursor of religion, or that religion differed from magic only in degree, for in essence they were both feeble attempts at understanding reality.

MAGIC AND SORCERY: UNIVERSAL PHENOMENA

Magic, sorcery, and witchcraft are a universal phenomena although most of the study has focused mostly on Africa. While other reasons explain the focus on Africa, on top of the list is British scholarship in the twentieth century, especially in the fields of anthropology and sociology. British social scientists invented and sustained an academic discourse on sorcery and witchcraft in Africa. Little, to nothing was written about these phenomena in Asia, the Americas, or the South Pacific, not to mention Europe. Research on sorcery and witchcraft elsewhere in the world is new. Until very recently, scholars neglected studies on witchcraft in South American, or treated them as part of the studies in shamanism. The nature and extent of witchcraft in South America was revealed only in 2004 by Neil Whitehead and Robin Wright, *In Darkness and Sorcery: the Anthropology of Assault Sorcery and Witchcraft in Amazonia*.[1] As in South America, so little too was known about sorcery and witchcraft in Oceania, but Mary Patterson's essay, "Sorcery and Witchcraft in Melanesia", enlightens us on practises of these universal phenomena there.[2] Sorcery and witchcraft practises in Melanesia are similar to those found elsewhere in the South Pacific. In his book, *Aboriginal Men of High Degree,* A. P. Elkin, documents similar practises of sorcery and witchcraft among the indigenous people of Australian as among the Melanesians.[3]

Recent studies on magic, sorcery, witchcraft show that there are different or regional perspectives to these phenomenon. For example, in his research in Sri Lanka, a largely Buddhist country, Bruce Kapferer has shown that sorcery and witchcraft are part of the people's religious world view connected with the deity *Huniyam*, who has a protective and positive side, but also has immense negative powers.[4] To the shrines of *Huniyam* go the victims of sorcery and those wishing to be protected from it. They go to curse their enemies and to throw back to them the force of their evil that is causing the victims distress and misery. Kapferer points out that in Sri Lanka, witchcraft is not hidden, but brought in the open and dealt with through rites of exorcism, *kapumas*, and the grand rite of *Suniyama*. These rites reconstitute or bring wholeness to the victim of sorcery, thus restoring the individual as a conscious being. Here we see how rooted is witchcraft into the religious cosmology is the Sinhalese. The Sinhalese rites of restoration are anchored in Buddhist cosmology concerning the place of individuals in the world and their consciousness in everyday life.

Most European scholars treat witchcraft as a historical fact of the early modern Europe 1450–1750. During this period witches, who were mostly women, attending meetings called *sabbats*.[5] European Christianity alleged that at such meetings witches flew on animals or broomsticks, performed incest, ate flesh of murdered babies, and worshipped the devil. Under the guidance or instructions of the devil they committed again persons and property. It was for these reasons that witches were apprehended, tried, and executed. The number of witches executed is a matter of controversy among historians, but twentieth century archival research by R. Briggs put the estimates at 40,000–50,000.[6] While most European scholars maintain a gender biased view of witches being women, Briggs argues that was not universal in Europe. In France, Briggs demonstrates, that of the 1,300 cases appealed to Paris Parliament, more than half were men. The percentages were also higher for male witches in Finland and Estonia although the more female witches in other countries in Europe.

The gender bias is also maintained by Lara Apps and Andrew Cow in *Male Witches in Early Modern Europe*.[7] Some scholars such as Ralph Austen maintain gender bias is also found in Africa because men there maintain authority, become diviners, healers, and control the scare resources. Austen implies that women become witches because they lack all these.[8] The preponderance of the claim that witches are women is not the knowledge of present writer. In the accounts of the 1930s witch hunts in Malawi written by playwright, Richard Paliani, shows that those accused of being witches and, or administered the poison ordeal, *mchape*, to cleanse them of witchcraft, were both male and female, often the elderly and children who had witchcraft substances put in them without their knowledge or consent.[9]

Witch hunts in the West ended for two reasons: (1) because accusations were being made upon the rich and powerful; (2) the accusations were made by girls who had been possessed so people concluded that it was the devil at work making the girls accuse innocent people.[10] Witchcraft disappeared in the West in the eighteenth century only to reappear in the nineteenth century through West's fascination with occult. The activities of contemporary Western witchcraft are diverse including: taro card reading, astrology, *wicca*, and ritual magic. Research in ritual magic in England in the last quarter of the twentieth century put the numbers in several thousands. According to Tanya M. Luhrmann there were some 80,000 practioners of *wicca* in America in the 1980s.[11] Anthropologist Susan Greenwood writes that in October 1993 she knew 11 witchcraft covens in London.[12] Most Westerners think of sorcery or witchcraft as of distant place and time. Anthropologist Jean Favret-Saada immersed herself in the study of contemporary sorcery of the Bocage region Normandy in France.[13] The people there practise occult activities explaining death, illness, and misfortune as caused by occult activities by neighbours and people seeking the services of "unwitchers" to undo the harm inflicted by others. Initially, the people did not accept Favret-Saada to study their practises because they thought she was like the French press that made fun of them and treated them as bizarre people. Once they found Favret-Saad was serious about them, she was initiated into the occult practises. She became caught up into occult practises of the Bocage region to the extent that she had to leave the field.

Most contemporary Western witchcraft is seen as New Age phenomenon and harmless, such as Satanists in the United States of America. However, it must be seen that contemporary Western witchcraft, regardless of how it is practised or treated by outsiders, it is a religious practise with rites, but no unified teaching or principle. Studies show that some groups of witches are open while others are closed and hierarchical.[14]

THE INTELLECTUALIST APPROACH

The study of magic focused on how the early humans came to magic. The approach of British anthropologists to the study of magic and religion was more like cultural psychology for the emphasis was on "primitivism". That is, the worldview of early peoples and how their thought process formulated their belief systems. This approach was crowned in another infamous European term, "noble savage", which portrayed early peoples as undeveloped philosophers. It is for this reason the Victorian theory of magic and religion is called "intellectualist". The British approach was later challenged by many scholars. The first criticism came from Lucien Lévy-Bruhl (1857–1939), a French sociologist who accused British anthropologists of treating all mind sets the same when in reality there are two different types of mind operations: logical and prelogical; scientific and mystical, each being socially determined and culture bound. Lévy-Bruhl credited the Western mind with logic and rationality while he assigned prelogical and mystical thinking to non-Western cultures.[15]

From Victorian anthropologists to the second third of the twentieth century, magic, sorcery, and witchcraft were topics of academic interest for various types of academics: anthropologists, theologians, scholars of religion, sociologists, or social scientists and philosophers. British anthropologists dominated the research and debate. This chapter is a quick exploration into the academic debate over magic, sorcery, and witchcraft. First, let us take a quick look at the writings of the Victorian anthropologists.

Tylor was the first to make a symbolic and an intellectualist approach to magic and religion. His interest in magic was to find why other cultures continued to believe in magic when to Western observers magic seemed false. He had three explanations: (1) that empirical evidence shows that magic worked; (2) rituals of rain are followed by rain, even though it may not come immediately; (3) explanation of failure of ritual is attributed to error in prescription, a spell, broken taboos or inadequate preparation for ritual; (4) evidence is not constant for judgement of success or failure is variable although magic itself is based on laws that are impersonal, constant, and universal.[16] Tylor postulated that there are three ways of looking at the world: through magic, religion, and science. Tylor drew from Hume's empiricist theory that there are three ways the mind makes sense of ideas: resemblance, contiguity in time and space, and cause and effect. Magic then, was to him rational and scientific, with the exception that the magician believes a causal connection between things is by resemblance and contiguity. Magic and science were to him involved in similar activities and both employed logic, the difference being in making association or establishing the link between the subject and object, understanding things as subjective and symbolic. Tylor made a sharp distinction between religion and magic.[17] This distinction lead scholars after him to argue that religion is always preceded by magic.[18]

Tylor's successor at Oxford, Robert Runalph Marett (1866–1943), saw his task as to correct what he perceived to be Tylor's overemphasis on the under-development of the intelligence of the ancients and contemporary non-European peoples. Tylor had postulated too, that the sense of religion among the ancients might have generated in the idea of spirit. Marett rejected Tylor's propositions suggesting that there must have been something before the idea of spirit that led to a sense of religion: fear, awe, wonder, or may be an instinct. He suggested that these feelings may have been generated by a sense of an impersonal power or force present in any unusual object such as a thunderstorm. His view was, therefore, that the people were able, at the emotional level, to distinguish between supernatural and ordinary phenomena. Therefore, Marett insisted that magic and religion should not be separated since both originate in mystery which is a matter of feeling.[19]

The Victorian scholar who popularised the study of magic was James George Frazer (1854–1951) in *The Golden Bough*, a twelve-volume encyclopedic study of magic and religion, with ethnographic materials drawn from a wide range of sources ancient and modern. Concerning magic he wrote:

> If we analyse the principles of thought on which magic is based, they will probably be found to resolve themselves into two: first, that like produces like, or that an effect resembles its cause; and, second, that things which have once been in contact with each other continue to act on each other at a distance after the physical have been severed. The former principle may be called the Law of similarity, the later the Law of Contact or Contagion . . . charms based on the law of Similarity may be called Homoeopathic or Imitative Magic. Charms may be based on the Law of Contact or Contagion may be called Contagious Magic.[20]

Moving from magic to religion, he saw the later as rejecting magic because magic follows "laws" of contact (for contagious magic) and imitation (for homeopathic or imitive magic based on the law of similarity). These laws, contact and imitation arise on the understanding that the real powers in the world are principles. Frazer followed Tylor's definition of religion as belief in spiritual beings, but while for Tylor religion resembled magic because of its uncritical association of ideas, Frazer was interested in the difference between religion and magic. He asserted that religious people do to not consider the power behind the natural world principles, but supernatural beings called gods and it is to these that religious people turn in prayer and pleading for favours and change. These supernatural beings have personalities and their personalities control nature. Frazer maintained Tylor's assertion concerning the logical nature of magical thought, but he condemned magic for its mistaken application of association of ideas: "All magic is necessarily false and barren; for if it were ever to become true and fruitful, it would no longer be magic but science. . . . Obviously, the conception of personal agents is more complex than a single recognition of the similarity or contiguity of ideas".[21]

Frazer believed religion to be above magic; it was an advance over magic because prayers and pleading, humans and not principles of natural order are involved in seeking explanation. While he considered religion above magic, he viewed it only as a step in the advance of human thought that he saw superseded religion in his own time. Magic as an art and a craft was to him "a false science as well as an abortive art" although it is nevertheless an attempt at science, that is, an attempt to establish cause and effect. "Whenever sympathetic magic occurs in its pure unadulterated from, it assumes that in nature one event follows another necessarily and invariably without the intervention of any spiritual or personal agency. Thus, its fundamental conception is identical; with that of modern science; underlying the whole system is a faith, implicit but *real and firm*, in the order and uniformity of nature".[22] So for Frazer, magic is logically wrong, while religion is factually in error, and science is correct and true thinking.

Bronislaw Malinowski (1184–1942), a Polish anthropologist who trained at the London School of Economics, was one of the distinguished twentieth century anthropologists. Malinowski, a disciple of Frazer, understood magic as serving psychological need and social functions. For him magic was a system of beliefs and practises that provide emotional responses to situations of frustrations. Malonowski argued against equating abstract terms such as power with metaphysical concepts. For him, magic provides answers for the "gaps" in technical and, or practical knowledge, or failure to control a situation. When such gaps occur, the individual's "nervous system and his whole organism drive him to some substitute activity". So magic serves to "bridge over the dangerous gaps in every important pursuit or critical situation", thereby giving the individual a feeling of confidence. "Magic flourishes wherever man cannot control hazard by means of science. It flourishes in hunting and fishing, in times of war and in seasons of love, in the control of wind, rain and sun, in regulating all dangerous enterprises, above all, in disease and in the shadow of death".[23]

Malinowski identified two main parts of magic: the spell and the material element. Malinowskin found that among the Trobriand Islanders among whom he did his field research, the spell, in a verbal form, command or incantation, was the most significant part of magic. The second part, the material or medicine is either placed on the path or in the front of the house of the subject of magic. Malinowski considered magic as a mode of behaviour than a philosophy. Comparing science and magic Malinowski writes:

> Science is born of experience, magic made by tradition. Science is guided by reason and corrected by observation, magic impervious to both, lives in atmosphere of mysticism. Science is open to all, a common good of the whole community magic is occult, taught through mysterious initiations, handed on in a hereditary, or at lease in a very exclusive filiation. While science is based on the conception of natural forces, magic springs from the idea of a certain mystic impersonal power which is believed in by most primitive people. This power is called *mana* by some Melanesians, *arueggultha* by certain *Australian* tribes, *Wakan, Orenda, Maritu*, by various Native Americans.[24]

SOCIAL ANTHROPOLOGISTS

Edward Evan Evans-Pritchard (1902–1973), is one of the most well-known social anthropologists whose work on magic and witchcraft among the Azande in Sudan dominated the discipline and beyond. Evans-Pritchard rejected the idea that the scientific understanding of cause and effect is evidence of superior knowledge. He argued that all knowledge was culture bound, but he maintained the distinction of scientific and magical societies. He concluded, therefore, that the scientific approach is much of a function of European culture as is the magical for non-European cultures. In a paper titled, "The Intellectualist (English) Interpretation of magic", Evans-Pritchard succinctly summarised the positions of Taylor and Frazer as follows.

> They considered that primitive man had reached his conclusions about the efficacy of magic from rational observation and deduction in much the same way as men of science reach their conclusions about natural laws. Underlying all magical ritual is a rational process of thought. The ritual of magic follows from its ideology. It is true that the deductions of a magician are false—had they been true they would have been scientific and not magical—but they are nevertheless based on genuine observation. For classification of phenomena by similarities which exist between them is the procedure of science as well as of magic and is the first essential process of human knowledge. Where the magician goes wrong is inferring that because things are alike in one or more respects they have mystical link between them whereas the link is not a real link, but an ideal connection in the mind of the magician. . . . A casual relationship exists in the mind but not in nature. It is a subjective and not an objective connection. Hence the savage mistakens an ideal analogy for a real connection.[25]

This essay was followed by a book, *Witchcraft, Oracles and Magic among the Azande*.[26] This anthropological study among the Azande deals with magical thought, focusing on empirical and mystical thoughts which are key words throughout the book. Evans-Pritchard says the Azande concept of witchcraft and magic differs from European understanding.

> When a Zande speaks of witchcraft he does not speak of it as we speak of the weird witchcraft of our own history. Witchcraft is to him a commonplace happening and he seldom passes a day without mentioning it. . . . To us witchcraft is something which haunted and disgusted our credulous fathers. But the Zande expects to come across witchcraft at any time of the day or night. He would be just surprised if he were not brought into daily contact with it as we would be if confronted by its appearance. To him there is nothing miraculous about it.[27]

Evans-Pritchard declares that the concept of witchcraft "provides them [the Azande] with a natural philosophy by which the relation between men and unfortunate events are explained and a ready and stereotyped means of reacting to such events. Witchcraft beliefs also embrace a system of values which regulate human conduct".[28] Evans-Pritchard insists that witchcraft is not a reality for the Azande, but a theoretical paradigm of explanation.

> It is an inevitable conclusion from Zande description of witchcraft that it is not an objective reality. The physiological condition which is said to be the seat of witchcraft, and which I believe to be nothing more than food passing through the small intestine, is an objective condition, but the qualities they attribute to it and the rest of their beliefs about it are mystical. Witches, as Azande conceive them, cannot exist".[29]

For the Azande witchcraft provides a theory of causation that supplements the theory of natural causation for things just do not happen, "death has always a cause, and no man dies without a reason", so maintain the Azande.[30]

Zande philosophy supplies a "missing link" for which witchcraft theory provides an explanation as to why certain particular acts, happen at a particular time. Evans-Pritchard argues, therefore, that empirical evidence does not contradict empirical knowledge of cause and effect:

> Witchcraft explains *why* events are harmful to man and not *how* they happen. Azande perceives how they happen just as we do. . . . He does not see a witch push over the granary, but termites gnawing away its supports. . . . His perception of how events occur is as clear as our own.[31]

Evans-Pritchard contends that once Zande witchcraft system is placed within the context in which it functions, and belief in witchcraft is transcended, certain striking similarities emerge between Zande theoretical system and scientific system; connections that are logical and consistent appear.

In an essay titled, "Understanding Primitive Society", social scientist Peter Winch, critises Evans-Pritchard's analysis of Zande thought, especially when Evans-Prtichard claims that "Azande do not perceive the contradiction as we perceive it because they have not theoretical interest in the subject and those situations in which they express belief in which witchcraft do not force the problem upon them".[32] Winch disagrees, arguing:

> the context from which the suggestion about the contradiction is made, the context of our scientific culture, is not on the same level as the context in which beliefs about witchcraft operate. Zande notions of witchcraft do not constitute a theoretical system in terms of which Azande try to gain a quasi-scientific understanding of the world. This in its turn suggests that it is the European, obsessed with pressing Zande thought where it would not naturally go—to a contradiction—who is guilty of misunderstanding, not the Zande. The European is in fact committing a category-mistake.[33]

John Beattie (1915–1990), like Evans-Pritchard, criticised the Victorian idea that the thought of non-western peoples was childish and that it failed to distinguish between mental associations and causal connections in the world. He argued that Victorian scholars and society failed to see that in non-scientific cultures people think in symbolic and literary terms. Furthermore, Beattie argued, symbolised things are about abstract concepts such as power, group solidarity, and familial or political authority: "symbolism is essentially expressive; it is a way of saying something which it is impossible or impractically to say directly".[34]

Mary Douglas (1921–), a student of Evans-Pritchard, in her book, *Purity and Danger: An Analysis of the Concepts of Pollution and Taboo*, says, "The European belief in primitive magic has led to a false distinction between primitive and modern cultures, and sadly inhibited comparative religion".[35] She suggests that European approach to magic and religion should not focus narrowly on spiritual beings, or be concerned with drawing boundaries between religion and magic, but should focus on comparing people's understanding of their destiny and their place in nature.

Up to this point, the discussion has so far been on magic and witchcraft and nothing much has been said about sorcery. There is a debate between sociologists and anthropologists over the nature of sorcery. The question is: Is sorcery magic or witchcraft? In his definition of sorcery, John Middleton, a functionalist sociologists, drew the distinction between anthropological and sociological understanding of sorcery. He wrote:

> A sorcerer is one who is thought to practise magic against others. The acts themselves are usually of such a nature that they can be performed by anyone. They are termed magical from the point of view of the anthropologist because there are no grounds in terms of Western science for believing them able to accomplish the ends claimed for them.[36]

It appears that the difference is subjective and according to one's discipline, and not in the nature of sorcery itself. However, in defining witchcraft Middleton and Winter were objective, saying witchcraft is "a mystical and innate power which can be used by its possessor to harm other people".[37] Historian Wolgang Behringer defines witchcraft as "a generic term" covering "all kinds of evil magic and sorcery as perceived by contemporaries".[38] Peter Geschiere on the other hand, cautions against making cut and dry distinctions between witchcraft and sorcery.[39] He says the Maka in Cameroon use the term *djaambe* to denote a force in a person's stomach that allows an individual to shift and perform some extraordinary feats. Geschiere argues that since *djaambe* is used to kill it would be translated witchcraft. The French translated *djaambe* as *sorcellerie*. Geschiere says both translations are wrong for they fail to capture the complexity of indigenous nuances. The Maka use *djaambe* to heal or to "affirm one's prestige" deep meanings with both witchcraft and French *sorcellerie* ignore.

RELIGION SCHOLARS

Evans-Pritchard, John Beattie, and Mary Douglas belonged to what was known as the Oxford Institute whose members maintained that magic and religion in non-

European cultures are rational within those cultures and that this rationality can be seen by a disinterested observer who places social and religious phenomena within their cultural environment and attempts to understand them from the local's perspective. We see that in the work of Placid Temples, a Belgian missionary to Congo. Temples main project was to refute Lévy-Bruhl's theory of "primitive mentality" and the anthropological use of such terms as *mana*, animism, fetishism, totemism, magic and dynamism to conceptualise African thought, society, and religion. He argued:

> What has been called magic, animism, ancestor-worship, or dynamism—in short, all the customs of the Bantu—depend upon a single principle, knowledge of the Inmost Nature of beings, that is to say, upon their ontological principle. For it is not by means of philosophical terms that we must express their knowledge of being, of the existence of things.[40]

He further claimed that "the key to Bantu thought is the idea of vital force, of which the source is God". Temples meant that Africans experience the world as an interrelation of forces. Force, he claimed, was the most fundamental term in African thought: "I believe that we should most faithfully render Bantu thought in the European language by saying that the Bantu speak, act, live as if, for them, beings were forces. Force is not for them an adventitious accidental reality. Force is more than a necessary attribute of beings: Force is the nature of being, force is being, being is force".[41]

For Temples then, the African world is based on this theory of forces. It is this theory, so Temples claimed, that makes Africans equate being with power. The theory of forces influenced the different ways in which Westerners and Africans perceived the world. Western epistemology considers power as an attribute of being while for the African to be is power—power is the essence of being. Temples explained:

> For the Bantu power is not an accident: it is more than a necessary accident; it is the very essence of being. . . . Being is power, power is being. Our notion of being is "that which is", theirs is "the power that is". When we think in terms of the concept of "being" they use the concept of "force". Where we see concrete beings, they see concrete forces. When we say that "beings" are differentiated by their essence or nature, Bantu say that "forces" differ in their essence or nature. They hold that there is divine force, celestial or terrestrial forces, human forces animal forces or mineral forces.[42]

While Temples made his refutation of the European mind from a philosophical-religious perspective, Robin Horton made his criticism by comparing science and African Traditional religion as two different modes of knowledge. Horton, a chemist by training, belongs to the group of European anthropologists scholars who dominated the discipline of African traditional religion. Here we will examine his much discussed essay "African Traditional Thought and Western Science", which first appeared in 1967 and has since been included in many other publications.[43] In this essays Horton establishes African religion and science as theoretical activities and as distinct from common sense. He notes that the African practise of linking disease or misfortune to spiritual agency does not make sense to Westerners, but, he argues, this is because they do not understand the idiom operative in the African cultural context. Horton argues that the contrast usually made between traditional African thought as non-empirical and scientific thought as empirical is misleading,

> because traditional religious thought is no more or less interested in natural causes of things than is the theoretical thought of sciences. Indeed, the intellectual function of its supernatural beings (as of too, that of atoms, waves, etc.) *is* the extension of people's vision of natural causes. In the second place, the contrast is misleading because traditional religious theory clearly does more than postulate causal connections that bear no relation to science. Some of the connections it postulates are, by standards of modern medical science, almost certainly real. To some extent, then, it successfully grasps reality.[44]

Horton puts magical systems versus scientific methods. The former uses words to control reality since words are inextricably bound up with reality and to know the name of a being is to have control over the being. The magician evokes spirits, which essentially means calling their names correctly and the control which that correct calling gives the caller. For the traditional thinker, it follows that contact with reality is only through words. Hence, no one in traditional society can escape the tendency to see the unique and intimate link between words and things. There is no way of imagining reality independent of words, or simply segments of independent reality. Here words are given enormous power.

Edward Geoffrey Parrinder (1910–2000) was a Methodist missionary who spent more than two decades in Africa, and later became professor of Comparative Religions at Kings College, University of London. Parrinder rejects Frazer's theory of magic. He dismisses Frazer's magic theory as "speculative". He argues:

> There is no evidence for the primary occurrence of magic. In addition, Frazer failed to take into account the spiritual character of magic, its constant belief in the power of dynamism behind things, in which it differs widely from modern science. In Africa, at least, it cannot be held (as some writers on comparative religion state) that magic is confined to mechanical actions and does not refer to the supernatural powers. The efficacy of magical practises does not merely reside in things done or said, but in the employment of a supernatural agency, a psychic power.[45]

Parrinder insists that the African world is a universe full of mystical powers and energy so that even the social system is based on the mystical plane. Europeans may have doubts about the validity of the spiritual approach to life, but, Parrinder insists, the African cannot evade the presence and importance to the whole society. He concludes by declaring:

> This world is a spiritual arena, in which is seen the interplay of psychic force. This is the African belief, and while its application may not always appear correct, the

religious man of any race will agree with the principle. The agnostic sociologist and psychologist may seek to explain away this belief and its rites as projections and symbols, social constructs which have subjective and not objective value. In the words of Edwin Smith, "In these matters I prefer to stand with the African".[46]

AFRICAN SCHOLARS

All the work that we have explored up to now has been by European anthropologists or religion scholars. We will now sample what African scholars say about magic, sorcery and witchcraft. Jomo Kenyatta was an ethnographer who studied at the London School of Economics in the 1930s under Bronislaw Malinowski who wrote the preface to Kenyatta's book, *Facing Mount Kenya*. In the book, Kenyatta dedicates a chapter on Magic and Medical practises. Kenyatta professes practicing magic and being an apprentice in the art as he reveals in the preface to the book:

> As for magic, I have witnessed the performance of magic rites many times in my own home and elsewhere. My grandfather was a seer and a magician, and in travelling about with him and carrying his bag of equipment I served a kind of apprenticeship in the principles of the art. I can therefore speak as a representative of my people, with personal experience of many different aspects of their life.[47]

The chapter on "Magic and Medical Practises", lists various types and methods of magical practises. The list of magical practises covers almost all areas of life and Kenyatta points out that magic and religion among the Gukuyu are difficult to separate. "Gikuyu religion", writes Kenyatta, "in the wider sense, enters into magical and herbal practises. In many cases magical practises and religious rites go hand in hand, and sometimes it is not easy to separate the two, especially with beneficial magical practises". He then lists Gikuyu magical practises:

1.   Charms or protective magic (*getheiito*).
2.   Hate or despising magic (*monuunga* or *roruta*).
3.   Love magic (*monyenye* or *moreria*).
4.   Defensive magic (*kerigiti, keheenga*).
5.   Destructive magic, witchcraft (*orogi*, i.e. poison).
6.   Healing magic (*kehonia, gethiito gia kohuuha morimo*).
7.   Enticing and attracting magic (*rothuko*).
8.   Silencing and surprising magic (*ngiria, itwanda*).
9.   Fertilising magic (*mothaiga wa anoru*).
10. Wealth and agricultural magic (*mothaiga was otonga*).
11. Purifying magic (*mokoora, mohoko*, or *ndahekio*).[48]

For Kenyatta magic is not a matter of academic inquiry and debate, but a practise of his life and of this people. Kenyatta points out the qualifications that made a magician credible: "The people respect and have confidence in a magician who has acquired the profession hereditarily and has gone through long years of training, at the end of which he has been initiated into the cult through payment of some sheep and goats or a cow, according to the amount required by the magician's initiating secret council".[49] One note worthy remark from Kenyatta is: a magician is duty bound "to defend the community from all dangers". A magician is critical to society, his or her business is secretive so much so that a novice takes a vow never to reveal magical secrets. Kenyatta gives several vows according to the type of magic. Here is an example of a vow for hunting magic:

> I promise you faithfully not to reveal the magical secret to anyone outside the magician's secret council. From now on, I am under the most solemn ties and engagements of honour, as well as the most religious and magical vows and protestations to conceal the secret formula of the magical power. I shall never sacrifice my honour or my religion.[50]

Kenyatta shows that magic is a specialty profession, the full knowledge of which is known only to those initiated into the magic guild. What clients know is that it works, but what is involved is secret knowledge.

Among the eminent African scholars who maintain the reality of magic is Mbiti. He rejects the Western theory of magic according to which African traditional religion is nothing but magic, or as some Europeans concluded that "Africans have no religion at all, only magic". Mbiti says, "Magic belongs to the religious mentality of African peoples. But religion is not magic, and magic cannot explain religion. Religion is greater than magic, and only an outsider could imagine that African religions are nothing more than magic".[51] In *African Religion and Philosophy*, Mbiti gives African ontology, which, according to Mbiti has five categories:

1. *God* as the ultimate explanation of the genesis and sustenance of both man and all things;
2. *Spirits* of extra human beings and the spirits of men who died long time ago;
3. *Man* including human beings who are alive and those about to be born;
4. *Animals and plants*, or the remainder of the biological life.
5. Phenomena and objects without biological life.

Later, Mbiti writes:

> In addition to the five categories, there seems to be a force, power or energy permeating the whole universe. God is the source and controller of this force; but the spirits have access to some of it. A few human beings have the knowledge and ability to tap, manipulate and use it, such as the medicine men, witches, priests and rainmakers, some for the good and other for the ill of their communities.[52]

Again he says, "African peoples know the universe has a power, force or whatever one may call it, in addition to the items in the ontological categories".[53]

Mbiti's ontology mirrors Tempel's foundation of African epistemology. There are significant differences between Temples and Mbiti, but it is outside the present study to get into them. I dealt with that in chapter five of *Africa's Agenda*. Mbiti's ontology does provide a key for understanding witchcraft. Mbiti, like Kenyatta has a chapter too dedicated to a discussion on magic and witchcraft. Mbiti says witchcraft is an everyday reality of an African in traditional society. He asserts:

> Every African who has grown up in the traditional environment will, no doubt, know something about this mystical power which often is experienced, or manifests itself, in the form of magic, sanctification, witchcraft and mysterious phenomena that seem to defy even immediate scientific explanation.[54]

Mbiti distinguishes between magic, sorcery, and witchcraft. Concerning magic, Mbiti writes about what he calls good magic performed by specialists: medicine persons, diviners, and rainmakers who manipulate the mystical power for welfare of their communities. He talks about healing and protective medicine or articles that individuals or babies wear to protect them. Mbiti is quick to point out that the wearers do not believe the power is inherit in the articles themselves, but from God, through the spirits, the living dead, that is, those recently departed whose memory is still alive among the living. The power in the articles may be through the "invisible force of nature in the universe". What distinguishes sorcery from magic is anti-social use of mystical power. The sorcerer practises bad magic, which include the use poison, among other ways, to harm others. Sorcerers are responsible for all evil and bad things that happen to people. On witchcraft Mbiti says:

> Witchcraft is a term used popularly and broadly, to describe all sorts of evil employment of mystical power, generally in a secret fashion. African societies do not often draw the distinction, sorcery, and evil magic, evil eye and other ways of employing mystical power to do harm to someone or his belongings. Generally the same word is used for all these English terms; and the same person is accused or suspected of employing one or more of these ways of hurting members of his community. In popular use the term "witchcraft' is designate to the harmful employment of mystical power in all its direct manifestations.[55]

Idowu, one of the early eminent African theologians and Patriarch of the Methodist Church in Nigeria, answering the question: "Do witches exist?" replied, "I will assert categorically that there are witches in Africa; that they are as real as murderers, poisoners, and other categories of evil workers, overt or surreptitious. This, and not only imagination, is the basis of the strong belief in witchcraft". He later on adds, "There is no doubt that there are persons of very strong character who can exude their personality make it affect other persons. Witches and witchcraft are sufficiently real as to cause untold sufferings and innumerable deaths".[56] Idowu's reality of witches is echoed by philosopher D. E. Idoniboye who says, "The point I want to stress here is that when Africans talk of spirits in the sense I have been discussing, they are not speaking metaphorically nor are they propounding a myth. *Spirits are as real as tables and chairs, people and places"*.[57]

Sociologist A. O. Sande compares scientific and magical knowledge and argues that magic is a way of knowing not inferior to science, but different. He argues:

> For one thing both science and magic are concerned with the task of exploring the vague, the unknown, and the problematic. Secondly, both science and magic attempt to control forces of nature through such knowledge. Thirdly, both science and magic assume the existence of an underlying order behind the apparent manifestations of various physical and social events. And both assume that there are certain laws which explain the assumed order and the general operation of nature; such laws when understood by either the scientist or the magician enable the problematic aspects of the physical and social events to be subject to manipulation by either the scientist or the magician.[58]

Sanda, therefore concludes:

> Magic instead of being downgraded as an unscientific way of knowing, may be studied more intimately from a less ethnocentric point of view, and with expectation of its possible contributions to knowledge about human groups. In addition, since both science and magic are cultural heritages as well as moulders of culture, it seems logical to expect that what is science or magic may vary from one period to another and besides, both aspects of knowledge always incorporate aspects of each other at every period in hsitory.[59]

Sanda rejects Malinowski's assertion about the superiority of science that it is "born of experience, magic is made by tradition". Sanda argues,

> If Malinowski was comparing ideals of science and magic, for it is evident that every branch of science is as guided by reason, experience, and observation as it is guided by tradition, subjective emotional states, and reflective (rather than empirically) based reasoning. And by the same token magical rites and beliefs may be based on empirical observation rather than on the concept of the supernatural or the mystical".[60]

Many people reject the existence of witchcraft and witches on the grounds that nothing can be proven, that is, empirically demonstrated or is observable as in scientific knowledge. In her essay, "On the Existence of Witches", philosopher Sophie Oluwole, debunks this view as we see in this rather extended quotation:

> Scientists today hold their hypothesis as a sort of religious dogma, and many cling fanatically to it as if it were the last word on possible knowledge. Until scientists accept that they have not discovered an indubitable method of knowing what is real, until they realise that science, being based on the generative theory of causal relationship which treats statistical evidence of succession as the basis of the hypothesis that a causal mechanism exists, is a direct consequence of our epistemological rather than an ontological requirement, so long will they give

room for being accused of "intellectual fraud"—"fraud for substituting the
epistemic for the ontic". As a matter of fact, this demand, this scientific hypothe-
sis, transcends experience. For nothing in our experience tells us that the real is
only the scientifically provable. Our consent to the occurrence of mysteries
confirm that *the mysterious is that which is not yet understood*, but not that which
is unknowable.

Hence, to declare something impossible just because "there is not place for
it in contemporary science" is to present a logically invalid arguement. . . . The
point, therefore, is that just as it is fraudulent to assert the existence of a power
whose nature we know nothing about, so also is it equally fraudulent to *deny the
occurrence* of an experience just because we do not understand it".[61]

A number of African philosophers have engaged in the debate over the reality
of magic or the rationality of witchcraft as a causal factor, or the African concept
of cause itself.[62] We will not get into that debate for it would take us too far into
technical philosophical language.[63]

MAGIC AND RELIGION

Let us conclude this chapter by once again reflecting on the relation between
magic and religion. Here we will look at what scriptures of select religions say
about magic. What we have seen in this chapter is that magic and religion always
exist side by side. It is because both operate on a deep belief which acts on
supernatural forces, or nature to achieve a desired end. Both religion and magic
share a common worldview in which forces interact with, and upon each other.
Through deep knowledge, the forces can be harnessed or manipulated towards a
desired goal or objective. Magic and religion have a great deal in common: both
operate from the mysterious, they are systems of thought each with its own
metaphysic, and they play a critical role in the life of their practioners.

A closer look at religions, one finds that magic exists in all religions and among
all believers. Often magic belongs to the office of priests, whose function is to call
forth, invoke forces from beyond the visible world. A priest says a prayer, or sings
as a ritual chant to invoke mysterious forces for the well being of the people.
Likewise, a magician chants, sings, or prays, to invoke mysterious forces for the
good of his or her clients. Concerning this closeness between magic and religion
Omosade Awolalu and Adelumo Dopamu say:

> In religious worship, it is sometimes difficult to tell where prayer (by way of
> supplication) ends and magic (by way of commanding) begins. For example,
> prayer may be regarded as efficacious only if certain aspects of it are repeatedly
> correctly. In that case, emphasis is on the formulae rather on the spirit and content
> of prayer. This fact can be illustrated with the practise of some Christian
> denominations which have to say certain rituals in a particular language without
> caring to have whether the worshippers understand what is being said or not. The
> same thing can be said of Islam where ritual must be said in Arabic.[64]

Magic is not only related to religion, but also to medicine. Thus, Awolalu and Dopamu say: " Now, since magic and medicine cannot be separated, and since what is common to them is also found in religion, it follows that magic, medicine and religion cannot be separated also. Magic and medicine form one aspect of religion and the three have coexisted throughout the ages. Any distinction made between them is that of approach and operation or technique".[65] Francis Arinze, currently Cardinal Arinze, makes an interesting observation on the relation between medicine and magic when he says that among the Igbo, "the word *ogwu* is used for charms for aspirin, and for penicillin injections. The Igbo word for 'hospital' is ụno-*ogwu* (medicine house) and the same Igbo word *dịbịa* can be applied to the diviner, the medicine man, and the elegant young man walking out of the University of London after seven years hard work with his M.D. certificate. The reason is that the Igbos do not sharply distinguish between the natural and the supernatural. The doctor and the patient never regard the treatment as purely material".[66]

Let us look at the relation between magic and religion in Christianity, Judaism, Hinduism, and Islam. Picture a Buddhist, a Hindu, and a Muslim attending for the first time the Christian ritual meal called the Last Supper or Eucharist. In the middle of this ritual, the celebrant stands up, makes invocations, chants, then says over bread and wine set on a table before the people. After the ritual prayer, the cleric says:

> On the night on which the Lord Jesus was betrayed he took bread. When he had given thanks and he broke and gave it to them saying: "Take eat this is body which is broken for you. Do this in remembrance of me". In like manner the cup, after supper, saying, "This cup is the new covenant sealed in my blood. Drink it in remembrance of me".

Then the cleric declares, "This is the body of Christ [Jesus]" referring to the bread, and "This is blood of Christ given for the forgiveness of our sins". The bread and the wine are circulated among congregation, or the people walk up to the priest in a single file. Both those sitting and those walking to the cleric, look contrite, they put the bread in their mouth, so does the cleric after which they drink the wine or grape juice in very tiny cups, or the cleric drinks from a highly polished silver or golden goblet. The celebrant says another prayer after which the people respond with one word, as they did after the chant or prayer. What will our first time visitors say about what the Christians are doing? How will they understand, rather, interpret the idea that what the congregation was eating and drinking were the body and blood of their convicted and executed leader, Jesus, 2,000 years ago? Is it not magic to eat a morsel of bread and claim eating a piece of human flesh? The very idea of eating human flesh and drinking human blood sounds bizarre. Does it not? How different is a prayer from a magician's chant or incantation? The magician's incantation invokes a mysterious power, so does the cleric's prayer.

Although by no means unique to Christianity, miracles are always difficult to understand. While the faithful see them as revealing divine presence, the non-religious person may dismiss them, or try to explain them away scientifically, as many do these days. However, there are many miracles that defy scientific explanation. Christianity has a few of those: that a young woman, Mary, gave birth without having met a man (the virgin birth: Matthew 2:18–24; Luke 2:1–20. Muslims also believe the virgin birth. *Qu'ran* 3:47); that Jesus rose from the dead (John 20:2–29; compare Matthew 28:9) having earlier raised his friend Lazarus from the grave (John 11:1–44), that Jesus fed more than 5,000 people with two fish and five loaves (John 6:1b, 3–6, 8–9, 12b, 14–15). Now, that is magic! Just a prayer and the fish and the loaves would not run out until everyone had eaten his or her fill?

Judaism abhors magic. In Hebrew scriptures magic is condemned as early as Deuteronomy 28:10–11 "No one shall be found among you who makes a son or daughter pass through fire, or who practises divination, or is a soothsayer, or an augur, or a sorcerer, or one who casts spells, or who consults ghosts or spirits, or who seeks oracles from the dead". Condemned too as idolatrous are the practises of diviners, astrologers, and exorcists (see 2 Kings 21:6; 2 Chronicles 33:6). See the strong condemnation in Exodus 22:18 "You shall not permit a female sorcerer to live". Yet behind this strong abhorrence of magic, the Hebrew Bible and indeed the whole of Judaism recognises the existence and reality of magic. Furthermore, there is the acceptance of good magic, or beneficial magical acts whether they be wrought by a priest or a prophet. These beneficial acts are called miracles, wonders, or signs of divine intervention by the religious, but to outsiders they are simply magical acts. A case in point: Moses, the founder of Judaism, engaged in magical competition with Egyptian magicians when he wanted to lead his people out of slavery in Egypt. The king of Egypt would not let Moses and his people go. So Moses, under divine instructions, performed wonders to the king of Egypt. The king called his own magician to match Moses' wonder.

> The Lord said to Moses and Aaron, "When Pharaoh says to you, "Perform a wonder", then you shall say to Aaron, "Take your staff and throw it down before Pharaoh, and it will become a snake". So Moses and Aaron went to Pharaoh and did as the Lord had commanded; Aaron threw down his staff before Pharaoh and his officials, and it became a snake. Then Pharaoh summoned the wise men and the sorcerers; and they also, the magicians of Egypt, did the same by their secret arts. Each one threw down his staff, and they became snakes; but Aaron's staff swallowed up theirs (Exodus 7:8–12).

The Hebrew scriptures are full of magical acts that are condemned and wonders that are sought and celebrated as signs of divine power to save or to heal. Perhaps the greatest of the healing wonders that leaves non Jews and non-religious believe it was a great "magical" feat was the healing of the Jews bitten by poisonous snakes. The account of the healing is narrated in Numbers 21:4–9, but here is the core of the wonder: "And the Lord said to Moses, 'Make a poisonous serpent, and set it on a pole; and everyone who is bitten shall look at it and live.' So Moses made a serpent of bronze, and put it upon a pole; and whenever a serpent bit someone, that person would look at the serpent of bronze and live" (Numbers 21:8–9).

Hinduism is one of the few religions that has sacred texts that discuss both good and bad magic. The *Atharva Veda* is a *Veda* that deals with *mantras* that can be used for both good and bad. This last recorded *Veda* of 760 hymns, called the *Veda* of priests, is a compilation of magical formulas and incantations to prevent disease and calamities. Let us sample some of the incantations.

Against sorcerers and demons.

1. May this oblation carry hither the sorcerers, as a river [carries] foam! The man or the woman who has performed this [sorcery], that person shall here proclaim himself!
2. This vaunting [sorcerer] has come hither: receive him with alacrity! O Brihaspati, put him into subjection; O Agni and Soma, pierce him through!
3. Slay the offspring of the sorcerer, O soma-drinking [Indra], and subject [him]! Make drop out the farther and the nearer eye of the braggart [demon]!
4. Wherever, O Agni Gâtavedas, you perceive the brood of these hidden devourers [atrin], do thou, mightily strengthened by our charm, slay them: slay their [brood], O Agni, piercing them a hundredfold! (I:8)

Atharva Veda has hymns against disease. The *Veda* provides prescriptions, sometimes involving the use of amulets such as the one below (2:9).

Possession by demons of disease, cured by an amulet of ten kinds of wood.
1. O [amulet] of ten kinds of wood, release this man from the demon (rakshas) and the fit (grââhi) which has seized upon .(gagrââha) his joints! Do thou, moreover, O plant, lead him forth to the world of the living!
2. He has come, he has gone forth, he has joined the community of the living. And he has become the father of sons, and the most happy of men!
3. This person has come to his senses, he has come to the cities of the living. For he [now] has a hundred physicians, and also a thousand herbs.
4. The gods have found thy arrangement, [O amulet]; the Brahmans, moreover, the plants. All the gods have found thy arrangement upon the earth.
5. [The god] that has caused [disease] shall perform the cure; he is himself the best physician.
Let him indeed, the holy one, prepare remedies for thee, together with the [earthly] physician!

In Holy *Qur'an* magic appears in several places: 2:102; 5:110; 6:7; 7:116; 10:76,77,81; 11:7; 15:15; 20:57–73; 21:3; 28:48; 34:43; 37:15; 43:30; 46:7; 52:15; 54:2; 61:6; 74:24. Interestingly, the story of Moses and Pharaoh's magician is repeated several times in the *Qur'an*: 7:112–126; 10:79–81; 20:69–70; 26:37–46; 79:23. Looking at the context of Pharaoh and his magician in Egypt, the *Qur'an* interprets their "great magic" as pure deception for the real victory was with Moses, because his staff, turned into a snake swallowed all their snakes.

Islam condemns magic considering it an act of blasphemy. The recurring point in all these references is that when unbelievers are told or shown the truth, they do not believe, calling miracles magic. The unbelievers call the truth magic because they are corrupt because they live in a distorted reality as 54:2 indicates: "Then they saw a miracle; but they turned away and said, 'Old magic'". The same sentiment is given in 61:6 which says people believed the miracles of Jesus were magic:

> Recall that Jesus, son of Mary, said, "O Children of Israel, I am GOD's messenger to you, confirming the *Torah* and bringing good news of a messenger to come after me whose name will be even more praised (Ahmad)". Then, when he showed them the clear proofs, they said, "This is profound magic".

Tracing the origin of magic the Holy *Qur'an* says:

> They followed what the evil ones gave out [falsely] against the power of Solomon: the blasphemers were, not Solomon, but the evil ones, teaching men magic, and such things as came down at Babylon to the angels Harut and Marut. But neither of these taught anyone [such things] without saying: "We are only for trial; so do not blaspheme". They learned from them the means to sow discord between man and wife. But they could not thus harm anyone except by God's permission. And they learned what harmed them, not what profited them. And they knew that the buyers of [magic] would have no share in the happiness of the Hereafter. And vile was the price for which they did sell their souls, if they but knew! (*Qur'an* 2:102).

Although the *Qur'an* disapproves the use of magic, however, in popular Islam and some quarters of Islamic mysticism, the use of magic is part of Islamic beliefs and practises. It must be empahsised though that the magical acts in Islam are usually pre-Islamic religious beliefs and practises such as *jinns* (demons). The *Qur'an* identifies a *jinn* as a fallen angel. *Sura* 18:50 says "We said to the angels, 'Fall prostrate before Adam'. They fell prostrate, except Satan. He became a jinn, for he disobeyed the order of His Lord. Will you choose him and his descendants as lords instead of Me, even though they are your enemies? What a miserable substitute!" Some of the Jihadist movements of the past took place to purify Islam's pre-islamic and local magical practises either through a local saint or in the tradition of the people.

What has been shown in this chapter is that religion and magic are very close to each other. Too often anthropologists and theologians have presented magic as a life style of people in prescientific age, or dismissed it as mere superstition. The subject is more complex as the discussion in this chapter has demonstrated. That is why this is still a subject of academic interest among African scholars of different training and expertise.

NOTES

1. Neil Whitehead and Robin Wright, *In Darkness and Sorcery: the Anthropology of Assault Sorcery and Witchcraft in Amazonia* (Durham, NC: Duke University Press, 2004).
2. Mary Patterson, "Sorcery and Witchcraft in Melanesia", *Oceania*, 2 and 3, 1974–75.

3. A. P. Elkin, *Aboriginal Men of High Degree* (St. Lucia: University of Queensland Press, 1945).

4. Bruce Kapferer, *The Feast of the Sorcery: Practises of Consciousness and Power* (Chicago, Ill: Chicago University Press, 1997).

5. The information in this section is gleaned from Mary Patterson, "Sorcery and Witchcraft", *Religion and Culture*, 2nd. ed. Raymond Scupin, ed. (Upper Saddle River, NJ: Pearson, Prentice Hall, 2008), 144–167.

6. R. Briggs, *Witches and Neighbours: The Social and Cultural Context of European Witchcraft* (London. Harper Collins, 1996).

7. Lara Apps and Andrew Cow in *Male Witches in Early Modern Europe* (Manchester: Manchester University Press, 2003).

8. Ralph Austen, "The Moral Economy of Witchcraft", *Modernity and its Malcontents: Ritual and Power in Postcolonial Africa*, J. Comaroff (Chicago, Ill: Chicago University Press, 1995).

9. Sylvester Paliani, *1930 Kunadza Mchape*. Blantyre, Malawi.

10. J. Demos, *Entertaining Satan: Witchcraft and the Culture of Early New England* (New York, NY: Oxford University Press, 1982).

11. Tanya M. Luhrmann *Persuasions of the Witch's Craft. Ritual Magic in Contemporary England* (Oxford, Blackwell, 1980).

12. Susan Greenwood, *Magic, Witchcraft and the Otherworld* (Oxford and New York, NY: Berg, 2000).

13. Jean Favret-Saada, *Deadly Words: Witchcraft in the Bocage* (Cambridge:Mason des Sciences de l'Homme and Cambridge university Press, 1980).

14. J. R. Lewis, ed. *Magical Religion and Modern Witchcraft* (Albany, NY: State University of New York Press, 1996).

15. Lucien Lévy-Bruhl, *Primitive Mentality* (New York, NY: Macmillian, 1923).

16. See my analysis of Tylor's work in *Theories of Religion in the Study of African Religions*, 44.

17. Edward B. Tylor, *Religion in Primitive Culture* (London: John Murray, 1871). 426.

18. James George Frazer, *The Golden Bough*, 12 vols. (London: Macmillan Press, 1980). Originally published 1890.

19. Robert Runalph Marett. *The Thresholds of Religion* (Methuen, 1909).

20. James Frazer, *The Golden Bough*. Part 1: *The Magic Art and the Evolution of Kings* (1932), 52.

21. James Frazer, *Encyclopedia Britannica*, 9th ed., S.V. "Taboo: Totemism" (London: Macmillan, 1976), 65, 71.

22. Frazer, *The Magic Art* I, 220.

23. Bronislaw Malinowski. *Sex, Culture and Myth* (London: Hart Davies, 1963), 261.

24. Bronislaw Malinowski, *Magic, Science and Religion and Other Essays* (New York, NY: Double Day Anchor, 1954), 19–20.

25. E. E. Evans-Pritchard, "The Intellectualist (English) Interpretation of Magic", *Bulletin of the Faculty of Arts*, 1 (1933): 282–311.

26. E.E. Evans-Pritchard, *Witchcraft, Oracles and Magic among the Azande* (Oxford: Claredon Press, 1937).

27. *Ibid.*, 64.

28. *Ibid.,* 63.

29. *Ibid.*

30. *Ibid.*, 111.

31. *Ibid.*, 72 Italics original.

32. *Ibid.,* 25.

33. Peter Winch, "Understanding a Primitive Society", *Rationality,* Brayan Wilson, ed. (Cambridge, MA: Blackwell, 1991, reprint. Original, 1970), 93.

34. John H. M. Beattie. *Other Cultures: Aims, Methods, and Achievements in Social Anthropology* (London: Cohen and West, 1964), 71.

35. Douglas, *Purity and Danger,* 58.

36. John Middleton, ed. *Magic, Witchcraft and Curing* (New York, NY: The Natural History Press, 1967), 3.

37. John Middleton and E. H. Winter, *Witchcraft and Sorcery in East Africa* (Londin: Routledge and Kegan Paul, 1963), 3.

38. Wolfgang Behringer, *Witches and Witch Hunts* (Cambridge: Polity Press, 2004).

39. Peter Geschiere, *The Modernity of Witchcraft: Politics and Occult in Postcolonial Africa* (Charlottesville, VA: University Press of Virginia, 1997), 13–15.

40. Tempels, *Philosophie Bantoe,* 22.

41. *Ibid.,* 22, 35, 36.

42. *Ibid.,* 36.

43. Robin Horton, "African Traditional Thought and Western Science", *Africa* 37, nos. 1 and 2 (January and April, 1967).

44. Robin Horton, African Traditional Thought and Western Science", *Rationality.* Bryan R. Wilson, ed. (Cambridge, MA: Blackwell Publishers, 1991), 132.

45. Edward Geoffrey Parrinder, *African Traditional Religion* (Westport, CT: Greenwood Press, 1970), 25–26.

46. Parrinder, *African Traditional Religion,* 28.

47. Jomo Kenyatta, *Facing Mt. Kenya* (New York, NY: Vintage Books, 1965), xix–xx.

48. *Ibid.,* 270–271.

49. *Ibid.,* 271.

50. *Ibid.,* 272.

51. John S. Mbiti, *Introduction to African Religions* (London: Heinemann, 1975), 10.

52. *Ibid.,* 15–16.

53. *Ibid.,* 192.

54. *Ibid.,* 189.

55. *Ibid.,* 197.

56. E. Boulaje Idowu, "The Challenge of Witchcraft", *Orita: Ibadan Journal of Religious Studies* 4, 1 (June 1970), 9, 88.

57. D. E. Idoniboye. "The Concept of 'Spirit' in African Metaphysics", *Second Order,* 2, 1 (January 1973), 84. Original emphasis.

58. A. O. Sanda, "The Scientific or Magical Ways of Knowing: Implications for the Study of African Traditional Healers", *Second Order: An African Journal of Philosophy,* 7, 1 and 2 (January and July 1978), 77–78.

59. Sanda, "The Scientific or Magical Ways of Knowing, 79–80.

60. *Ibid.,* 78.

61. Sophie B. Oluwole, "On the Existence of Witches", *Second Order: An African Journal of Philosophy,* 7, 1 and 2 (January and July 1978), 28, 31. Italics in the original text. The quotation is from J. R. Symythies, "Is ESP Possible?" in Smythies, ed. *Sceince and ESP* (London Routledge and Kegan Paul), 5. Oluwole's essay was republished in Albert G. Mosely, *African Philosophy: Select Readings* (Englewood Cliffs, NJ: Prentice Hall, 1995), 357–270.

62. See, for example, Kwame Gyekye, *An Essay on African Philosophical Thought: Akan Conceptual Scheme* (New York, NY: Cambridge University Press, 1987); Barry Hallen

and J. O. Sodipo, *Knowledge, Belief and Witchcraft* (London: Ethnographica, 1986); J. O. Sodipo, "Notes on the Concept of Yoruba Thought", *Second Order*, 2, 2 (1973); D. A. Masolo, *African Philosophy in Search of Identity* (Edinburgh: Edinburgh University Press, 1994), 124–146.

63. Those philosophers include, among others, J. O. Sodipo, P. O. Bodunrin.

64. J. Omosade Awolalu and P. Adelumo Dopamu. *West African Traditional Religion* (Ibadan, Nigeria: Onibononaje Press, 1979), 243.

65. *Ibid.*, 244.

66. Francis A. Arinze, *Sacrifice in Ibo Religion* (Ibadan, Nigeria: Ibadan University Press, 1970), 22.

8
Sacred Time, Objects, and Space

In our exploration of myth we found that myth sets apart, or turns the ordinary to the sacred, beginning with the origin of the myth itself which becomes a sacred origin: its time, sacred time; the place, a holy place, so holy too is the person(s) and things involved. Every religion has sacred places, time, and rituals. This chapter is dedicated to a further exploration of the sacred through space, time, and art.

Sacred Time

We touched upon the concept of time as being linear and cyclical time earler in this book. Whether time is understood as linear or cyclical, time is never perceived as a flitting moment, rather as a key to knowledge of what constitutes people. This is to say that time gives people their identity and meaning in life. That time gives identity and meaning is clear in rituals of liminality, but also festival rituals. It is time that gives rise to ritual; conversely, ritual celebrates time. Rituals celebrate a particular time, a time of action, a time when things happened in the primordial past at a sacred time. All rituals mark sacred time. Nowhere is this expressed with greater clarity than in the Dreamtime ritual of the indigenous people of Australian. Their myth called the "Dreamtime", is the overarching myth about all creation and existence: the beginning of all things, stories of their ancestors, the origin of death, and about power and life. Dreamtime was not a time of sleeping and living in an unrealistic, illusory time. Dreamtime was the time before everything, when creative powers emerged to bring into being the universe and everything that exist. It was in Dreamtime that the ancestral spirits came on earth and gave everything that exists including human life and culture. When the ancestral spirits came on earth, they established relations among all creatures, so that indigenous Australians believe that everything in the universe is interconnected because of their origin in Dreamtime. That is to say, everything is part of the unchanging network of relations that goes back to the time of the ancestral spirits, the time of the beginning of knowledge and the laws of existence. Everything is unchanging because it comes from the same source, Dreamtime. Indigenous Australians consider Dreamtime as something that continues in the spiritual life of the people.

Dreamtime is the primordial, dynamic time; action time that continues to inspire the living to be alive to the spirit and in the world. Thus, for Australian "Dreaming" is being alive in the spirit, spirituality, or set of beliefs (that inspire). Dreaming is sacredness of the earth; dreaming is seed power, a state of consciousness attuned to the potency of the earth. So the Australian Dreamtime ritual is the attempt to capture, or rather invigorate the primordial potency or consciousness. It appears that rituals in marking time, they are like indigenous Australian Dreamtime, they raise consciousness of sacred time, original time.

Sacred time is a time to remember, reflect on life, and to visualise destiny. It is time to get in touch with one's deep self, and to make a transition as the time may demand. Sacred time may be a particular time of transition or shifts in harmony with nature or natural events. Many religions mark sacred time with celebrations such as the native American Sun dance performed at summer solstices, the agricultural rituals of South Africa, the Christian Good Friday, Muslim holy month of Ramadan when Allah revealed the first verses of the *Qur'an* in 610. The holy month ends with the festival of *Eid al-Fitr* (Literally the "Festival of Breaking the Fast"). Sometimes Jewish New Year, *Rosh haShana* coincides with Muslim Ramadan. *Rosh haShana* is a sacred time of a ten-day period of reflection, repentance, and celebration ending at the Day of Atonement of *Yom Kippur*. Jewish sacred times also include Festival of Booths, *Sukkot,* a time reminding the Jews of their time in the wilderness when they slept in tents. There are other sacred times in Judaism than space allows for discussion in this book. For Islam and Judaism, as it is for Christianity, their weekly days of celebration and divination, Friday, Saturday, and Sunday, respectively, is a sacred time.

Sacred time is also marked by rituals of liminality as a candidate transition into another, or higher stage of life. Initiation rituals are makers of sacred time. The Ndebu ritual of liminality mentioned earlier in the book, or the Shinto purification rituals are rituals that mark sacred time.

Wearing a *Yajnopavita* is a very holy and sacred ceremony among Hindu boys ages of between five and eight. By this ceremony, they become fit for the repetition of *Gayatri*. A Brahmin becomes a true Brahmin only after this ceremony.

Sacred times inspire calenders. Almost all the calenders of various religions are based on sacred times, when major events in the people's lives started. The Jewish year begins with the celebration of *Rosh haShana*, the Muslim calender begins with the year of Muhammad; the Buddhist calender begins at Buddha's death or his entrance into *nirvana* (eternal bliss). Thus the Thai calender starts at 543 B.C.E. While the Buddhist calender begins at his entrance in *nirvana* his *Vesak* (Buddha day) is the most important sacred time in Buddhism when devotees around the world celebrated Buddha's birth, enlightenment and death all in a single day, the first full moon day in May. The Buddah's first sermon, or the turning of the wheel of the Dharma is celebrated in July.

While focusing on sacred time, it should not be concluded that other times are not sacred. In religions of structure, there is no bifurcation of time: there is no sacred and profane time. All time is sacred, but that the set times are times of heightened perception and experience of ultimate reality or the divine. During sacred times humans step out of themselves, to see themselves as who and whose they are, or to whom they belong as individuals and communities are transported by rituals to the origin, when things started, were ordered or were given. Sacred time can be a time of self-discovery.

Almost all religions of structure view time in two ways: (1) as abstract in the sense of being eternal, or open ended, and unfolding, and (2)actual, as a moment in which events happen. However, while recognising the abstract, unfolding nature of time, emphasis is placed on the two dimensions of time, the present and the past because of particular events they embody. In other words, time is when a particular event(s) happens. The event defines the time so that people understand or think about the time in relation to the event that took place at a particular a moment. Thus, the concept of time as a continuous abstract and empty of events, is unknown to Africans and others in religions of structure. For Africans, time is an attribute of the event that it embodies, for without the attribute it would not be possible to separate the unbound, linear abstract, to have the present and the past, or the future to which people are bound. Events measure time, its length, beginning with the present, the shortest length of time, the extended past limited by memory, and the unmarked future, empty, and less meaningful. In contrast, the future with its definite end is critical and meaningful in religions of salvation. In brief, time as a metaphysical concept is not an important category, or a key concept towards understanding religions of structure.

Sacred Space

Sacred places inspire awe and reverence, not only because of their size, but the myth of their origin, the founding event that people reenact in ritual. Holy places are not all grandiose, some are simple shrines at which prayers are said and sacrifices offered.

Mountains

Religions of structure consider all space as sacred space, yet there are sites set apart as holy places. The title of Kenyatta's book, *Facing Mount Kenya*, points to a sacred place, Mount Kere-yanga, the place of origin of Gikuyu, the founding ancestor of the Gikuyu, the place of creation, the resting place *Mogia* (the divider of the Universe) on his inspection tour of Gikuyu land. Kere-yanga, Mount Kenya, is a holy place. Gikuyu elders say their prayers facing Mount Kenya because before Mogai departed he told Gikuyu that "whenever he was in need he should make a sacrifice and raise his hands towards Kere-yanga (the mountain of mystery) and the

Lord of nature will come to his assistance".[1] The Gikuyu received blessings and instructions for life and Mount Kenya, the Gikuyu centre of the universe. So no ritual of celebration can be complete without facing Mount Kenya, the place of creation, of the first ancestor, of divine authority, of security and blessing.

What Mount Kenya is for the Gikuyu, Mount Kilimanjaro is for the Changa who live on the slopes of the highest mountain in Africa, and so too, is Mount Fuji to the Japanese who believe the spirits of the ancestors dwell on Mount Fuji. Mount Sinai is a holy place for the Jews for it is here that they received the Ten Commandments or instructions for living with each other and their God. Over time the awe over Mount Sinai moved to Mount Zion, or Jerusalem, the city of their beloved king David. Mount Zion became the centre of Jewish life, just as Mount Sinai had been. On Mount Sinai, Moses received the Law; David brought the Ark of Covenant, or the box containing the Ten Commandments, to Jerusalem, thereby making Mount Zion a holy place, the abode of YHWH (God) and the centre of Jewish life, the place of blessing and security.

> Great is the Lord and greatly to be praised
> in the city of our God.
> His holy mountain, 2beautiful in elevation,
> is the joy of all the earth,
> Mount Zion, in the far north,
> the city of the great King.
> 3Within its citadels God
> has shown himself a sure defence.
>
> 9We ponder your steadfast love, O God,
> in the midst of your temple.
> 10Your name, O God, like your praise,
> reaches to the ends of the earth.
> Your right hand is filled with victory.
> 11 Let Mount Zion be glad,
> let the towns; of Judah rejoice
> because of your judgements (Psalm 48:1–4, 9–11).

The understanding that Jerusalem was the abode of their God, made the Jews localise him to the extent that they believed God only existed in Zion, thus Israel. The temple, built on Mount Zion, became the centre of Jewish universe, worship, and ritual practises: offerings and sacrifices. The temple on Mount Zion regulated the activities of seasons, and thus organising Jewish life. Mount Zion became the key to Jewish cosmogony, the very centre of the world as a rabbinic texts states:

> Just as the navel is found at the centre of the human being, so the land of Israel is found at the centre of the world . . . and it is the foundation of the world. Jerusalem is the centre of the land of Israel, the Temple is at the centre of Jerusalem, the Holy of the Holies is at the centre of the Temple, the Ark is at the

centre of the Holy of the Holies and the foundation stone is in front of the Ark which spot is the foundation of the world.[2]

It was only on Mount Zion that Jews could experience the fulness of God's presence, or have the most profound religious experience. So when the Jews were taken into exile into Babylon, roughly modern day Iraq in 580, they found it hard to praise their God in a foreign land. In other words, God had been left in Judah, at Mount Zion. Psalm 137 expresses the sense of loss and of being disconnected to their God that the Jews experienced in exile.

By the rivers of Babylon—
there we sat down and there we wept
when we remembered Zion.
2On the willows there
we hung up our harps.
3For there our captors
asked us for songs,
and our tormentors asked for mirth, saying",Sing us one of the songs of Zion!"

4How could we sing the Lord's song
in a foreign land?
5If I forget you, O Jerusalem,
let my right hand wither!
6Let my tongue cling to the roof of my mouth,
if I do not remember you,
if I do not set Jerusalem
above my highest joy (Psalm 137:1–6).

Mount Zion, with its temple was so central to Judaism and Jewish life that when it was destroyed by the Roman in 70 C.E., Judaism was no longer the same. With the temple gone, the centre of Jewish religious life moved to the synagogue (Greek for assembly). Unlike the temple, sacrifices are not offered in the synagogue, but still the visual centre of the space for worship has the ark (*aron kodesh*) containing the *Torah* scrolls. *Aron kodesh* is not the Ark of Covenant with the Ten Commandments. *Aron kodesh* is always in the wall facing east towards Jerusalem and Mount Zion.

Rivers, Lakes, and Seas

Not only mountains are sacred sites, but bodies of water as well are the abode of ancestral spirits, thus places of ritual, sacrifice, and celebration. In the past many African groups offered their sacrifices at river banks; they prayed standing on the beaches of lakes and invoked their ancestors and God on the shores of the sea. In the past, a Chopi chief in South Africa made a national offering sacrifice at a river bank. He would offer a sacrifice with eyes turned towards the river and then place the cut meat on the bank of the river. While mountains are holy places because of their majesty, bodies of water are sacred because they represent the origin of life, but also their cleansing or purifying power. The Ganges river, the most sacred of the seven sacred rivers of India, is to Hindus the place of purification in life and in death. The desire of every pious Hindu is to be purified by the holy waters of the Ganges, a river whose source is believed to be in heaven in the hair of the Lord Shiva. The river itself is a goddess. Thousands of pious Hindus travel long distances to north-central India to the holy city of Varanasi on the bank of the Ganges for purification in the holy river. Many pious Hindus bring their dead to be cremated on the banks of the holy river and for their ashes to be spread on the river for eternal purification.

Churches and Temples

It is not only a natural phenomenon that provides humans a sense of the sacred, but also spaces created by humans such as churches, temples, and shrines. These sacred places are of various designs and sizes, and sometimes they reflect the period and culture of the people. For example, the Gothic architecture was the design of the twelfth to the sixteenth century Europe, while the Byzantine architecture with its massive dome at the centre reflects the design of Byzantine empire or of the eastern (orthodox) churches. Russian architecture reflects Byzantine influence as the onion domes seen on the Kremlin in Moscow, Russia. Byzantine architecture with its distinctive dome style is similar to Islamic architecture which also has domes as the Dome of the Rock in Jerusalem. The Bacilicas architecture with its vaults and large roofs such as found in both Catholic and Orthodox churches reflects the design of the early or mediaeval church. Bacilicas architecture developed from Roman architecture of public buildings. St Peter's Bacilica in Rome, Italy, is the most well-known bacilica architecture.

Shrines

While some religions build big and magnificent structures for places of worship, in other religions they have simple structures where prayers, offerings, and sacrifices are given to a deity or honour to a holy person, or a hero. The word shrine is from the Latin word *scrinium*, meaning a container, a box, if you will, containing the valuables and itself made of valuable materials. Originally, *scrinium* contained sacred articles such as a relic, that is, something belonging to a dead holy person which was more than a memorabilia, but supposed to have the power to produce unusual effects, a healing miracle, for example, when touched or placed on the sick. Besides relics, a *scrinium* would also contain religious objects or articles. A Shinto shrine is a good example on this point for it houses the *Kami*.

Shrines may be found in variety of ways: a mound in a hut, an enclosure in room, a homestead, or outside, on a tomb or grave site, or in the forest. Shrines may be private or family, or public or communal. Often, offerings of water, food, beer, or animal sacrifices of chicken, goat, or sheep are made at the shrine. Some shrines are beautifully decorated while others are plain and simple. Besides offering prayers, shrines may be places of celebration, with people bringing food to eat or beer to drink at the shrine.

Graves

In many places and religions people go to the graves on certain celebrations and there eat and drink with the spirits of the ancestors. In Sufi Islam, people celebrate their saints at their graves with food and singing. In Chinese religions with their great respect for the elders or ancestors, bring their families to the cemetery where they eat and drink with the ancestors. In Africa, graves may be treated as shrines or shrines are built on them. Upon the shrines pieces of food are offered or a libation is poured, invoking the ancestors to mediate their prayers to God.[3]

A Vodun shrine. Vodun is a new religion, a hybrid religion between West African religion (Togo, Benin, and among the Yoruba in Nigeria) and Catholicism in the Americas. This religion of African origin was brought over to the new world by enslaved Africans who were then baptised Catholics without their consent. The Africans did not want to forget their religion, so they mixed Catholic practises with their traditional African religion. Vodun is practised by more than 80 million people.

A Vodun shrine in Haiti, New Orleans, New York and elsewhere, is beautifully decorated, graced with a variety of food items. Let us take a brief look at ritual at the shrine of this hybrid religion. As we look at the Vodun shrine, we see: (1) patterns of maize (corn) flour on the floor unique to the particular deity or *loa* to whom the ritual at the shrine is dedicated; (2) the purified ritual rattle and drums; (3) various food items on the shrine itself; (4) the animal sacrifice; (5) the priests, male *houngan*, and female, *hounsis* and perhaps their students who will dance to the sound of the rattle and the tom-tom beat of the drum, the sound rises to a crescendo and one person is possessed by *loa* and falls to the ground, the body taken over by the spirit.

A Hindu shrine. In most Hindu homes they have a room or space set apart as a shrine for daily celebration ritual, or the honouring of gods, *puja*. At the shrine is a tray with seven sacred objects used in celebrating the divine: a bell, Diva light, incense holder and incense, water container and a spoon, a container for *kum kum* powder, and an offering of food called *prashad*. Dominating a Hindu home shrine is a *murti*, images of various gods such as Lord Krishna or Lord Ganesh. Along with images of divinities, there may also be a *mandala*, a symbolic representation of the universe.

Hindu acts of celebration, the *puja*, involves images (*murtis*), prayers (*mantras*) and diagrams of the universe (*yantras*). *Puja* may be done in private or with one's family at the family shrine in the home, offering divinities water, fruit, flowers, and incense. While they may have their prayers at the family shrine, Hindus attend the temple where a priest recites the *Vedas*, although technically any "twice-born" Hindu may read scriptures.

When an individual or family comes to a shrine, the head of the household rings the bell as an invocation, or inviting God in the home. A lamp is lit, symbolising divine presence. The light is passed around or waved before the Deity. This denotes that the Lord is *Jyotis-Svarupa*, who is all-light. The devotee then says: "O Lord! You are the self-effulgent Light of the universe. You are the light in the sun, moon, and fire. Remove the darkness in me by bestowing your divine light. May my intellect be illumined". The devotee then lights an incense stick, *Dhupa*, not simply to purify the air with its aroma, but to symbolise divine presence which is all pervading in the universe. The devotee prays: "O Lord! Let the *Vasanas* and *Samskaras* dormant in me vanish like the smoke of this *Dhupa* and become ashes. Let me become stainless". Water is offered using the spoon. After prayers a paste sandal paste, is made with *kum kum* power to mark the forehead as a sign of receiving blessings. Finally, food offering, *prashad* (fruit, sweet rice, butter, or sugar) is offered to the Lord after which the food is shared by all. Here we see that sacred places often imply sacred objects.

Most of the Hindu sacred objects are also found in other religions: a bell, light (or fire), incense, water, food offering, and images of the divine.

Sacred circle

Talking about architecture, the Lakota Native Americans see sacred space as a circle. To the Lakota's the circle represents the earth, the path of the sun around the earth, and the circle of life through which all things must pass. This cosmogony informs how they build their homes and their villages. Their homes, called *tipis* are round and so are their villages so that everything in concert with the universal forces that more in circular motion of the universal circle. Their most sacred ritual dance, *Wiwanyang Wacipi* (the sun dance), lasting four or more days, is done in a place that is circular with a double ring of sticks erected around the holy place. The dancers wear rings of sage on their heads and around their wrists and ankles. The sun dance is an important ritual dance for many other Native Americans in the central plains in north America.

The dance is held in the spring or summer solstice. The ritual dance fittingly takes place in the spring for it is about renewal, celebrating new life, a renewal or rebirth of the spiritual life of individuals and the community, a regeneration of mother earth and all nature in it, a harmony between of the cosmos. This ritual dance involving sacrifice is about reconciliation of individuals within the community.[4]

Sacred Ritual Objects

Buddhism

Buddhism is one of the religions with many sacred objects which include the following: Begging bowl, Buddha image, incense burners, *mala* (prayer beds), monks' robes, *stupas* and *pagodas*. *Stupas* and *pagodas* are shrines containing sacred relics and appear in many sizes and styles throughout the Buddhist world. The *mala*, or rosary, has 108 beads or more. Buddhists believe going 200 rounds of prayer using the 108 beads of the *mala*, one will have said a prayer for each breath of a day. In other words, 200 *malas* of *Japa* (prayers using *mala*) is equal to the total number of human breaths a day, 21,600 breaths. Each *mala* has the *meru*, the central bead that signals to the faithful that they have completed one round of prayer using 108 beads that they have moved along their spiritual path, thereby dispelling ignorance.

In Tibetan Buddhism the *mandala* is the most important sacred object. Also very important is the singing bowl used as an aid in meditation. The bowl makes a resonant sound when it is rubbed by a *puja* stick. The sound produces a calming effect necessary for meditation. Tibetan Buddhists have a prayer wheel, a metal cylinder on a rod containing tightly wound printed *matras*. The prayers on the wheel are believed to be released into the universe when the wheel is spinning. Spinning the wheel is like saying a prayer. That is why it is known as the wheel of transformation. The wheel has a hub which represents discipline and eight spokes which point to the eight directions, thus representing the eightfold path: right understanding, right thought, right speech, right action, right livelihood, right effort, mindfulness, and concentration.

Thangka. In Tibetan home shrines and at altars in monasteries they hang a ceremonial banner or painting carried out by priests. The flat banner represents the eight ways of conquering sin and desire: the development of knowledge, wisdom, compassion, meditation, and ethical vows; taking refuge in the Buddha; abandoning false views; generating spiritual aspiration, skillful means, and selflessness; and the unity of the three principles: emptiness, formlessness, and desire-less-ness.

Kapala or skull cup, is used in Tibetan Buddhism for libation during rituals associated with wrathful deities in art. The cup is said to be normally made from a human skull. The cup is an object used in Tibetan rituals.

Phurpa or ritual weapon is used in Tibetan Buddhism by high-level Tantric practitioners to conquer evil spirits, ignorance and to destroy obstacles.

Dorje. This is a small sceptre that Tibetan *lamas* hold in their right hands during ceremonies. *Dorje* is considered indestructible and it can dispel ignorance.

Musical instruments. The sacred objects in Tibetan Buddhism include sacred musical instruments: Bells, drums, trumpets and horns are used in many religions including the following: esoteric Buddhism to symbolise mantras and dispel evil.

Judaism

There are a number of ritual objects in Judaism beginning with *tallit*: a prayer shawl. Every devout Jew from the age of 13 for boys and 12 for girls put on a rectangular prayer shawl before prayer with 613 fridges called *tzitzit*, which represents the 613 commandments they are to keep. The *tzitzit* were commanded by God in the Jewish holy book, *Torah* which says,

> The Lord said to Moses: Speak to the Israelites and instruct them to make for themselves fringes on the corners of their garments throughout the ages; let them attach a cord of blue to the fringe at each corner. That shall be your fringe; look at it and recall all the commandments of the Lord and observe them, so that you do not follow your heart and eyes in your lustful urge. Thus you shall be reminded to observe all my commandments and to be holy to your God. I, the Lord, am your God, who brought you out of the land of Egypt to be your God: I, the Lord your God (Numbers 15:37–41).

The *tzitzit* reminds Jews of the commandments of God. Devout Jews wear *tallit* for morning prayer, but also during the week as well as on Shabat and high religious holidays. During Sabbath and holiday evening prayers, only the cantor (a prayer leader) and *Torah* readers wear a *tallit*. The prayer shawl is not worn anyhow. The wearing itself is ritualistic. Several steps are taken:

1.   The shawl is opened so that the colour is seen.
2.   The devotee recites a prayer, a *berachah* whose transliteration runs as follows: *Baruch ataadononai Elohaynu melech haoloma asher kid'shanu b'mitzvotav vtzivanu l'hitatayf batzitzit* (Blessed you are you, Lord God, ruler of the universe who makes us holy with the commandments, and has commanded us to wrap ourselves in the *tzitzit*).
3.   The devotee then kisses the end of the *atarah* where the last word of the blessing is embroidered and then the beginning where the first word is.
4.   The devotee wraps the *tallit* around the shoulders, holding it over the head for a moment of individual meditation.
5.   The devotee adjusts the *tallit* over the shoulders comfortably.

The *tzitzit* is kissed several times during the whole celebration:

1.   The *tzitzit* is kissed three times at the recitation of the third paragraph of the *shema* (creed) (Numbers 15:37–41).
2.   When the devotee reads the word *tzitzit*
3.   When the *Torah* is carried out of the Ark and moved around the synagogue in a procession called *hakafah*. Devotees close to the *Torah* in *hakafah* touch the *Torah* with *tzitzit* and then kiss the *tzitzit* as a sign of love of the *Torah*.[5]

Yarmulke also called a *kippah* is a small thin, slightly-rounded cloth scull cap that often, but not always every Jewish male devotee uses to cover the head. The head covering is to remind Jews that they are always to follow God's commandment at all times in all places.

Tefillin or phylacteries, are two small black leather boxes worn on the left arm and forehead by observant adult male Jews. The boxes have long leather straps for tying them to the arm and the forehead. The leather boxes of the *tefillin* contain scrolls of *Torah* passages specifically Exodus 13:1–10, 11–16 and Deuteronomy 6:4–9, 11:13–21. Deuteronomy 6:4–9 includes the *shema*:

> Hear, O Israel: The Lord is our God, the Lord alone. 5You shall love the Lord your God with all your heart, and with all your soul, and with all your might. 6Keep these words that I am commanding you today in your heart. 7Recite them to your children and talk about them when you are at home and when you are away, when you lie down and when you rise. 8Bind them as a sign on your hand, fix them as an emblem on your forehead, 9and write them on the doorposts of your house and on your gates.

A *Kittel* is a white linen robe worn by Jewish men on special occasions to signify purity, holiness, a *Kittel* nd new beginnings. Traditionally, a Jewish man first wears a kittel on his wedding day, thereafter on *Rosh Hashanah*, *Yom Kippur* and *Passover*, and ultimately as a burial shroud. *Kittels* are worn by Orthodox Jews although conservative and reformed Jews wear it too.

Mezuzah. The box on the left is to remind the devotee of God's law as the heart is on the left while the box on the forehead is to remind devotees to concentrate on the commandments of God with all their mind. Jews are to remember the commandments not only by wearing them for ritual prayer or ritual acts, but also by putting them on their doorpost. Every devout Jewish home has a *mezuzah* (from the Hebrew for doorpost) which is a small parchment or *Torah* passages in Hebrew, a small parchment containing two sections from the Deuteronomy (6:4–9 and 11:13–21). The *Torah* parchment is rolled up in a decorative case and placed on the doorpost of observant Jews.

The Aron Ha-kodesh. It has already been indicated that the central part of a synagogue is the Ark of covenant containing the *Sifrei Torah* (*Torah* scrolls). A *Ner Tamid* (eternal light) hangs outside and above it. The faithful face in their common celebration and divination. The Ark cabinet is not exposed, but is separated from the people by a curtain called a *parochet*.

Menorah (candelabrum) is a ritual seven-candle holder in a Jewish home reminding Jews of the seven-branched candle holder that used to be in the Temple. The *menorah* is a sign of hope that one day the temple will be rebuilt. The instructions for making the *menorah* are given in the *Torah* Exodus 25:31:40. Note that the nine-branched candle holder used at *Hannukkah* is not the same as the *menorah*.

Shofar. This is a "trumpet" made of a ram's horn used to call the faithful to service on the morning of high holy days of Rosh Hashanah and Yom Kippur. It is also used the month before Rosh Hashanah. *Shofar* is also a musical instrument for religious purposes. *Shofar* finds its scriptural grounding in Genesis 22:13 "And Abraham looked up and saw a ram, caught in a thicket by its horns. Abraham went and took the ram and offered it up as a burnt-offering instead of his son", and Zechariah 9:14

Then the Lord will appear over them,
and his arrows go forth like lightning;
the Lord God will sound the trumpet
and march forth in the whirlwinds of the south.

Sikhism

It is mentioned elsewhere in the book that the most sacred object in Sikhism is the *Guru Granth Sahib*, the holy book in Sikhism. It has also been pointed out that whenever the holy scriptures are read, a fly whisk is used as a sign of veneration of the holy book, but also to fun the reader(s).

That fly whisk is called a *chauri*. Other Sikh objects include the Five Ks: *Kesh* (Turban), *Kachh* (cotton underwear), *Kara* (bracelet), *Kangha* (a comb), *Kirpan* (a steel dagger).

Kesh is uncut hair, a sign of saintliness and deep spirituality in Sikhism as one seeks to live according to God's will. It is from this understanding of hair that gave rise to Sikh turbans. The turban helps in keeping long hair tidy and clean.

Kangha (comb). A Sikh is expected to keep the long hair neat and clean. Thus he is supposed to comb the hair twice a day and tie the turban neatly.

Kara is a steel bracelet worn on the right wrist symbolising restraint from evil deeds, reminds a Sikh of belonging to God and therefore allegiance to God. The steel bracelet also serves to remind individual Sikhs not to do anything that would bring shame or disgrace to them personally and to *Khalsa*

Kacch are white cotton shorts that a Sikh must wear all the time as an undergarment. *Kacch* are a soldier's short, practical in battle, and therefore symbolises commitment moral strength, chastity, and procreation.

Kirpan is a steel dagger, a symbol of courage, resistance against evil and self-defence of truth. Therefore *kirpan* is a symbol of commitment defend and serve the poor, the weak and the innocent.

Hinduism

The Hindu ritual of the *Yajnopavita,* or the sacred thread is worn by the Brahmins, Kshatriyas and the Vaisyas. It is worn across the chest and rests on the left shoulder. The first time it is worn, it is made of three threads that are tied together in a knot called *Brahma-granthi*. The three threads symbolise a variety of triads, among them that one should be a *Brahmachari* in thought, word and deed. Each thread represents a *Veda*, viz., the *Rik, Yajus* and *Sama*. Each thread also represents the three Hindu divinities: Brahma, Vishnu and Siva. The knot in the middle represents the formless Brahman, the Supreme Principle. *Yajnopavita* also represents the three conditions of Sat, Chit and Ananda or being consciousness and Bliss the creation, preservation and destruction of the universe the three qualities of Sattva, Rajas and Tamas of the Trigunatmika Maya, and the knot represents the Isvara who controls Maya. The three threads stand for three states of waking, dreaming and deep sleep and the like and the observation by the wearer of the triple control over mind, speech and body, or of thought, word and deed.

Gerua (the Ochre Cloth) is the dress of a *sannyasin*, someone who has renounced the world. It is a sign of purity. The Ochre Cloth indicates that he is as pure as fire itself; he shines like the burnt gold, free from all impurities of desires and Vasanas. The cloth reminds a *sannyasin* that he cannot be involved in things of this world of which he has renounced.

Native Americans

The sacred pipe. Among the most sacred objects in Lakota religion is the sacred pipe. Every Lakota must smoke a sacred pipe before considering any matter of importance such as a vision quest, or engaging in any ceremony. The Lakotas believe the spirit in the pipe smoke is pleasing to *Wakan Tanka* and all the spirits. The spirit is smoothed by smoking the pipe, for the spirit of God is the spirit from the pipe. The Lakota say the pipe was given to them by God.

Drum and rattle. Like the sacred pipe, the drum and the rattle please the *wakan*. These two sacred objects are used in almost all major Lakota ceremonies: the Sun Dance, the *Hunka*, and the Buffalo ceremony. A shaman has a drum and two rattles that he sounds in healing the sick. Someone else may sound the drum and the rattle when the Shaman is performing a ceremony.

African Religion

Apart from the drum, it is virtually impossible to list the sacred objects in African religion. There as many sacred objects in African religion as there are different peoples and their religious practises. Sacred objects in African religion include divination stones, beads, masks, sculptures, metal artifacts, costumes, textile, bundles, horns for storing medicines or as objects of divination, or used in libations. In short, African religion may have the largest number of sacred objects. This is what led Europeans to call all sacred objects fetishes. The various sacred objects are to be found at shrines or in homes.

NOTES

1. Jomo Kenyatta, *Facing Mount Kenya* (New York, NY: Vintage Books), 5.

2. *Midrash Tanhuma, Kedoshim*, Vol. 10. A. Herzberg, *Judaism* (New York, 1963), 143.

3. John S. Mbiti, *Introduction to African Religions* (London: Heinemann, 1975).

4. David M Jones and Brian L Molyneaux, *Mythology of the American Nations* (London: Hermes House, 2006).

5. See Jacob Neusner, *The Enchantments of Judaism: Rites of Transformation From Birth Through, Death* (New York, NY: Basic Books, 1987).

9

Living Within The Sacred

For most people religion means morality or ethics. In fact, most people collapse religion into morality to the extent that the two are inseparable. To show that the two are separate, we will need to define what each means and also investigate the meaning of ethics. The word religion derives from two Latin words *religare*, to "bind oneself", *relegere* "scrupulous observance". We note a sense of action from these two origins of the word religion: binding and observing. The words bind and observance indicate that religion is not an article of faith, but action. True religious people, therefore, are those who are active in their religion because religion is a doing word, a verb, that calls for action for religion to be meaningful. The founder of Christianity, Jesus of Nazareth, made it clear that religion is not an article of faith but action when he said to his followers: "Not everyone *who says* to me, 'Lord, Lord', will enter the kingdom of heaven, but only one *who does* the will of my Father in heaven" (Matthew 7:21. Emphasis added). Religion is action. Jesus also taught his followers that people will be judged on their action.

> Then the king will say to those at his right hand, 'Come, you that are blessed by my Father, inherit the kingdom prepared for you from the foundation of the world. 35for I was hungry and you gave me food, I was thirsty and you gave me something to drink, I was a stranger and you welcomed me, 36I was naked and you gave me clothing, I was sick and you took care of me, I was in prison and you visited me (Matthew 25:34–26).

The word morality is from the Latin *moralis*, meaning the customs of the people. Morality pertains to accepted conduct or character according to custom of a particular society. Morality is, therefore, behaviour according to the manner of living proper to a specific society. As based on custom, morality is handed down; its authority is from time immemorial. Ethics derives from the Greek word for custom or character, *ethos* which also is the root for the word ethnic, which means common culture. Ethics then, is the character or custom of a group of people sharing a common culture. Both morality and ethics refer to common cultural behaviour or practises rooted in, or rising from the cosmogony of a particular people.

Each culture has acceptable and prohibited behavioural practises. The unacceptable or prohibited behavioural patterns are in some cultures called *taboos*. Doing what is morally acceptable and commendable, or achieving moral excellence is called virtue. In other words, virtue is moral ideal. Aristotle differentiates between two types of virtues: "Virtue of the thought and virtue of character. Virtue of thought arises mostly from teaching, and hence experience and time. Virtue of character [i.e., *ēthos*] results from habit [*ethos*]; hence its name ethical, slightly varied from *ethos*".[1] Virtue is acquired by practise, or habituation as Aristotle puts it, so that moral excellence can properly be called "habits of the heart", by which it is meant moral excellence has been so habituated as to become second nature to an individual. Aristotle says, "Virtue . . . we acquire, just as we acquire crafts, by having previously activated them".[2]

Individuals who make moral ideals their second nature, their habit of the heart, so to speak, become moral exemplars whom people seek to emulate. Founders of religion, and other dedicate religious individuals, are people of highest moral excellence or virtue. People with such moral excellence include, the Buddha, Jesus, Muhammad, the saints, or individuals like Gandhi, Martin Luther King, Jr., among others. Moral exemplars do not point to moral guides, they embody virtues in themselves so that they are themselves the guide. That is why they attract others to look up to them as moral guides. The power of their persuasion lies in their moral excellence demonstrated in the cardinal virtues: courage, compassion, generosity, equanimity, patience, justice, kindness, and wisdom. People of great virtue in religion also depict theological virtues: faith, hope, love, fortitude, prudence, temperance, and justice.

The relation between morals or ethics and culture is also seen in the fact that religious practises are interwoven into the fabric of cultural practises. For example, Judaism is essentially a religion for the Jews and embodies Jewish cultural practises; Confucianism is a Chinese religion with Chinese cultural practises, Buddhism is an Asian religion expressed in various Asian cultural idioms and practises. Religion and culture are intrinsically interwoven to the extent that it is sometimes impossible for religion to rise above certain cultural practises. Culture certainly defines the nature of religion. For example, South American Catholicism, is different from Irish Catholicism. While both are Catholics, and share the same beliefs, they practise the religion differently for they emphasise cultural practises that are unique to each of them.[3] This is also true for Protestants in north America where African American religious practises are very different from Caucasian Protestants. Their celebrations are vastly different as Caucasian maintain their European religious cultural practises, which Black people consider cold, an enthusiastic and stale as compared to their dynamic, spirit-filled, and emotional religious experience. Religion is cultural and culture bound for religious beliefs and practises are expressed in cultural thought, idiom, and practise.

Ethics is a rational interpretation and evaluation of morality. Ethics is thinking about common cultural behavioural practises. Morality is about what everyday life is; ethics is about what ought and not to be or done. We can, therefore, say that morality reveals the nature of religion, or more precisely, the nature of cosmology giving rise to certain behaviour, while ethics articulates the virtues embedded in morality. This also means that morality appeals to cosmogony for authority. Simply, individuals do certain things, behave in a certain way, or live a certain manner of life because it is ordered by their cosmogony. Ethics builds a rationale for what is enjoined by a particular cosmogony.

Here religion and ethics have been cast within cosmogony, but it is wrong to conclude that those who do not have a religion are immoral and unethical. The non-religious individuals have morals and ethical because they too, have a cosmogony and an ultimate concern that dictate their manner of living. This is to assert that there is no individual with an ultimate concern who is without morals and ethics. For example, those who negate the existence of a divine being and maintain humanity as the ultimate concern, atheists, are usually very ethical people because their focus is on what the human condition ought to be, thereby they reject the existential depravation of human life. In their rejection of the current poor state of the human condition, atheists develop a dynamic understanding of human interaction, morals and ethics, to promote human goodness, thus humanity itself, their ultimate concern.

The point is that morality and ethics become religious, or are religious only when their source of authority is religious. This means that there are two sources of authority for morality and ethics, religious and social. There is religious morality or ethics, just as there is social morals and social ethics. While the two sources of moral and ethics seem clear-cut, in practise it is not always easy to keep the two separate. To illustrate, all societies and religions abhor killing of another human being. Yet some religions will endorse killing for religious reasons. The Hebrew Bible, the Christian Old Testament, and the *Qur'an* say that their forefather, Abraham, was told to kill his son as a sacrifice because God told him so. He almost slit his son's throat when God stopped him. Abraham was not a murderer, but a religious man, who, at the command of God was willing to kill his own offspring as a sign of total obedience to God. No scriptures condemn him. Instead, Abraham is celebrated by the three Semitic religions as a great man of faith. Instances of God commanding his people to kill abound in the Hebrew Bible and a few injunctions are found in the *Qur'an*.

A moral dilemma may arise because of a conflict between the two forms of morality and ethics. Christian ethics promotes love, peace, and justice, and condemns killing vigorously, but Christians do not hesitate to send their sons and daughters to die in war, not for religious reasons, but ideological. Christians send their children to the war front and then finds a theological justification for their children's death. Christians who claim the Ten Commandments as the basis of their moral and ethical code, have no problems with capital punishment, yet one of the commandments says "Do not kill".

REASONS FOR MORALITY AND ETHICS

Why be moral? From what has been stated here, it is clear that whatever religion may mean to different individuals, whatever ultimate concern individuals may have, morality is the practical guide of that religion or ultimate concern, and ethics is the reflection on both the guide and the cosmogony. For example, Christian ethics is a reflection on Christian teachings concerning on how Christians ought to live. So it is too, with Islamic or Buddhist ethics. Being moral then, is to live within the sacred, or the ultimate concern.

Living within the sacred first means that people are inspired by their future, or what they see as their destiny. For religious people that future or destiny is being with God. For non-theistic religions—Buddhism, Confucianism, Hinduism, Jainism—the destiny is entering the *nirvana* or being integrated into the cosmos through enlightenment thereby no longer suffering the pain of continued re-incarnations. In both theistic and non-theistic religions entering eternal bliss depends on how one lives this life. Through morals, one can avoid eternal returns or re-incarnations because of *karma*, collected bad deeds, or eternal banishment in the presence of God in theistic religions. Morality, therefore, is critical for eternal destiny, since morality is a guide to proper behaviour towards eternal integration into the universe and bliss, avoiding eternal condemnation.

It seems to be too individualistic to be a moral person or moral agent for self-interested reason, to be saved. In as much as it seems empty and unethical to be moral because of self-interest, religions of salvation do not have an ethical problem because they maintain that individuals and not groups will be saved. In religions of salvation, the good one does, or one's morality gains one salvation. This approach to morality leads to a wrong understanding of the meaning and nature of religion. Religion becomes "doing" things for merit. This misconception was articulated much better in the New Testament. A rich young lawyer comes to Jesus and asks him, "What should I do to inherit eternal life" (Matthew 19:16). The answer Jesus gives the young man highlights the misconception on the nature of religion and meaning of religion so that it is worth reproducing it here:

> 17And he said to him, "Why do you ask me about what is good? There is only one who is good. If you wish to enter into life, keep the commandments". 18He said to him, "Which ones?" And Jesus said, "You shall not murder; You shall not commit adultery; You shall not steal; You shall not bear false witness; 19Honour your father and mother; also, You shall love your neighbour as yourself". 20The young man said to him, "I have kept all these; from my youth; what do I still lack?" 21Jesus said to him, "If you wish to be perfect, go, sell your possessions, and give the money to the poor, and you will have treasure in heaven; then come, follow me". 22When the young man heard this word, he went away grieving, for he had many possessions (Matthew 16:17–22).

Notice how the young man keeps saying: "I have done all that. Tell me what I need to do next if there is anything else. I am perfect" The young lawyer believes religion is about doing something to earn one's place with God. Note that Jesus tells him that religion is not about doing something and being perfect; religion is about "being" with God. Jesus tells the young man, go sell all your possession so that you do not depend on your ability to do something, but on being with God. As a respectable young person, he believes on earning something, and he has an impressive, near perfect moral record, "I have kept all these; from my youth; what do I still lack?" Jesus reminds the young man what is written in the Book of the Law, and the Jewish creed, *Shema* as important moral grounds, he nonetheless underscores that religion is not doing, but living within the sacred. In fact, the *shema* says true religion is allowing God be in one's very being:

> 4 Hear, O Israel: The Lord is our God, the Lord alone. 5You shall love the Lord your God with all your heart, and with all your soul, and with all your might. 6Keep these words that I am commanding you today in your heart. 7Recite them to your children and talk about them when you are at home and when you are away, when you lie down and when you rise. 8Bind them as a sign on your hand, fix them as an emblem on your forehead, 9and write them on the doorposts of your house and on your gates (Deuteronomy 6:4–9).

Note all the action words connected with loving God: keeping, reciting, binding, fixing, writing. The *Shema* shows that religion is being in and with God.

While maintaining that people will be saved as individuals, Christianity and Islam maintain that becomes a moral person as a sign of love and gratitude to God. Moral goodness is a response to God's love. This is an attempt to ensure that morals are not for self-interested reasons. Confucianism explains much better why be moral. In Confucianism, *li* or proper behaviour, is about living a good life, this life. There is no heaven, after life, or salvation in Confucianism. Accordingly, this life is very important in itself to be human destiny. Ethics then, has to do with proper behaviour in politics, or the common life and the common good. *Li* (ethics) is about harmony of human life and society. The concept of morals or virtue in Confucian mirrors that of religions of structure where being moral is not for gaining eternal bliss.

SOURCES OF MORALS AND VIRTUES

Morals have their origin in beyond time; they rooted in the cosmogony of different people. All religions assign the elders a critical role in promoting morals and virtues through writing them into a book or mediating through narrative. In this way, the elders are elevated to the status of moral exemplars. This is more so in religions of structure, because in religions of salvation the moral example is the founding leader: Moses in Judaism who received the Ten Commandments from God, as was Mohammed long after him and the Buddha long before Moses and Muhammad. The moral code of Judaism as received by Moses runs as follows:

You shall not make for yourself an idol, whether in the form of anything that is in heaven above, or that is on the earth beneath, or that is in the water under the earth. 5You shall not bow down to them or worship them; for I the Lord your God am a jealous God, punishing children for the iniquity of parents, to the third and the fourth generation of those who reject me, 6but showing steadfast love to the thousandth generation of those who love me and keep my commandments.

7 You shall not make wrongful use of the name of the Lord your God, for the Lord will not acquit anyone who misuses his name.

8 Remember the sabbath day, and keep it holy. 9For six days you shall labour and do all your work. 10But the seventh day is a sabbath to the Lord your God; you shall not do any work—you, your son or your daughter, your male or female slave, your livestock, or the alien resident in your towns. 11For in six days the Lord made heaven and earth, the sea, and all that is in them, but rested the seventh day; therefore the Lord blessed the sabbath day and consecrated it.

12 Honour your father and your mother, so that your days may be long in the land that the Lord your God is giving you.

13 You shall not murder.

14 You shall not commit adultery.

15 You shall not steal.

16 You shall not bear false witness against your neighbour.

17 You shall not covet your neighbour's house; you shall not covet your neighbour's wife, or male or female slave, or ox, or donkey, or anything that belongs to your neighbour.

Beyond the decalogue or the Ten Commandments, there are other numerous places in the Hebrew Bible from which Jews can draw inspiration for a moral life. In fact, Jews say the first five books of their Bible are Books of the Law (Genesis, Exodus, Leviticus, Number, Deuteronomy), meaning Books of moral instruction such as the following passage from Exodus 23:1–9.

You shall not spread a false report. You shall not join hands with the wicked to act as a malicious witness.

2You shall not follow a majority in wrongdoing; when you bear witness in a lawsuit, you shall not side with the majority so as to pervert justice;

3nor shall you be partial to the poor in a lawsuit.

4 When you come upon your enemy's ox or donkey going astray, you shall bring it back.

5 When you see the donkey of one who hates you lying under its burden and you would hold back from setting it free, you must help to set it free.

6 You shall not pervert the justice due to your poor in their lawsuits. 7Keep far from a false charge, and do not kill the innocent or those in the right, for I will not acquit the guilty. 8You shall take no bribe, for a bribe blinds the officials, and subverts the cause of those who are in the right.

9 You shall not oppress a resident alien; you know the heart of an alien, for you were aliens in the land of Egypt.

Christianity

While Christians also follow the moral precepts in Judaism, they also draw moral inspiration from the words of Jesus who said:

3 Blessed are the poor in spirit, for theirs is the kingdom of heaven.

4 Blessed are those who mourn, for they will be comforted.

5 Blessed are the meek, for they will inherit the earth.

6 Blessed are those who hunger and thirst for righteousness, for they will be filled.

7 Blessed are the merciful, for they will receive mercy.

8 Blessed are the pure in heart, for they will see God.

9 Blessed are the peacemakers, for they will be called children of God.

10 Blessed are those who are persecuted for righteousness' sake, for theirs is the kingdom of heaven.

11 Blessed are you when people revile you and persecute you and utter all kinds of evil against you falsely on my account. 12Rejoice and be glad, for your reward is great in heaven, for in the same way they persecuted the prophets who were before you (Matthew 5:3–12).

These verses are called the Beatitudes, meaning the attitudes Christians need to maintain. Take note here that Jesus defines religion as a state of mind that leads to action. That is why some Christians call these verses the *Be*-attitudes. Elsewhere in the New Testament, Jesus insists on the fact that religion is not a matter of following moral precepts, but maintaining a proper attitude of mind as th In Mark 7:18–23 shows:

18He said to them, "Then do you also fail to understand? Do you not see that whatever goes into a person from outside cannot defile, 19since it enters, not the heart but the stomach, and goes out into the sewer?" (Thus he declared all foods clean.) 20And he said, "It is what comes out of a person that defiles. 21For it is from within, from the human heart, that evil intentions come: fornication, theft, murder, 22adultery, avarice, wickedness, deceit, licentiousness, envy, slander, pride, folly. 23All these evil things come from within, and they defile a person".

Confucianism

The source of virtue in Confucianism is in cosmic or natural law as the various writers of the Chinese classics maintain. Lu Hsiang-Shan maintains:

The moral principle inherent in the human mind is endowed by Heaven and cannot be wiped out. Those who are clouded by material desires so as to pervert principles and violate righteousness, have become so because they do not think, that is all. If they can turn truly to the true selves and think, their sense of right and wrong and their ability to chose write and wrong will have the qualities of quiet alertness, clear-cut intelligence and firm conviction.[4]

Another early contributor to the Chinese classics, Mencius, writes:

No man is without a sense of compassion, or a sense of shame, or a sense of courtesy, or a sense of write or wrong. The sense of compassion is the beginning of righteousness [*i*]; the sense of courtesy is the beginning of decorum [*li*] and the sense of right and wrong [*chih*] is the beginning of wisdom. Every man has within himself these four beginnings just as he has four limbs.[5]

In Chinese classic as in Aristotle's ethics, virtue is developed by habituation. In Chinese classics that habituation is done through education. The role of education is produce individuals of moral excellence or virtue demonstrated in *ren*, which is translated variously as excellence, benevolence, kindhearted, or humanness.

African Religion

Moral excellence among Africans is given by the ancestors, who are the moral exemplars. The continuation of generations, is a testimony to the moral life of the ancestors. However, the moral precepts mediated by the elders with the help of the ancestors have their source outside the human circle of the living and the dead. Moral principles were given by the Creator. The ontological principle for a moral life lies in two concepts *umunthu* personhood or humanness and *moyo*. For the African, the criterion for ethical principle is *munthu,* the human and in the light of *moyo*. What is bad or good is measured by its ability to enhance or destroy human life, *moyo*.[6] This anthropocentric view does not in any way put humans above nature for humans are themselves within and part of nature. *Munthu*, as a species being, is nature being.

In the African world, virtue does not to earn one merit for eternal life. The world will not end in African cosmogony. The goal and role of moral excellence or virtue is for good human life, *moyo* as that is measured by *munthu*. Thus Africans understand virtue as *umunthu*, character or behaviour befitting *moyo* of *munthu*, a human being. Accordingly, in African society generosity is virtue par-excellence for it assures security, mutuality, and communication elements critical for circulation of available resources and benefits so that none suffers need in society and *moyo* is promoted. *Umunthu* and *moyo* are the keys to understanding moral excellence and virtues in the African world.

NOTES

1. Aristotle, *Nicomachean Ethics*, Terrence Irwin, trans. (Indianapolis, ID: Hackett Publishing) 13:2, 1.

2. *Ibid.*, 13:2, 2.

3. For Latin American Catholicism and cultural practises see Harvey J. Sindima, *The Gospel According to the Marginalized* (New York, Peter Lang, 2008), chapter 1.

4. Theodore DeBary, et al. *Sources of Chinese Tradition*, 568.

5. *Ibid. The Mencius*, II, A:6, 105.

6. I have explored fully the concepts of *umunthu* and *moyo* in many writings including the following among others: "Bondedness, *Moyo* and *Umuthu*: Organising Logic and Principle of Life", *Ultimate Reality and Meaning: Interdisciplinary Studies in the Philosophy of Understanding*, 14, 2 (1991); "Community of Life", *Ecumenical Review*, 14, 4, (1989); *Africa's Agenda: The Legacy of Liberalism and Colonialism in the Crisis of African Values* (Westport, CT: Greenwood Press, 1995), 201–214.

Works Cited

Alexander, Philip S. ed. *Textual Sources for the Study of Judaism*. Chicago, ILL: Chicago University Press, 1984.

Alston, P. William. "Religion", *The Encyclopedia of Philosophy*, ed. Paul Edwards. New York, NY: Macmillan, 1967.

Apps, Lara and Andrew Cow in *Male Witches in Early Modern Europe*. Manchester: Manchester University Press, 2003.

Arinze, Francis. A. *Sacrifice in Ibo Religion*. Ibadan, Nigeria: Ibadan University Press, 1970.

Aristotle, *Nicomachean Ethics*. Translated by Terrence Irwin. Indianapolis, ID: Hackett Publishing.

Awolalu, I. Omosade and P. Adelumo Dopamu. *West African Traditional Religion*. Ibadan, Nigeria: Onibononaje Press, 1979.

Austen, Ralph. "The Moral Economy of Witchcraft", *Modernity and its Malcontents: Ritual and Power in Postcolonial Africa*. Edited by Jean Comaroff and John Comaroff. Chicago, Ill: Chicago University Press, 1995.

Baker, Samuel W. "The Races of the Nile Basin", *Transactions of the Ethnological Society of London*, n.s. 5 (1867).

Beattie, John H. M. *Other Cultures: Aims, Methods, and Achievements in Social Anthropology*. London: Cohen and West, 1964.

Behringer, Wolfgang . *Witches and Witch Hunts*. Cambridge: Polity Press, 2004.

Beidelman, T. O. "Swazi Royal Ritual", *Africa*, 32 (1966): 374–75.

Boesak, Allan. "Wholeness Through Liberation", *Church and Society* (May–June).

Bodurine, P. O. "Witchcraft, Magic and E. S. P.: Defence of Scientific and Philosophical Scepticism", *Second Order: An African Journal of Philosophy*, 7, 1 and 2 (July and January, 1979): 36–49.

Boulaga, F. Eboussi. *Christianity Without Fetishes: An African Critique and Recapture of Christianity*. Translated by Robert Barr. Maryknoll, New York: Orbis Books, 1984.

Briggs, R. *Witches and Neighbours: The Social and Cultural Context of European Witchcraft*. London. Harper Collins, 1996.

Brown, Joseph Epes, ed. *The Sacred Pipe. Black Elk's Account of the Seven of the Oglala Sioux* Norman, OK: University of Oklahoma, 1953.

Comaroff, Jean and John Comaroff., eds. *Modernity and its Malcontents: Ritual and Power in Postcolonial Africa.* Chicago, Ill: Chicago University Press, 1995.

DeBarry, Theodore W. ed. *Sources of Indian Tradition* I. New York, NY: Columbia University Press, 1966.

Demallie, Raymond J. and Elaine A. Jahner, eds. *Lakota Belief and Ritual.* Lincoln, NB: University of Nebraska Press, 1991.

Demos, J. *Entertaining Satan: Witchcraft and the Culture of Early New England.* New York, NY: Oxford University Press, 1982.

Doniger, Wendy and Brian Smith. Translated. *The Laws of Manu.* London: Penguin Books, 1991.

Douglas, Mary. *Purity and Danger: An Analysis of the Concepts of Pollution and Taboo.* London: ARK, 1986.

Durkheim, Emil *Elements of Religion.* London: Allen & Unwin, 1964.

———. *Elementary Forms of Religious Life* (1915). London: Allen & Unwin, 1964.

Ejizu, Christopher I. *Ofo: Igbo Ritual Symbol.* Enugu, Nigeria: Fourth Dimension Publishers, 1986.

Eliade, Mircea. *Shamanism: Archaic Techniques of Ecstasy.* Original 1907. London, England: Arkana, 1989.

Elkin, A. P. *Aboriginal Men of High Degree* (St. Lucia: University of Queensland Press, 1945.

Evans-Pritchard, E. E. *The Nuer.* Oxford: Claredon Press, 1940.

———. *Witchcraft, Oracles and Magic among the Azande.* Oxford: Claredon Press, 1937.

———. "The Intellectualist (English) Interpretation of Magic". *Bulletin of the Faculty of Arts,* 1 (1933): 282–311.

Favret-Saada, Jean. *Deadly Words: Witchcraft in the Bocage.* Cambridge: Mason des Sciences de l'Homme and Cambridge university Press, 1980.

Feraca, Stephen E. *Wakinyan: Lakota Religion in the Twentieth Century.* Lincoln, NB: University of Nebraska Press, 1998.

Frazer, James George. *Encyclopedia Britannica,* 9th ed., S.V. "Taboo: Totemism". London: Macmillan, 1976.

———. *The Golden Bough,* 12 vols. London: Macmillan Press, 1980. Originally published 1890.

———. *The Golden Bough.* Part 1: *The Magic Art and the Evolution of Kings.* London: Macmillan, 1932.

Gardener, John and John Maier, trans. *Gilgamesh.* New York, NY: Vintage Books, 1985.

Gaster, Theodore. *Thespis: Ritual, Myth, and Dram in the Ancient Near East.* New York, 1961.

Geertz, Clifford. "Religion as a Cultural System", *Reader in Comparative Religion: An Anthropological Approach* Lessa Willia *Antebellum South*. New York, NY: Harper and Row, 1979.

Geschiere, Peter. *The Modernity of Witchcraft: Politics and Occult in Postcolonial Africa*. Charlottesville, VA: University Press of Virginia, 1997.

Glazer, Nahum N. ed. *The Passover Haggada*. New York, NY: Schoken Books, 1953

Griaule, Marcel. *Conversation with Ogotemmêli: An Introduction to Dogon Religious Ideas*. London: Oxford University Press, 1965.

Gyekye, Kwame. *An Essay on African Philosophical Thought: Akan Conceptual Scheme*. New York, NY: Cambridge University Press, 1987.

Greenwood, Susan. *Magic, Witchcraft and the Otherworld*. Oxford and New York: Berg, 2000.

Hallen, Barry and J. O. Sodipo. *Knowledge, Belief and Witchcraft*. London: Ethnographica, 1986.

Heid, Stephen. *Celibacy In The Early Church: The Beginnings Of A Discipline Of Obligatory Continence For Clerics In East And West*. San Francisco, CA: Ignatius Press, 2000.

Herzberg A. "Midrash Tanhuma, Kedoshim", Vol. 10. *Judaism*. Brooklyn, NY: 1963.

Horton, Robin. "African Traditional Thought and Western Science", *Africa* 37, nos. 1 and 2 (January and April, 1967).

———. "African Traditional Thought and Western Science", *Rationality*. Edited by Bryan R. Wilson. Cambridge, MA: Blackwell, 1991.

Idoniboye, D. E. "The Concept of 'Spirit' in African Metaphysics", *Second Order*, 2, 1 (January 1973).

Idowu, E. Boulaje. "The Challenge of Witchcraft", *Orita: Ibadan Journal of Religious Studies*, 4, 1 (June 1970).

———. *African Traditional Religion: A Definition*. London: SCM Press, 1973.

———. *Olódùmarè: God in Yoruba Belief*. London: Longman, 1962.

Iwu, Maurice M. *African Ethenomedicine*. Enugu, Nigeria: SNAAP, 1986.

Jenkins, C. ed., "Origen on I Corinthians", *Journal of Theological Studies* (Old Series) 9 (1908).

Jones, David M. and Brian L Molyneaux, *Mythology of the American Nations*. London: Hermes House, 2006.

Kapferer, Bruce. *The Feast of the Sorcery: Practises of Consciousness and Power*. Chicago, Ill: Chicago University Press, 1997.

Kaplan, Mordecai. *Judaism as a Civilisation: Toward a Reconstruction of American Jewish Life*. New York, NY: Jewish Publication Society of America published, 1994. First published 1934.

Kenyatta, Jomo. *Facing Mt. Kenya*. New York, NY: Vintage Books, 1965.

Kitagawa, Jospeh M. *The Religious Traditions of Asia*. New York, Macmillan 1989.

Kuper, Hilda. An African Aristocracy. London: Oxford University Press, 1947.

Lambo, Adeoye T. "Traditional African Cultures and Western Medicine". Edited by F. N. L. Poynter. *Medicine and Culture*. London: Wellcome Institute of History of Medicine, 1969.

Lessa, William A. and Evon Z. Vogt, eds. *Reader in Comparative Religion: An Anthropological Approach*. New York, NY: Harper and Row, 1979.

Lévy-Bruhl, Lucien. *Primitive Mentality*. New York, NY: Macmillian, 1923.

———. *How Natives Think*. London: Allen and Unwin, 1926.

Lewis, J. R. ed. *Magical Religion and Modern Witchcraft*. Albany, NY: State University of New York Press, 1996.

Lienhardt, Godfrey. *Divinity and Experience: The Religion of the Dinka*. London: Oxford University Press, 1961.

Livingston, James. *Anatomy of the Sacred: An Introduction to Religion*. 5th. ed. Upper Saddle River, NJ: Pearson, 2005.

Luhrmann, Tanya M. *Persuasions of the Witch's Craft. Ritual Magic in Contemporary England*. Oxford, Blackwell, 1980.

Maimela, Simon. "Theology and Politics in South Africa", *Chicago Theological Seminary Register* (Spring 1979)

———. "The Concept of Israel", *Africa Theological Journal* 15, 2 (1986).

Malinowski, Bronislaw. *Magic, Science and Religion and Other Essays*. New York, NY: Double Day Anchor, 1954.

———. *Sex, Culture and Myth*. London: Hart Davies, 1963.

Marett, Robert Runalph. *The Thresholds of Religion*. London: Methuen, 1909.

Marvic, B. A. *The Swazi*. London: Cambridge University Press, 1940.

Mason, Herbert. *Gilgamesh: A Verse Narrative*. New York, NY: Penguin Books, 1972.

Masolo, D. A. *African Philosophy in Search of Identity*. Edinburgh: Edinburgh University Press, 1994.

Mbiti, John S. *African Religions and Philosophy* 2nd. ed. London: Heinemann, 1990.

———. *Introduction to African Religions*. London: Heinemann, 1975.

Mei, V. P. trans. William T. Bary, ed. *Sources of Chinese Tradition*. New York, NY: Columbia University Press, 1960.

Metuh, Emfie Ikenga. *God and Man in African Religion*. London: Geoffrey Chapman, 1981.

Middleton, John. ed. *Magic, Witchcraft and Curing*. New York, NY: The Natural History Press, 1967.

——— and E. H. Winter, *Witchcraft and Sorcery in East Africa*. London: Routledge and Kegan Paul, 1963.

Morgan, Kenneth. ed. *The Path of the Buddha*. New York, NY: Ronald Press, 1956.

Mosely, Albert G. *African Philosophy: Select Readings.* Englewood Cliffs, NJ: Prentice Hall, 1995.

Müller, Max. *Introduction to the Science of Religion.* London: Longmans, Green and Co., 1873.

Nath, Shri Surender. *Jaap Sahib.* rev. ed. New Dehli, India: Gobind Sadan Institute for Advanced Studies in Comparative Religion, 1996.

Nehardt, Nicholas and John G. *Black Elk Speaks: Being the Life Story of a Holy Man of Oglala Sioux.* New York, NY: William Morrow. Pocket Books ed., 1932.

Neusner, Jacob. The Death and Birth of Judaism.New York, NY: Basic Books, 1987.

———, *The Enchantments of Judaism: Rites of Transformation From Birth Through, Death.* New York, NY: Basic Books, 1987.

Niangoran-Bouah, Georges "The Talking drum: A Traditional African Instrument of Liturgy and Mediation with the Sacred", *African Traditional Religions in Contemporary Society.* Edited by Jacob K. Olupona. New York, NY: Paragon, 1991.

O'Flaherty, Wendy Doniger. Trans. *The Rig Veda.* London, Penguin Books, 1981.

Olupona, Jacob K. ed. *African Traditional Religions in Contemporary Society.* New York, NY: Paragon, 1991.

Oluwole, Sophie B. "On the Existence of Witches", *Second Order: An African Journal of Philosophy,* 7, 1 and 2 (January and July 1978).

Origen, *Homilies on Genesis and Exodus.* Ante-Nicene Fathers. Vol. 4.

———. *Contra ,* I.42. Translated by Henry Chadwick. Cambridge, Eng: Cambridge University Press, 1965.

———. *On First Principles* vol. 4. Peabody. Massachusetts: Hendrickson, 1994.

Otto, Rudolf. *The Idea of the Holy.* London: Oxford University Press, 1923.

Mosely, Albert G. *African Philosophy: Select Readings.* Englewood Cliffs, NJ: Prentice Hall, 1995.

Paliani, Sylvester. *1930 Kunadza Mchape.* Longmans. Blantyre, Malawi.

Parrinder, Edward Geoffrey *African Traditional Religion.* Westport, Connecticut: Greenwood Press, 1970.

Patrinacos, Nicon D. "Celibacy", *Dictionary of Greek Orthodoxy.* Pleasantville, NY: Hellenic Heritage Publications, 1987.

Patterson, Mary. "Sorcery and Witchcraft in Melanesia", *Oceania,* 2 and 3 (1974–75).

———. "Sorcery and Witchcraft", *Religion and Culture,* 2nd. ed. Edited by Raymond Scupin. Upper Saddle River, NJ: Pearson, Prentice Hall, 2008.

Paul VI. Pope. *Sacerdotalis Caelibatus.* 24 June 1967.

Poynter. F. N. L., ed. *Medicine and Culture.* London: Wellcome Institute of History of Medicine, 1969.

Powers, Marla. *Oglala Women: Myth, Ritual, and Reality.* Chicago, Illinois: Chicago University Press, 1986.

Raboteu, Albert J. *Slave Religion: The Invisible Institution in the Antebellum South.* New York, NY: Oxford University Press, 1980.

Sanda, A. O. "The Scientific or Magical Ways of Knowing: Implications for the Study of African Traditional Healers", *Second Order: An African Journal of Philosophy*, 7, 1 and 2 (January and July 1978): 20–35.

Scupin, ed. Raymond. *Religion and Culture*, 2nd. ed. Upper Saddle River, NJ: Pearson, Prentice Hall, 2008.

Sindima, Harvey J. *Drums of Redemption: An Introduction to African Christianity* Westport, Connecticut: Greenwood Press, 1995.

———. *Africa's Agenda: The Legacy of Liberalism and Colonialism in the Crisis of African Values.* Westport, Connecticut: Greenwood Press, 1995.

———. *The Legacy of Scottish Missionaries in Malawi.* Lewiston, New York: Edwin Mellen Press, 1990.

———. "Bondedness, *Moyo* and *Umunthu* as Elements of Achewa Spirituality, Organizing Logic and Principle of Life", *Ultimate Reality and Meaning: Interdisciplinary Studies in the Philosophy of Understanding* 14, 1 (March, 1991).

———. *Religious and Political Ethics in Africa: A Moral Inquiry.* Westport, Connecticut: Greenwood Press, 1998.

———. *Theories of Religion in the Study of African Religions.* Forthcoming.

———. "African Religion and Medicine". Unpublished Essay.

———. *Reclaiming Christianity in the Twenty-First Century: Building a Spiritual Power House.* Blantyre, Malawi: Africa Academy Press, 2008.

———. *The Gospel According to the Marginalized.* New York, NY:, Peter Lang, 2007.

———. *I Believe: Creeds, Confessions, and Statements from the First to the Twenty-first Century.* Forthcoming.

Smith, Robertson. *Religion of the Semites* 3rd. ed. London: Macmillan, 1927.

Sodipo, J. O. "Notes on the Concept of Yoruba Thought", *Second Order*, 2, 2 (1973).

Symythies, J. R. "Is ESP Possible"? *Science and ESP*. Edited by J. R. Symythies. London Routledge and Kegan Paul, 1967.

Temples, Placid. *Bantoe Filosofie.* Antwerp, Belgium. 1946.

Turner, *Drums of Affliction: A Study of religious Processes of the Ndembu of Zambia.* Oxford: Claredon, 1968.

Tylor, Edward B. *Religion in Primitive Culture*, 2 vols. London: John Murray, 1871.

Van Gennep, A. *The Rites if Passage* (1908). London: Routledge and Kegan Paul, 1965.

Walker, James R. *Lakota Belief and Ritual.* Translated and Edited by Raymond J. DeMallies and Elaine A. Jahner. Lincoln, NB: University of Nebraska Press, 1991.

Whitehead, Neil and Robin Wright, *In Darkness and Sorcery: the Anthropology of Assault Sorcery and Witchcraft in Amazonia.* Durham, NC: Duke University Press, 2004.

Winch, Peter. "Understanding a Primitive Society", *Rationality*. Edited by Brayan Wilson. Cambridge, MA: Blackwell Publishers, 1991, reprint. Original, 1970.

Wilson, Brayan, ed. *Rationality*. Cambridge, MA: Blackwell, 1991.

Yinger, J. M. *Religion, Society and the Individual*. New York, NY: Macmillan, 1957.

Young, William A. *The World's Religions: World views and Contemporary Issues* 2nd. ed. Upper Saddle River, NJ: Pearson/Prentice Hall, 2005.

Ziervogel, D. *Swazi Texts*. Pretoria: Van Shaik, 1957.

Zuesse, Evan M. *Ritual Cosmos: The Sanctification of Life in African Religions*. Athens, Ohio: Ohio University Press, 1985.

Index

African religion 15; monotheism 20; and magic 24, 111, 127, 129; traditional religion 26, cosmology 41; symbols 46, 67–69; prayer in 51–52; healing rituals 54; 65, 67; religious functionaries 105; and medicine 111, 113, 116; and science 129, 131; sacred objects 153, moral excellence 158, 164, 165

Agni, Lord 33, 47, 56, 137

Akan, The 34, 84, 140, 170

Alston, William 22, 28, 29, 168

Ananda, The 80, 81, 86, 154

Apache, The 35, 42, 43

Arinze, Cardinal Francis 135, 141, 168

Beatitudes 164

Beattie, John 126, 127, 140, 168

Behringer, Wolgang 127, 140, 168

Bible, Holy 2, 4, 45, 58, 72–75, 77, 79, 84–86, *See also* Hebrew, Old Testament, New Testament

Brahman 90, 117, 154

Brahmin 33, 47, 144

Buddha, The 30, 38, 39, 47, 80, 81, 86, 94, 144, 150, 151, 158, 161, 172

Buddhism Incarnation 19, 26, 38, 156; non-theistic religion 21, 22, 50; enlightenment 29–30; 31; no cosmogony 38–39; creed 60; scriptural interpretation 74, 78–80; functionaries 89; monasticism 92; celibacy 99; sacred time 142; sacred objects 149;

Pali canon 79, 80, 84, 85; Tibetan 154; Theravada 79, 80

Canon Qur'an 72–74; Buddhist 79–80, 89; Chinese 79; Christian 76–78; pseudo-Canon of Nicaea 97, Canon law 103, 105; of Constantinople 103–105; of Trent 106

Celibacy 100; Hindu 101; Christian 103–107, 118, 170, 172 *See also* monasticism; celibate priesthood 106; Hindu monks 99, 100, 117

Chukwu 52, 53, 67, 68

Confucianism 26, 31, 38, 39, 41, 73, 85, 158, 160, 161, 164

Cosmogony 33–36; African 165; Shinto 33–35; Native American 34–35; Dogon 35; Hebrew 36, 37, 146 Sumerian 36, 37–38; Jain rejection of 38; Buddha rejection of 39–40, 41; Lakota 150; and ethics 158–161. *See* cosmology

Cosmology 16; African 24; Shinto 34–35; Native American 34–35; Dogon 35; Hebrew 36, 37; Sumerian 36, 37–38; Jain rejection of 38; Buddha rejection of 39–40, 41

Culture and education, 4; African 5, 7–9; Arab 8; Jewish 73, 99; Indian 33; Modern 126; non-European 24, 122, 125, 126, 133, 172; preliterate 79; and ethics 157–158, and religion 148 and theory in religion 46, 122, 125–127; scientific 126.

Dan Fodio, Usman 5

de Brosses, President Charles 23

Dinka, The 51, 52, 69, 170

Divination 49, 50, 54, 58–60, 62–68, 75, 76, 90, 91, 107, 108, 136, 144, 153, 155

Diviners 89, 107, 108, 113, 117, 121, 132, 136

Dogon, The 35, 47, 170

Dopamu, Adelumo 67, 69, 134, 135, 141, 168

Douglas, Mary 24, 28, 127, 140, 169

Dreamtime 143–144

Drum and healing rituals 7–8, 45, 108–112, 121, 140, 173; in African religion 57–62; as text 82–86, 172

Durkheim, Emil 11, 17, 21, 28, 169

Eastern Orthodox 96–97, 103, 117

Ejuzi, Christopher 41

Elders 4; Jewish 30; Giguyu 112–114, 145; Chinese 149; African 161, 165

Ethics 17, 18, and religion 157–161, 164, 165, 168, 173

Eucharist, The 32, 133

Evans-Pritchard Nuer religion 13–14; Azande magic and witchcraft 23–24, 122–125, 137

Five Pillars, The 62

Frazer, James 23, 28, 123–125, 129, 139, 169

Functional, theory 21, 27

Geertz, Cliford 22, 28, 170

Geschiere, Peter 127, 140, 170

Gikuyu, The 25, 112, 130, 145, 146

Gilgamesh 36–38, 47, 169, 171

Grath Sahib 76, 86

Hadith, The 74

Halakhah 91–93

Healers 108–112, 121, 140, 173 *See also* medicine men

Hebrew Bible 45, 58, 73, 74, 79, 86, 136, 159, 162

Hermeneutics Biblical 78–81; Buddhist 79–81, 85.

Hinduism 19 classes 33; the body 50, 56, poetry and hymns; liturgy 63, 67, 89; scripture 71, 72, 74; in religious studies 83; functionaries 84, 93, 99; magic in 135, 137; sacred objects 154–155, 160

Horton Robin 128, 129, 140, 170

Hsü Tzŭ 39, 41

Idowu Boulaje 20–21, 26, 28, 132–133, 140, 170

Igbo, The 41, 48, 51, 52, 67, 68, 135, 169

Incarnation, Hindu view of 19, 27, 38, 162

Indra, Lord 33, 47, 56–58

Inspiration, mechanical 72–73; 78, 87, 164, 165

Islam, reasons for studying 2–5, 10; and African culture 7–10; Wahabbi 16; and salvation 19; monotheism 20; creed 61–62; scripture 71, 74, 75, 82, 85; functionaries 91, 93; liturgical language 134; and magic 135, 137, 138; liturgy 144; architecture 149; ethics 161

Iwu, Maurice 110, 118, 170

Jaap Sahib 54, 68, 69, 172

Jainism, religion of salvation 9, 26, 31; cosmogony 38–39; the body 50; scripture 85; monasticism 93, 100, 101

James, William 25, 28; Walker 34, 47, 48, 87, 118, 118, 123, 139, 169, 171, 174; Young 47, 48, 172.

John, Pope Paul II 107

Judaism 3, 10, 17, 19, 20, 23, 26, 31, 58, 60–62, 68, 74, 74, 75, 82, 85, 86, 91-93, 101, 118, 135, 136, 144, 147, 151, 155, 156, 158, 161, 163, 168, 170, 172; Judaism Orthodox Judaism 92;

Reconstructionist Judaism 93; Reformed Judaism 93

Kaba, The 63

Kami 34, 47, 148

Karma 38, 39, 47, 160

Kenya 2, 5, 10, 25, 28, 51, 63, 112, 118, 130, 140, 145, 146, 155, 171

Kenyatta, President Jomo 25, 28, 112, 113, 118, 130–132, 140, 155, 171

Kere-Nyanga 113. *See also* Mount Kenya

Kwoth nhial 51, 52, 68

Lakota, The 31, 47, 51, 113–115, 118, 150, 155, 169, 174

Lambo, Adeoye 111, 118, 171

Libation 26, 27, 41, 49, 52, 57, 63, 64, 66, 68, 149, 151

liminality 42, 43, 47, 59, 112, 143, 144

Liturgy 62–64; and African 63–66, 87, 107; Hinduism 90; Islam 92; Judaism 90–92; and Ethiopian monastic life 98, 99; 172

Magic 21, 23–25, 27, 28, 90, 109, 111, 112, 119–125, 127–140, 168–171

Malawi 2, 4–6, 17, 26, 63, 68, 121, 139, 163, 172, 173

Malinowski, Bronislaw 124, 130, 133, 139, 171

Mbiti, John S. 25, 28, 51, 69, 111, 118, 131, 132, 140, 155, 171

Medicine men 113–115, 131; *See also* healers

Meditation 55, 75, 76, 86, 102, 151, 152

Mediums 89, 107–109, 113

Mencius 164, 165

Middleton, John 127, 140, 171

Missionaries Christian 6–8; and language 13–14; in Africa 17, 59, 82, 83, 109, 173

Monasticism 93; Buddhist 94–95; Christian 95–96, Catholic Monastic Process 96; Eastern Orthodox church 96–97; Ethiopian church 97–99; Hindu 99; Jain 100–102

Monotheism 16, 20, 27, 82

Morality 9, 10, 21, 157–160

Mount Sinai 92, 146

Mount Zion 59, 146, 147

Moyo 17, 165, 173

Mount Kenya 25, 28, 140, 171

Muhammad, Prophet 10, 16, 31, 61–63, 71, 144, 158, 161

Müller, Max 13, 17, 82, 172

Myth 30, 31, as structure of reality 33–36, and ritual 40; of White Painted Woman 42; and symbols 45, 46, 48; Australian aboriginal Dreamtime 143–145

Nanak, Guru 31, 54, 55, 68, 76

Narrative 12, 31, 46, 47, 77, 161, 171

Native Americans 113, 114, 124, 150, 155; shamanism 114–117, 155; sacred circle 150; sacred pipe 31, 68, 155, 169. *See* Lakota, Apache

New Testament 72–74, 106, 160, 164. See also Holy Bible

Neusner, Jacob 92, 118, 156, 172

Ndembu, The 43, 48, 173

Ngai 112, 113

Niangoran-Bouah Georges 83, 84, 87, 172

Nigeria 5, 20, 41, 48, 69, 118, 132, 141, 149, 168–170

Nuer, The 13, 44, 51, 52, 68, 69, 108, 169

Ofo ritual 41, 48, 169

Ogotemmêli 35, 47, 170

Old Testament 72–74, 77, 78, 159. *See also* Holy Bible

Olódùmaré 20, 21, 27

Oluwole, Sophie 133, 140, 172

Otto, Rudolf 21, 22, 28, 50, 68, 89, 118, 172

Parrinder, Edward Geoffrey 129, 140, 172

Paul VI, Pope 106, 107, 118, 172

Philokalia 96, 117

Pius XII, Pope 106

Prayer 22, 22, 24, 31, 41, 49, 51–55, 57, 62, 63, 65–68, 74, 75, 76, 91, 93, 96, 97, 99, 103, 123, 134–136, 150–153

Profane 22, 25, 27, 49, 145

Prophets 58, 61, 62, 73, 89, 107, 108, 163

Puja 63, 67, 68, 90, 149, 151

Qur'an 2,4, 34, 62, 63, 72, 73, 93, 139–141, 146, 1161

Religions of salvation 19, 22, 42, 49, 51, 67, 71, 74, 93, 101, 109, 145, 160, 161

Religions of structure vii, 19, 20, 24, 42, 46, 49–51, 68, 81–83, 89, 107, 113, 145, 161

Revelation 16, 71–73, 82, 86

Rig Veda 47, 56, 57, 74, 172

Rituals; 16, 22, 24, 25, 28, 32, religious 41, 67, 149–151; liminal 42–43, 107, 110–114; sacrificial 40–43; healing 45, 112–115; seasonal rituals 43; and myth 45–48; purification 62–63, 144; and magic 111, 121–125; and time 143–147, in Vodun 149; ritual objects 153–154.

Robertson Smith 21, 28

Sacred 17, 22, 25, 30; poems and hymns 33, 58; stick 41; rituals 43; Oglala holiness 51; animals 57; writings 56, 71, 73–75, 79, 86; time 143–145; space 145–150; circle 150; pipe 31, 68, 155, 169; objects 22, 108, 149–151, 155

Sacrifice 16, 25, 27, 32, 33, 38, 44, 45, 47, 49, 56, 57, 65, 66, 90, 117, 131, 141, 145, 147, 149, 150, 159, 168

Sadhana 99, 117

Sadhu 99, 101, 117

Salat 62, 63, 68

Scripture 4, 17, 33, 49, 55, 59, 62; mechanical inspiration 71–73; uses of 77–78; interpretation 78–80; oral scripture 83–85; types of 89, 91, 92, 98, 100, 106. *See* hermeneutics

Seder, meal 32

Shadada, The 61, 68

Shamanism 114–117, 155

Shema 60, 62, 68, 152, 153, 161

Shia 62, 63

Shinto 85, cosmogony 34–35, 87, 146, 150

Shiva, Lord 30, 47, 56, 148

Shrines 67, 75, 120, 145, 148, 149, 151, 155

Sikhism 31, 54, 55, 68, 71, 76, 85, 91, 154, *Grath Sahib* 78; reading scripture 93; sacred objects 156

Singh, Baba Virsa Singh 30, 54

Smith, Robertson 21, 28, 35, 47, 130, 169, 173

Sorcery 23, 110, 117–120, 125, 128, 130, 136–138, 167–170

Spirituality 23, 112, 119–122, 127, 130, 132, 138–140, 170, 172, 174

Sudan. 5, 23, 108

Swazi, The 43, 48, 168, 171, 174

Symbols 7, 12, 22, 45, 46, 54, 130

Tanak 2, 4, 73, 74, 85, 86 *See also* Hebrew Bible, Torah

Tanzania 2, 5, 63

Taoism 85

Tapas 99, 117

Tempels 24, 28, 140

Ten Commandments 146, 147, 159, 161, 162

Theology 6, 16, 17, 55, 82, 163, 171

Tolerance 11

Torah 30, 58, 61, 62, 71, 73, 74, 86, 91, 92, 138, 147, 152, 153. *See also* Hebrew Bible, Tanak

Transcendence 11, 16

Turner, Victor 43, 48, 173

Tyler, William 60

Tylor, Edward 23, 28, 60, 122, 123, 139, 173

Umunthu 9, 17, 165, 173

van Gennep, Arnold 43, 173

Veda 33, 47, 56, 57, 71, 73, 74, 85, 90, 99, 102, 137, 149, 154, 172

Vanaprastha 102, 117

Virtues 4, 9, 113, 158, 159, 161, 165

Wahhabi 8, 16

Wakan Tanka 34, 51, 114, 115, 124, 155

White Painted Woman 42, 43

Witchcraft 23, 24, 27, 28, 119–122, 125–127, 130, 132–134, 138–141, 168–172, 174

Yinger, Milton 21, 175

Yom Kippur 45, 47, 144, 153

Zionism 93

Zuesse, Evan 19, 28, 40, 42, 46, 48, 174